Jack
CHARLTON
THE AUTHORISED BIOGRAPHY

Jack
CHARLTON
THE AUTHORISED BIOGRAPHY

BY COLIN YOUNG

HEROBOOKS

HEROBOOKS

HERO BOOKS

PUBLISHED BY HERO BOOKS
1 WOODVILLE GREEN
LUCAN
CO. DUBLIN
IRELAND

Hero Books is an imprint of Umbrella Publishing

First Published 2016

A CIP record for this book is available from the British Library

ISBN 9781910827017

Printed in Ireland with Print Procedure Ltd
Cover design and typesetting: Jessica Maile
Cover photograph: Sportsfile
Photographs: The Charlton family collection and Sportsfile

To Lesley and my great friend Danny Fullbrook

CONTENTS

FOREWORD

By Jack Charlton

IT WAS the morning after the night before. After Italia 90, we had the open top bus and the reception outside the Bank of Ireland building.

A million people lining the streets of Dublin… Tricolours, green shirts everywhere! I've never seen so many smiling faces. Women, men and children of all ages; babies held up in the air to all the lads on the top of the bus.

I got the flight back to Newcastle the next morning. Dennis Woodhead, an old friend, the former commercial manager at Sheffield Wednesday, passed now, he picked me up. He'd booked the ferry from Stranraer to Larne that afternoon.

I had enough time to kiss Pat on the cheek, pick up the bag of clean clothes she'd sorted and chuck the fishing gear in Dennis' boot. There was a mountain of mail in the office. Pat had sorted them into piles; letters from all over the world, postcards from Italy, a few bills. It could wait. I had a river to get to.

It's a good three hours drive to Stranraer. The ferry crossing is another two-and-a-half hours and then we had to drive for nearly four hours over the border to Ballina.

I have a rule. I only drink Guinness in Ireland. I've tried it back home and it doesn't taste the same. It doesn't feel the same. If I go to John's pub on the beach at Blyth, I'll have a John Smith's.

There's a pub, Furey's I think, just over the bridge at Sligo, which is about an hour from the house we bought in Ballina. I was desperate for a pint. We decided to call in.

As we got to the front door a fella in his 60s came out. Grey hair, ponytail; he looked merry. He clocks me.

'Ah, Jack,' he says. 'It's so good of you to come to me retirement do. Thanks for coming. Now… can I get you a pint?'

IT'S ONE of the stories that stands out. When I look back at that wonderful time with Ireland, and all the fun we had, the people always stand out. I love them and I know they love me. And you can't beat that.

From day one, the Irish people made Pat and myself welcome. We go back now, and the response from everyone never ceases to amaze us.

I love the way they just accepted us for being us. I never had to change when I went to Ireland. Some might say that's not a good thing, but I know I always felt at home, relaxed and comfortable in the beautiful surroundings. And among beautiful people.

And I'll tell you what; we had some fun, some great memories. I said we'd stick it up 'em if they listened to me. And I was right.

Before I took the Ireland job, I had looked at European and world football and all the best teams. I knew there was no way we could enter the fray against them, play them at their own game, and expect to be successful. Ireland had tried it for years and it had never worked.

So we invented a game that was totally different to everything world football had ever seen before. And we turned the game on its head.

Nowadays, every team in Europe does what we did back then. But they have a different name for it now, because it sounds better. When you go to FIFA meetings and conferences now they call it 'pressing'.

They've given it a fancy name because they don't want to tell us that we started it and we brought it into international football. Ireland. But we did. They might call it 'pressing'. We called it… 'put people under pressure'. Easiest game in the world in international football. All these ball-playing defenders were used to having all the time in the world. So we went after them. And they didn't like it.

And it worked, of course. I don't think any of us could have predicted how far it would take us, but we gave it a go and we upset a few of the big guns along the way. No one liked playing Ireland. They used to dread coming to Lansdowne Road.

I'll take that.

TEN YEARS was enough.

I had done everything I wanted to do with Ireland by then, I think. Though it was a blow missing out on Euro 96 in England. We would have brought a lot to that party. I didn't enjoy watching that tournament. In fact I missed most of it.

After that, we had to let the players I'd had for 10 years go, and new players had to come in and there was a need to rebuild the team.

Realistically, it needed a new man to do that job. I'm glad Mick got it. And he did a great job. Not as good as me, mind, but he did well for Ireland.

It can't be easy following me, y'know.

The plan was just to take a break. And I was offered jobs. Wales asked me, and I had Celtic on the telephone. But nothing took me fancy. Nothing that could match what we had with Ireland. Nothing to take me away from the fishing in Ireland and Northumberland, and from Pat and the grandkids for days on end.

I was in football from the age of 15. It was all I ever knew. But I needed the break, and I enjoyed it.

I still grafted. After dinner speaking; four, five times a week, all over the country! My son John and I would be in Brighton one night, Barrow the next, Bristol two nights later. Just telling the stories. Recalling some of those wonderful memories. And I still have my own favourite players, games, all sorts of different things.

We had some great days, some great nights and we all have some great memories.

I know that the people of Ireland cherish them and I know they enjoyed the days when they did something they'd never done before, like going to a World Cup a couple of times, and the European Championships. I know they enjoyed that.

And I'm looking forward to hearing other people's memories of some great times.

I know that much has been written about me and my life, and our kid Bobby, winning the World Cup in '66; Leeds United, Boro, Sheffield Wednesday, Newcastle United, then Ireland.

I've said all I need to say.

So we're happy to let people we've met along the way tell their stories. Because, it's about them as much as me.

THERE ARE simply too many people for me to thank. It would fill the entire book and I'd still forget someone and get into trouble.

So the best way to deal with that is to thank everyone who has played a part in my story, and this story.

So, to all the teammates who played alongside me, and all the lads who played for me, and all the staff and the helpers who worked alongside us, thank you.

And thanks too to all my family, and particularly my wife Pat who has been beside me every step of the way.

Hopefully you'll all enjoy reading this book as much as I've enjoyed living my life.

Jack
September 1, 2016

INTRODUCTION

By Colin Young

JACK CHARLTON is sitting in the back of his friend Bill Logan's four-wheel Truckman. He picks up another small trinket filled with fishing flies from his collection and opens the lid. He has packed 13 in three separate bags… 'and there's millions at 'ome', he says.

This hand-size box is silver and inscribed, "Jack, from the Legion Social Club, Cork, 1989". This one may contain the fly he knows he needs for this particular pond. If he has to look through them all, more than once or twice, he will.

He knows what he needs.

The fish are not biting like they did the last time they were here, and he is a little fed up, judging by his humorous and numerous expletives. He stares intently at the small feathery objects that are mainly yellow, orange, red and/or black. Nothing. He lets out a long breath, blinks hard a couple of times and huffs again.

'This is bloody hard work,' he says. 'The last time we came we caught five and we had to stop.'

The first couple of hours of this particular day's fishing in Northumberland have not been successful by any stretch, but certainly not by the standards set the last time they came to his friend's pond near Jack's home.

We'd set out from Matfen, 10 miles west of Newcastle, bought three steak and gravy pies at the WMH butchers in Haydon Bridge and headed to a stretch of the River Tyne nearby which Jack has fished on with friends for years. There has been rain overnight, which was encouraging news, as the Tyne has been too low for salmon movement, and fishing, for days. But the deluge in the early hours has brought 'silt and s****' and as soon as we turn the corner on to a bridge, Jack's face falls and he curses.

'Look at the bloody colour of it,' he says as the three of us take in the flowing, bubbly chocolate-coloured torrent below us.

'We won't be bloody fishing in that.'

Still, Bill does as he is instructed by his passenger and slowly guides his vehicle down a track towards a railway bridge, which is their usual starting point. A fortnight ago, you could count the rocks on the bank on the other side and walk across the river to them. Today the bank is covered by a surging, murky mess full of detritus and whole trees. There may be salmon in there too, but we won't be seeing any and they won't be seeing us.

We descend from the car and stand on the bank where Jack had hoped to fish; Bill standing to his left for balance, as he casts from the right. He stares at his beloved Tyne for some considerable time.

'I've never seen it like that,' he says, although that seems hard to believe. He points out the areas of the river that are usually perfect for salmon. To the left of a small island is an inlet that attracts the fish. Last time, they could walk to it; today Olympic kayakers would struggle to get there.

He has not caught one this year and that won't be changing today. He knows it but there's no rush and plenty to admire and aspire to, so we drive to three different locations along a half-mile stretch of river in this most stunning part of England, where Jack Charlton feels most at home. Given the ferocity of the water, and its deep, dark, depressing colour, it is no surprise that the original verdict on fishing here remains the same.

An hour later, the decision is made to head to the trout pond near Ryall. His friend has a lake there and he knows the place well as he has also been shooting in the woods regularly for the past decade. The salmon heading up to the Northumberland hills have had a lucky escape again today.

And then it is the turn of the trout to defy Jack Charlton.

And that's why we are back at the car boot, putting off the pie-eating while Jack finds the right fly and casting line. The yellow and black one he started with is placed back among his enormous collection when he clocks a small black and white fly on a single. It is smaller than the tip of the finger that has been missing from Jack's right hand for many years. With the dexterity and skill that he has had since then, Jack ties the fly to his line.

It is a fiddly, painstaking skill, particularly when he has to use his teeth rather than the scissors we all forgot to bring, but he still has it. Like his casting, and the release of his line on his long rod through his fingers and thumb, it comes naturally, as it always has.

He huffs a few times in frustration when he misses the small hole at the top of the fly, but that is a rare event. When that thinnest of lines pops through the hole, he gently wraps it four times back round the line and ties a minute knot.

He has his dropper. He repeats the exercise with a second, bushier, brighter fly and he is ready. We walk across to the new wooden gangplank; Bill at his side as ever, and he casts away to his heart's content. One flighty trout away to our right flips up a few times to break the silence and remind us he's here but we all know he is too far away. Jack wants to stay on the gangplank and he's rewarded within five minutes with a firm bite.

Bill goes to get the net from the boot, positioning me closer to the fly-fisherman among us. And then Jack is ready.

Now, excuse my ignorance here, but this is where you earn your fish. I'd always assumed you reeled the thing in as soon as you have hold of it and hauled it ashore in an instant. But there is a skill to landing a fish that doesn't want a hook in its mouth and would prefer to stay in the water.

Jack once had a beautiful salmon virtually in his grasp, on the section of river we've just left behind. It flipped away in the last seconds of his battle with Jack, missing the net Bill was holding. It is an incident his friend has never been allowed to forget.

For several seconds, Jack gives his slippery adversary the line to swim of its own accord, and then, while Bill hovers above the water, he gently guides it in, pulling and pushing it towards the net. But before it reaches the surface of the water, it squirms free and escapes. All three of us let out an instinctive… 'Oh… no'.

I was filming with my phone at this point, hoping to record Big Jack landing a Big Fish. When he stops, I stop, regrettably. Because that's when he says, quite calmly but quite loudly… 'Fooking hell'.

And then we all laughed.

It's not Bill's fault today, and certainly not Jack's. The jinx is 'the laird in the back', as Jack now calls me, but in my brief time in fishermen's company, I have found they like their excuses. There are several more attempts over the next half an hour, and one more bite resulting in the loss of two flies, which is not well received, before the final casts with a stronger line and the single flies. But there is nothing today.

I listen again to the tale of the five fish on this very pond, just a few weeks ago. At one point, Jack stares out in to the pond, casts again, and shakes his head. He spies me watching him, as I have all afternoon, and he looks at me.

And his face lights up with the most wonderful, beaming smile; his blue eyes sparkling beneath his spectacles and flat cap.

The pub at Stamfordham was shut, so Jack insisted on a John Smith's back at the house. After returning the rods, bags and boxes to the den, he shows me his greenhouse, constructed by Bill and some friends.

'Well…' he says. 'It's a wooden house with windows,' before opening the door to reveal six healthy, tall tomato plants with plenty of very green fruit.

'What else do you grow?' I ask.

'Whatever the wife tells me to grow,' he says, as he waters a solitary cucumber plant on the shelf. And outside to the left is the messy bit of the garden, as Pat calls it, where he has potatoes and onions flourishing in the sunlight. She looks after the rest of the couple of acres, while Jack tends to his pond.

It is immaculate. And the veg plot is a bit of a mess in comparison. Jack fetches the beers and we sit round the kitchen table with Pat and Bill, explaining to her the lack of fish for tea. It has not been a good day.

But it has been one of the best of my life.

I first met Jack when the North East Football Writers' Association honoured him at our annual dinner at the Ramside Hall Hotel in Durham. My colleague Ray Robertson, who had covered Jack's Middlesbrough years for the town's *Evening Gazette*, made the introduction for our John Fotheringham Award, which is always kept secret from the recipient.

Ray became good friends with Jack, as many journalists have over the years, and he made a very personal and heartfelt speech about the great man. He'd managed Boro players, many from the region, who had gone on to great things.

And he knew John well, as a hard-working, old school scribe who had brilliant contacts, like Jack. After we'd shown a short video of Jack's incredible career, including the actual footage of his infamous 'black book' interview for Tyne Tees Television, our Player of the Year, Niall Quinn then followed that with his own tribute to his former Ireland manager, delivered as only Niall can, before presenting our Guest of Honour with a silver bowl.

Jack, who had been enticed to the annual bash on the pretence of doing an after-dinner turn, proceeded to ignore the presentation and launch into his act. He was about halfway through it when he realised he still had the bowl in his right hand.

He looked at it, paused, held it up, and said... 'What was this for again?'

A few weeks later, we were on the same flight from Newcastle to Dublin and when he spotted me on landing he insisted I took a lift in his chauffeur-driven car to the centre. As we walked together through the airport, everyone seemed to part before us, everyone knew him, and he just cheerily waved and said hello and they waved and smiled back.

And he never stopped talking for the whole journey, pointing out landmarks from that memorable open top bus tour in 1990. He was still talking about having to warn those kids away from the wheels.

I missed out on Jack's years.

When I started covering the Republic of Ireland, Mick McCarthy was starting his second campaign. But that walk and car journey were at the start of my own wonderful adventure with Ireland. It didn't take me long to appreciate what Jack meant to the people of Ireland and why they mean so much to him.

When I met Mick to interview him for this book, I'd just started and made the mistake of bemoaning the task I'd taken on and the work involved.

'But it's an honour, right?' he questioned.

And as ever with Mick McCarthy, particularly on the subject of Jack Charlton, he was right. That day fishing with Jack and Bill was towards the end of writing this book and it was just a joy to spend time in their company, watching Jack enjoying himself. And that smile...

It has been an honour. It has been a laugh. And I hope the final result goes some way to offering a fitting tribute to a wonderful man.

Colin
September 1, 2016

PROLOGUE

JACK CHARLTON is playing noughts and crosses with his grandkids Dylan, John, Niamh and Roisin.

And he's cheating.

It is very difficult to cheat at noughts and crosses but Jack manages it. Or tries to. He cheats at everything because he still hates losing. The grandkids, the kids, his wife Pat, the players, the teammates, the friends. They all know it.

And his mother Cissie – shortened from Elizabeth – knew it pretty much from the day he was born. It will come as no surprise to all the above that Jack was regarded as 'a livewire' by Cissie from a very young age.

He was 'a buggah'.

Cissie Charlton wrote an autobiography. In it she said, 'From the time he could walk Jack was full of devilment. I would often say to myself, "God give me strength".'

Jack was just two, and dressed in only his nappy when he toddled out of the house and joined a passing funeral procession marching proudly behind the Salvation Army band.

As he got older, Jack had a host of money-schemes including a milk round, Sunday morning paper round which he organised like a military operation, deliveries for a local grocer, making pig swill for his father Bob and collecting used timber from the colliery where Bob worked, which he then chopped up and sold on. He was a runner for his grandfather Jack "Tanner" Milburn, one of the town's local bookies, and his sidekick Uncle Buck, Jack's favourite relative and a man who once got stuck in the toilet window of the local greyhound track when one of his schemes backfired.

In the spring Jack would pinch daffodils and sell them round the houses and he even once helped himself to a neighbour's allotment and attempted to sell the loot back to the same man. Fortunately the neighbour Mr Curtis and his wife had taken Jack under their wing, and forgave and laughed at the indiscretion.

When he wasn't trying to earn extra money, Jack was out in the fields or on the beach, in a river or fishing by a lake. There is no record of when, but it was probably not long after the funeral incident that the obsessions started. The outdoors, wildlife fascinated and engulfed him then, and still does to this day.

Jack could be gone for hours roaming the unspoilt countryside, firing his catapult, studying wildlife traps, ratting, poaching, fishing or just walking, lost in his own big world among the fields, woods and streams of Northumberland. One of his favourite places was a local swamp called Sandy Desert where he would attempt to catch rats. Then he got his first rod, a split-cane salmon rod he bought from his friend Ronnie Goldsworthy.

He cut the fifteen-foot rod down to size so he could use it for sea fishing off Newbiggin, another of his favourite haunts to this day. If Jack was gone all night fishing, Bob and Cissie were never concerned. His mother's only worry was that he was wrapped up sufficiently, and she would ensure he had three or four layers of jumpers, trousers and socks to keep him warm overnight.

HE WAS born into North East football royalty.

Four of Cissie's brothers, Jack, George, Jimmy and Stan, became professional footballers. Like Jack, Uncles George and Jimmy played for Leeds United.

One summer George came back from Yorkshire with a proper leather ball which was one of Ashington's most prized possessions, not just among the young Charlton boys. Normally the kids had to use tennis balls. When George and Stan joined Chesterfield Cissie would have no hesitation in putting the two oldest boys on a bus to Saltergate where George would meet them. One of Jack's fondest childhood memories is of playing football on the Chesterfield pitch in one of the drastically oversized first team strips, with George playing in goal.

Jack treasured his first pair of football boots for years.

They were purchased for Christmas just before the end of the Second World War, when he was seven. Cissie had seen an advert in the local paper and sent Jack round to the address with her savings of ten shillings, a substantial amount of money. Jack came away with a pair of shiny Mansfield Hotspurs, and two shillings in his pocket for Cissie after negotiating a better deal.

The real star of the family, and star of Ashington and the whole region, was Cissie's cousin Jackie Milburn. The Newcastle and England star, who remained in the area, scored twice in the 1950 FA Cup final and he followed that with two more cup winners' medals a year later and in 1955.

Cissie regularly took her boys to St James' Park. Bobby was still a baby in her arms when he made his first visit and occasionally they would meet up with Jackie Milburn, who would take them down the tunnel and they would stand behind the dug out during the game.

Cissie was, in her own words, 'a football addict' and she knew her football. Her husband Bob, on the other hand, had no interest in the game. Indeed he missed the 1966 World Cup semi-final between England and Portugal because he had a shift at the local pit. Cissie, who didn't miss a game as her sons went on to lift the Jules Rimet Trophy, did persuade him to attend the final. Bob, who was quite at home with the wives at the after-match celebrations, did not regret the trip.

When Cissie wanted to go to Leeds to watch her brothers Jack and George, Bob would look after the children, but never travelled with her. Jack's wife Pat and Cissie became regular travelling companions when Jack's career took off with Leeds and England. Bob was happier in his garden or at the allotment, and in his spare time he would take his faithful whippet Bonny out or pop down to the nearby working men's club for a pint.

His sporting passion was boxing. He sparred himself as a young man in boxing contests, earning the money to buy Cissie's wedding ring. Bob tried to get Jack into boxing, but his son didn't like the cliques at the boxing club and he discovered most of his peers didn't want to fight him because he was too big.

Jack did regularly spar for his school but, to his father's disappointment, could not muster the same enthusiasm for the sport. Nevertheless, Bob and Jack had a close bond thanks to their outdoor pursuits. When he reached his teens, Jack was allowed to use his father's gun and would head out shooting for ducks near Cresswell. The pair would walk for several miles up the Northumbria coast late at night and sit together in the sand dunes as the sun came up, attempting to shoot ducks for the kitchen table.

Bobby was much closer to Cissie, whereas Jack often said he spent his entire life seeking his mother's approval. 'I always knew I was not her favourite,' he admitted in a BBC radio interview in 1989.

BOBBY CHARLTON was born on October 10, 1937 nearly two years after Jack. On the day their brother Gordon was born, seven years later, Cissie sent Jack and Bobby out with half a crown to go to the cinema, and when the boys returned they had a brother. The baby of the family Tommy was born two years after that.

As they grew up Cissie would regularly ask Jack to take his younger brother out on his adventures. The pair both hated it. If they made it beyond the end of the street it was a miracle because Jack was notorious for clipping Bobby round the ear very early in their excursions, and his younger brother would head home in tears.

When he was 13, Jack discovered there was trout in the Wansbeck River at Bothal, near the family home. He would regularly head out and poach up to a dozen fish at a time, staying out of sight after dropping his line into the river. One day Bobby went out with him and almost caught a fish, only to lose the trout at the last moment.

Jack was not very happy.

And not just because Bobby had lost what was a large fish, but because his brother then made him re-cast the line with another worm because he couldn't stand worms.

Bobby did like the outdoors, but only to play football. He wanted to play football or read about it, poring over the football results and match reports in the evening paper and vowing, if he didn't make it as a footballer, that he was going to be a football journalist.

Cissie sent Bobby down to Chesterfield to spend time with her brothers during the school holidays. Jack was too busy in the countryside. If they were picking teams for one of their marathon matches down at Hirst Park, Bobby was always picked before his older brother; always. Bobby went on to play for East Northumberland, Northumberland and England schoolboys, often with Jack watching. Jack never represented any such teams as an adolescent, although interestingly, he did sign pro forms before Bobby. When the offer came from Leeds United after Jack had been spotted playing for Ashington YMCA however, Cissie was convinced they had the wrong son.

On one of the occasions Bobby did go to watch his older brother on the Ashington Colliery Welfare Ground, Jack made an error that cost his side the game. When he got home, Bobby pointed out how the 'stupid' mistake had marred his performance. He received a ferocious punch to the head for his insolence. Bob sorted Jack out after that.

It is a myth that Cissie trained and coached Bobby, or Jack for that matter. She would have had no qualms going for a kick-about but she left the real coaching to her father "Tanner". A ruthless trainer of local sprinters, and tough taskmaster, he worked on Bobby's natural pace but also talked endlessly about his grandson not wasting his talents. He made an enormous impact on the young boy, and when he died Bobby said he felt like he had lost his best friend.

The brothers would both save money from their paper round to go to St James' Park. But when he went to Leeds, Jack handed over control of his beloved enterprise to Bobby. On his first break from Elland Road, he returned to Ashington to discover Bobby had not only wrecked the bike Jack had given him, but had given up the paper round too.

Academically, they were different. Jack failed his Eleven-Plus exam, so went to Hirst Park Secondary Modern School. He was forever getting a clip round the ear from teachers for allowing his attention to wander, as he stared out of the windows.

Bobby passed his Eleven-Plus two years later, first earning a place at King Edward VI School in nearby Morpeth. When Bobby and Cissie discovered King Edward was a rugby school and didn't play football, they were mortified. With the support from Mr Hamilton, the head teacher at Hirst North School, Cissie wrote to the education authority, explaining her son had exceptional ability at football, and needed to go to Bedlington Grammar School instead. She won her case and Bobby went to Bedlington. Bobby, the model student, just got good grades.

And when his football stalled, because his studies were getting in the way, Cissie acted again. This time she employed the services of Jack's head teacher at Hirst Park, Mr Hemmingway. He arranged for his old friend Joe Armstrong, the local Manchester United scout, to take a look at the young Bobby Charlton in a game for East Northumberland Boys. After the game, Bobby was offered the chance to join Manchester United when he'd finished school.

Then, after starring for England schoolboys in a win over Wales at Wembley, Beatrice Street was besieged with scouts, some offering serious backhanders, and as much as £800 to sign Bobby. Several teams were dismissed, most notably on the Charlton's doorstep.

Bobby Charlton joined Manchester United for £10 in 1953, aged just fifteen. But even then, Bedlington headmaster Mr James was unimpressed that his schooling had not finished before he headed west. He was to attend Stretford Grammar School as a compromise before he was released from the constraints of the North East.

'I DON'T care how small a pay you bring home. After seeing what you have to go through to get it, I won't complain.'

That's what Cissie Charlton said to her husband after she had experienced a visit to Woodhorn Colliery with her friend May Hill. Today Woodhorn, which closed as a working pit in 1981, is a superb museum and memorial to the men who worked the seams, as well as the North East's once proud coal industry itself. It once held a 1966 exhibition, showing off Jack's medal and his Football Writers of the Year award which was presented a year later.

Bob Charlton worked as a coal cutter at Linton, three miles from Ashington. May Hill's husband Bob was an overman at Woodhorn and had invited the women to see where he worked. It was a rare visit, as some miners believed women underground brought bad luck. And, like virtually every colliery, Woodhorn had had its fair share of misfortune and disaster. Thirteen men lost their lives in an underground explosion on August 13, 1916.

The women, wearing pit helmets to protect them from timbers and low roofing, were taken 800 feet down to the shaft bottom in the steel cage. The sheer force of the blast of air that greeted them stunned Cissie, who was terrified and hated every second of the experience.

They walked for miles through the gloomy, uneven galleries, spooked by the mice, which Cissie hated, and the shadows and echoes. They had to negotiate the low galleries, cracking their heads and backs against the roof. Cissie would clean and bathe her husband's scrapes and scabs with extra care after her visit. A pony, attracted by the visitors' lights, latched onto the group until they reached the coalface.

And there Cissie saw a miner, stripped to the waist, his bait hanging in mid-air in a tin away from the rodents. She recognised the equipment and the work he was doing. It was exactly the same back-breaking work, after the walk through those dark and dusty tunnels, that her husband did every day on an identical black wall of coal.

They returned to the surface, grimy and blinking at the strength of the daylight. Desperate to get rid of the coal dust that clung to the top of their mouths, the women were delighted to be offered a cup of tea and supper in the colliery canteen.

When Cissie asked where the canteen was, their guide said, 'Through that door there, hinny'. Of course the door didn't lead to the canteen at all. They walked straight into the pit baths, which was full of cheering, naked miners.

AT THE age of 15, Jack started work at Linton Colliery, where dad Bob worked, having turned down the opportunity to go to Leeds United to join the ground staff. Deep down he didn't think he was good enough to make it as a footballer, and neither did Cissie, and he had always assumed he would follow his dad down the pit.

He took the 'tankie', the special train from town to Linton, and for the first few weeks he was on the 'screening' part of the operation.

This was where the beginners, the old and injured miners worked. Their task was to sift through coal on the surface as it came along the conveyor belts, and sort and throw out the stones and debris. It was long, boring work and Jack asked to be moved on.

He was transferred to the weigh-cabin where the wagons of coal were weighed and registered. Jack enjoyed working there, setting up traps for rabbits during his shifts to sell to the miners and he became adept at etching wildlife on the larger stones.

But the idyllic work-life was interrupted when he was selected to go on a sixteen-week training course to become a fully-fledged miner. He didn't get past the induction.

He felt exactly the same as Cissie when he took that first horrible journey into the depths of the Northumbrian earth. Jack was appalled by the experience.

'I watched them bore a hole into the coal and place explosives there. When the moment came to blow out the coal, everybody had to get back thirty yards. Then came the shout, "Hands over ears".

'I've never, ever experienced anything like it. There we were, crouched on our hands and knees four hundred feet underground, and then suddenly this vast sound nearly takes our heads off. And then the dust! You couldn't see your hand for the dust – it's in the air, it's in your eyes, it's in your lungs. I don't mind saying that my first inclination was to bolt for the lift to get to the surface.

'Later, they showed me a draughty, dimly lit place where two haulage ways met. Here the coal tubs coming from different directions were sent to the shaft head – they called it "hanging on and knocking off". And I said to the miner who was showing me the place, "Am I to be here eight hours a day?"

'He said, "Yeah".

'Five and a half days a week?'

'And he went, "Yeah".

'And I said, "Nah – I'm not going to do it". I went and put my notice in and I left.'

Jack was told he would never work in the mine again by the colliery manager, but he wasn't bothered. Whatever happened, Jack Charlton would never be a miner.

When he told Cissie, she said, 'If that's what you want to do Jack, you do it'.

Bob was disappointed, but he understood.

ON FEBRUARY 6, 1958 chartered British European Airways flight 609 carrying the Manchester United team crashed on its third attempt to take off in a blizzard at Munich-Riem airport. There were eventually 23 fatalities, including eight of the team and eight sports writers.

Miraculously, some of the 44 passengers survived after being thrown from the plane, including Bobby Charlton and manager Matt Busby. Still strapped to his seat, Bobby's only visible injury was a gash to his head.

As news filtered through from Germany, Cissie was naturally fraught with worry. At first radio and television reports said there were no survivors. Then local newsagent and friend Ted Cockburn got news and before putting the *Evening Chronicle* placards in front of the shop, he turned up in the yard at the house. Bobby was alive.

Jack and Pat headed straight to Ashington, as Cissie knew they would. They had received the same news on arriving in Newcastle. Although he was not given permission for leave by Leeds United, as soon as he heard the news in the dressing room he had picked up Pat and got the first train home. Before they got the connecting bus to Ashington from Haymarket Station, Jack saw a late edition of the *Chronicle* confirming Bobby was among the survivors. The couple did a little jig of celebration at the bus station.

Before Jack arrived at Beatrice Street, local policeman Bob Turbill turned up with a telex from the Foreign Office.

'Alive and well, see you later.' It was signed 'Bobby'.

Cissie was forbidden by her doctor to travel to see Bobby recovering in hospital because she was just getting over a mastectomy. So she missed the chartered flight with the other relatives but a few days later she hitched a lift on a newspaper delivery van to Manchester to get through the snow. She helped stand-in manager Jimmy Murphy out at Old Trafford as he attempted to keep the club, and the team, running.

The bodies of the victims were kept in the club gym, and it was Cissie who was on hand to show the relatives the caskets. She attended the funerals of David Pegg and Eddie Colman on Bobby's behalf. Two months earlier, the excited young pair were among a group of Manchester United teammates who had stayed over, with Bobby, at Cissie's and Bob's on the way back from a game in Scotland when the team bus had broken down.

When Bobby was eventually well enough to return home he arrived at Liverpool Street Station in London with Cissie and Jack waiting. They gave pressmen the slip and headed to Jack and Pat's house in Leeds. After an overnight stay, Bobby moved back to Ashington where he recuperated for several weeks. Cissie and Jack said he talked about the crash only once.

While Bobby was there, and twenty days after the tragedy, Duncan Edwards died. It was a massive blow and Cissie had tried to keep the news from him.

The recovery was slow, painful and difficult. Pressmen persisted in trying to talk to him, but he refused until one day Cissie reminded him he too had wanted to be a reporter, and it could have been him stood on the doorstep. When he'd done his first interview, complete with a photo of him kicking a ball, Bobby said he was giving the game up.

But with gentle persuasion from Cissie, a couple of chiding letters from Jimmy Murphy, and the help of family doctor Dr McPherson, Bobby was soon on the train back to Manchester and reviving that great career of his. Incredibly, three months after the Munich Air Disaster, Bobby Charlton and Manchester United won the FA Cup.

As for Jack, he reckoned Bobby was never the same. 'He stopped smiling,' he said, 'a trait which continues to this day. Friends occasionally come up to me and say, "Your Bob goes around as if he has the weight of the world on his shoulders" – and I have to agree. He had had a great playing career, a good life and his business is doing well. I would say that he doesn't smile as much as somebody in his position should'.

THERE ARE much more esteemed writers than this author who have tried to analyse the alleged 'fallout' between Jack and Sir Bobby Charlton

For the record, there is no rift. And there was never really a 'conflict'. They just fell out like two silly old stubborn Milburn 'buggahs'.

They talk now and they do meet up, although usually at funerals. Then there's the 1966 get-togethers, of which there were numerous in the 50th anniversary year in 2016. But even the annual golf match is proving difficult for the older members of the squad now. Once the players used to take it in turns to host the event at their local golf club; nowadays only a handful can complete a round.

Jack and Bobby Charlton achieved football's ultimate prize together. They knew their lives would change forever the moment Bobby said to Jack… 'What about that kidda?' on the Wembley turf. 'Nobody can ever take this moment away from us.'

And there's the rub for Jack and 'Our Kid' as he will forever call him. Everyone expects them to share that glorious moment forever.

They are different and always have been. Jack is the extrovert who shoots from the hip and the lip, and is less concerned by any collateral damage. Bobby has always been more introverted.

They had different interests as youngsters and they have different interests and pleasures, more importantly, now. They don't mix in the same circles, never have, and a foursome with Jack, Pat, Bobby and Norma in the 113 years of marriage between them, is a rare event indeed.

Jack and Bobby remained close in their early playing years. Cissie would remind Jack to 'go easy on our Bobby' although he never had to 'man-mark' him. When they were married, they drifted apart. And while Pat and Cissie became regular travelling partners and avid followers of Jack on his travels, Norma and Cissie were never as close. As Bobby said, 'I never questioned any of this even when I felt myself obliged to defend the feelings and status of a wife whom I loved dearly and who would always do so much to enhance my life'.

Alike in so many ways, and almost telepathic, Jack and Cissie had a close bond. They laughed and joked, sparred and quarrelled and Jack would despair of his mother and her wicked sense of humour, in much the same way his family treat him now.

He bought his parents a house with his £1,000 World Cup winnings – and called it Jules Rimet. It was a step up from the house in Beatrice Street where Jack and Bobby had shared a bed and outside toilet but Cissie preferred the simplicity of her original home. He then moved his parents into the farmhouse in the Yorkshire Dales before Bob's death in 1982. Cissie moved back to Ashington and, at first, she lived close to the former family home in Beatrice Street, but after a number of falls, she reluctantly agreed to be moved to a home in Newbiggin up the Northumberland coast.

Jack, Pat and the grandkids, as well as numerous friends, were always on hand to keep her entertained and take her for days out.

Bobby, and Norma, stayed away. Even when he once held a coaching school just 250 yards from Cissie's flat, Bobby didn't visit. He opened a local supermarket; nothing. Jack called Bobby and told him to go and see her.

When he met ex-teammates, he'd often say, 'If you see Our Kid, tell him to go see Our Mother'. Although Jack always took the view that Bobby was missing out more than Cissie, it hurt him. And Cissie.

He was very happy that Bobby was at Cissie's funeral to carry the coffin. She died at the age of 84 in 1996, just four months after Jack quit the Ireland job.

It would be several years before the two brothers forgave each other and started talking. It is not a date that is recorded, because it was really no big deal. It just happened.

It does in families.

But not many brothers have won the World Cup together.

In his latest book, Bobby says, 'In our different ways, we offer thanks that the divisions which once spilled into the open, and made us appear in the eyes of the world brothers at war rather than the ones who embraced so warmly on the most wonderful sporting day of our lives, have softened down through the passing years. And to the stage where we know that, in the end, we have more to celebrate in each other than set us apart.

'There were, to be honest, some points in our lives when such a perspective seemed remote, if not impossible. So often it could be said that we may have been united by our blood but not our natures. This may have been exaggerated to some degree, as is the case so often in lives which are at least to some extent under the gaze of the public, but then again it would be wrong to minimise the differences between us.'

The esteemed sports writer James Lawton and Bobby Charlton wrote that in 2016 and no one I've spoken to disagrees.

ONE OF the Charlton brothers still plays football.

Tommy Charlton is 70. Every week, he goes down to Eastwood Trading Estate in Rotherham and plays for 90 minutes with his mates. Walking football. Tommy commands centre defence, just like Jack in his heyday.

'I let the young 'uns go up-field,' he says.'We play on an artificial pitch which came from Chelsea, so I tell people I play on the same pitch as Drogba.' Tommy was the youngest brother, and like Jack, more interested in using the outdoors for more than just football as a kid. He did play the game to a decent non-league standard, but knew he would never match his famous older brothers.

'As a young fella, to be honest, it was easier not to compete because everybody expected me to play like Bobby and Jack but I couldn't do that. I loved playing, and I still do; I have never felt fitter and I absolutely love the walking football, and I would go anywhere to play it, if anybody offered me the chance.

'But nobody ever showed me how to play. And I certainly didn't have Tanner Milburn telling me how to work on natural speed, like he did with our Bobby.

'I had to live with physical and verbal abuse because of my famous brothers. When I was at college, one guy just came up and hit me in the face; he never did tell me why. But there's a lot of people who are stupid and jealous.'

Tommy remembers his grandfather "Tanner" Milburn well, and the regular visits of Uncle Stan, one of four Milburn boys who played professionally.

'Footballers were not paid during the close season in those days, so Stan used to stay at our house with his whole clan. I remember sitting at the table one day and saying, "Uncle Stan, how come you have no neck?" and he said, "Heeding the ball lad, heeding the ball".

'Stan was a very good sprinter and, this is a sad story, but he was asked to run in a race by "Tanner", who was a bookie and knew a good sprinter when he saw one. And "Tanner" put lead weight in his shoes. Stan lost and my grandad cleaned up. He vowed never to run again.'

Unlike Jack, Tommy was destined to follow Bob down the pits and became a renowned mining rescue expert in the South Yorkshire coalfield before his retirement. Tommy still lives and plays football near Rotherham, and is married to Carol, with son Andrew and daughter Lisa, who is a nurse at the Royal Hallamshire Hospital in Sheffield. 'I did an apprenticeship at the pit as a mechanic and had lots of jobs before ending up in mines rescue as assistant superintendent, running my own station, at Denby Grange.

'Jack was never going to be a miner in the long run. The opportunity to play football and work in the pit didn't come into it then. It was one or the other. If you saw the jobs Jack had to do, you knew it wasn't going to last long.

'One was sticking pieces of paper on the side of wagons. Now that was not

Jack. He was never going to make a career out of that. He didn't like it, so he walked away from it. He was destined to be a footballer and a football manager.

'I used to love going to Ireland with him. Irish people and people from the North East are very similar people. And you cannot help but warm to Jack. The Irish people loved him and he was always the same.

'But what helped was being successful. His knowledge of football was unquestionable, so there was a good start, and he's a big fella who creates a good atmosphere around him and who knows everything about football, or so he believes. If you are a footballer, you're not going to argue with him. He could work out the charlatans and the pretenders. If anybody was going to succeed with Ireland, it was Jack.'

DAVIDSON'S BAKERY, Darras Hall, near Newcastle-upon-Tyne and owner Trevor Davidson is waiting for royalty. North East and Irish football royalty.

He's known as Big Jack round these parts but Jack Charlton OBE – 'Other Buggers' Efforts' he's always called it – is on his way to deliver some tea.

There's no red carpet in the bakery of course. But the silver spoons are out, a pot of Northumberland Tea is brewing and there's a plate of delicious shop-made chocolate cookies on a table in front of a display of tea depicting the beaming Guest of Honour.

Northumberland Tea – or Jack's Tea as it is increasingly becoming known – is the brainchild of Bill and Helen Logan who launched the company three years ago to help raise funds for the Sir Bobby Robson Foundation.

The former Newcastle manager, who was Jack's close friend, launched his foundation in 2008 to fund cancer research and trials at the city's Freeman Hospital and set out with a £500,000 target. It has now surpassed £10 million.

When the Logans approached their friend and Bill's long-time fishing companion to be the poster boy for their "Best Cup Since 1966" campaign, Jack was only too happy to oblige. His only condition was for Bill to accompany him on trips to the lakes and rivers around Northumberland for fishing.

The pair travel together to the Jack Charlton Disabled Anglers Association fishing days and Jack still helps out with anglers of all ages on their fishing days throughout the UK and Ireland. Jack also insists on being a passenger whenever Bill makes his deliveries to the shops and bakeries near the Charlton family home and son John's pub on the coast near Blyth.

'The customers love seeing him,' says Bill. 'He goes into the shops and meets the staff, sits himself down, gets a cup of tea. And I have never seen him refuse anything in pastry or batter.

'He does his bit and carries the tea in, signs the boxes for customers and I think he likes seeing himself on the posters on the wall. And then as long as we get our fish and chips on the way home, he's had a great day out. He's always on at me to take him.'

Helen adds, 'To us he's just Jack... but the effect he can have on people is amazing. The kids absolutely love him and he always has the most time for them. They have absolutely no idea who he is, but I've seen their fathers or grandfathers weeping behind him, just thrilled that they're talking to Jack.'

When he arrives for the pending photo-shoot with wife Pat, Bill and Helen, he is looking fit and dapper in flat cap, scarf and a blue and red tie, not dissimilar to the one he wore at his feisty first press conference as Ireland manager more than 30 years ago. He's ushered to his table where the pot of tea awaits.

He's soon into the cookies.

He quizzes Bill about his latest fishing trip.

Bill then reveals, to Jack's great amusement, that the pair have devised a cunning two-man hugging stance to adapt to the river fishing, which seems to involve a lot of work for Bill's arms, to prevent Jack falling in the river. Jack's daughter Debbie has bought him a seat for the lake fishing and they are due to go out as soon as the season starts shortly. Jack's legs may no longer cope with fly-fishing's endurance tests but the dexterity to prepare his casts remains.

'It is quite simply unbelievable,' says Bill. 'The way he ties the fly is so fast and soft at the same time. I still don't know how he does it so quickly.'

The man himself is in great form despite a fall the previous night. Nothing broken this time but it's another reminder that the 80 year-old is not as steady on his feet as he used to be. Nothing wrong with his mind, though.

'Right. What we doing?' asks Jack, to anyone who'll listen. With that, the photographer arrives and duly keeps Jack in situ, takes a few photos of Jack in front of photos of Jack before taking him outside for some more.

Several minutes of chaos ensue when Pat leaves proceedings to buy a sympathy card for the family of one of Jack's former Friday night drinking pals.

It all goes slightly awry when Jack heads behind the counter for one final picture with the staff. His attention is inevitably drawn to the vast array of sausage rolls, pies and cakes within his eye-line and the queue of customers is out of the door by the time he is satisfied he has thoroughly inspected the bakery's entire range and can pose for the staff pictures.

Eventually he returns for a second cuppa and cookie, a chance to reminisce on those incredible 10 years at the helm of Irish soccer.

'We did well. We were a good little team, you know. We qualified for the European Championships in 1998 and two World Cups and we beat some good teams. People didn't like to play against us.

'We didn't win anything but that wasn't necessary.

'We had some fun along the way.'

It started in Euro 88 and Stuttgart where Ireland beat Bobby Robson's England. They met again in Cagliari when Kevin Sheedy struck to cancel out Gary Lineker's early bobbly opener. The pair, who first met on a coaching course at Lilleshall, remained close friends and Charlton frequently visited Robson while he was working as a consultant to Republic of Ireland manager Steve Staunton.

'He was under a lot of pressure when we played in Italia 90. The stick he got from the English press was terrible.

'But he's the most successful England manager since Sir Alf and he got the England team to the semi-finals... just those penalties... and the Germans.

'Bob was a great friend of mine and I did some work with him when he was manager at Newcastle and working with Ireland. He and Lady Elsie had a place near us and we spent a lot of time together and we discussed how I could do some work with him for the foundation. Unfortunately Bob died.

'Helen lost both her parents very quickly one after the other and they want to put something back to the foundation and the Freeman. And for me it's a lovely way to keep in touch with people, and go out and see them and have a nice cup of tea.'

When I mention I was in Rome for the quarter-final defeat to the hosts and had waited behind the goal for the lap of honour, Tricolour in one hand, tinny in the other, the smile which Ireland fans remember fondly returns.

'Were you in Rome?' he says. 'Good laird.'

Pat is close by to prompt and the pair recall that memorable meeting with Pope John Paul II. Pronounced 'Po-Ep'.

'Mick Byrne kept asking me, "If we get to Rome will you take us to see the Po-Ep?" so of course I just said yes to shut him up. What I didn't realise was that the quarter-final was going to be played in Rome. And of course as soon as we beat Romania, Mick's in my ear, telling me we're going to see the Po-Ep.

'Monsignor Liam Boyle, he sorted it with Bishop Tony Farquahar. I don't know how they pulled it off but Mick was delighted and of course all the lads were too.'

Jack met the Pontiff during the photo-call.

'I know who you are… you're The Boss,' His Holiness is said to have said to the Ireland boss.

'All true,' Jack says.

Pat recalls watching horrified as her husband struggled to keep his eyes open throughout the two and a half hour Mass. Having dozed off at one point, he awoke convinced the 'Po-Ep' was waving at him. Jack half stood up and waved back.

'I didn't really understand what was going on but it went on for a long time,' he says. 'But aye… I thought he was waving at me.'

Pat giggles at the memory.

'That definitely happened… I saw that.'

'Hee… hee,' says Jack.

'Always in the background.'

EMMA WILKINSON

Over the years my grandad has met, worked with, and befriended a remarkable number of people. I never cease to be amazed by the volume of Christmas cards that adorn the walls and windowsills of my grandparents' house each year. Many of the senders will appear in this book. Many will share memories of their friend 'Big Jack' – a tough-tackling footballer, a straight-talking manager, a practical joker and a thoroughly honest man.

He is all of these things and more. At his core, he is a proud, protective, generous and deeply loving family man.

Decades ago, grandad bought a rural farmhouse in the Yorkshire Dales for his parents to live in. His dad had spent many years working down the coalmines of the North East. The clean air, beautiful scenery and peaceful silence of this new home would be a dream place for them to spend their later years. And they loved it there.

In the years since, 'the farm' has continued to be a place filled with happy memories for our family. My mum Debbie, and uncles John and Peter spent many long weekends playing in the open fields and empty barns as children – although not always as harmoniously as my grandparents would've liked. Winding each other up is a long-held family tradition that endures to this day.

The next generation – my siblings, Christopher, Kate and Tom and my cousins John, Niamh, Roisin and Dylan have also whiled away hours in tree houses and on rope swings there. I have particularly fond memories of grandad's unconventional fishing lessons. He was less than impressed at the number of times I managed to cast the line into the tree behind me and my refusal to pick up the fish I did eventually manage to catch. I felt I experienced something akin to the dressing-down he reserved for his players after a miserable first-half showing. But with some 'gentle' encouragement on his part, and a measure of queasiness on mine, ten year-old me triumphantly trudged back to the car with my fingers through the gills of a sizeable rainbow trout. The image of us in matching green overalls, fishing rods in hand, is one I still hold dear.

The farm is a special place for us.

So it was particularly special for my grandad to see the isolated farmhouse he bought so many years ago play host to a family wedding. When my now-husband and I discussed possible places to get married, there seemed no better venue. It's a place that had made an impression on him too.

When the day came in August, 2015 my grandparents looked on from the front row with pride. The spotty teenager I'd introduced to them with some trepidation ten years previously had stuck around! The initial relentless and unforgiving mickey-taking from my grandad and uncles – that was a staple of any family get together – thankfully didn't scare him off. He gave as good as he got in these early exchanges and from there on grandad has always enjoyed his company and made him feel not just welcome, but part of the family.

Grandad is never one to admit to getting emotional, but I'm sure I saw the quiver of a lip and a tear in the eye that day. Not that he would ever admit that.

The few times he's been snapped looking slightly emotional, such as carrying the 2012 Olympic torch through Newcastle, or walking onto the pitch at the Ireland v England friendly in the Aviva Stadium in 2015, he's been adamant that it was the 'wind in his eyes'. One thing he can't deny though, is that he certainly made the most of having everyone together at the farm.

After a few wines and whiskeys, he danced the night away with a big smile on his face – even more wobbly than normal but still able to pull out some of the old moves. I'm told when he was finally helped into bed – a bit worse for wear – he was still chuckling away.

In many ways, grandad has led a very atypical life. But to us he has only ever been grandad. A man who mastered international football management, but still can't operate the television remote. A man who has been lucky enough to be exposed to the finer things in life but still can't accept that a battered haddock and bag of chips is going to set him back more than £2.50.

And a man who will hold his grandchildren back from the road before they have looked both ways, whether they are four or twenty-four.

Fame has not changed him and is a concept that he still finds endearingly novel. Nothing is ever too much to ask and whether he is sent something to sign in the post, or someone wants to reminisce with him in a restaurant or pub about Leeds, Ireland, the World Cup or anything else for that matter, he is always obliging. He feels fortunate to be in the position that he is, and he is hyper-aware of the future down the pit that may have awaited him had circumstances been different.

Much has been written about the role my great-grandma Cissie played in altering this path but she is not the only woman to have played a pivotal role in his life. He owes a great deal to my grandma Pat, who with love and a dash of exasperation has supported him unconditionally for more than 50 years.

So, before you go on to read a variety of anecdotes and interesting insights into my grandad as a friend, colleague, sports personality, and much more besides, I am pleased to have described him to you as the kind, humble and loving husband, father and grandfather that I, and the family, know him to be.

JACK AND PAT Charlton were only the seventh and eighth people to be presented with honorary Irish passports.

Irish President Mary Robinson presented them to the pair at Áras an Uachtaráin.

'Every country needs inspiration and leadership, heroes and heroines,' President Robinson told them, '… and you, in your time, provided it.'

Jack and Pat then travelled to a reception hosted by Tanaiste, Dick Spring at Iveagh House, where the official presentation of the documents was made.

The couple received their Irish passports on Sunday, December 8, 1996 less than a year after his resignation as Ireland team manager. 'This is one of the best days of my life, maybe even the best,' Jack declared. 'I am conscious of the honour which has been conferred on Pat and myself, and we both feel privileged and proud.'

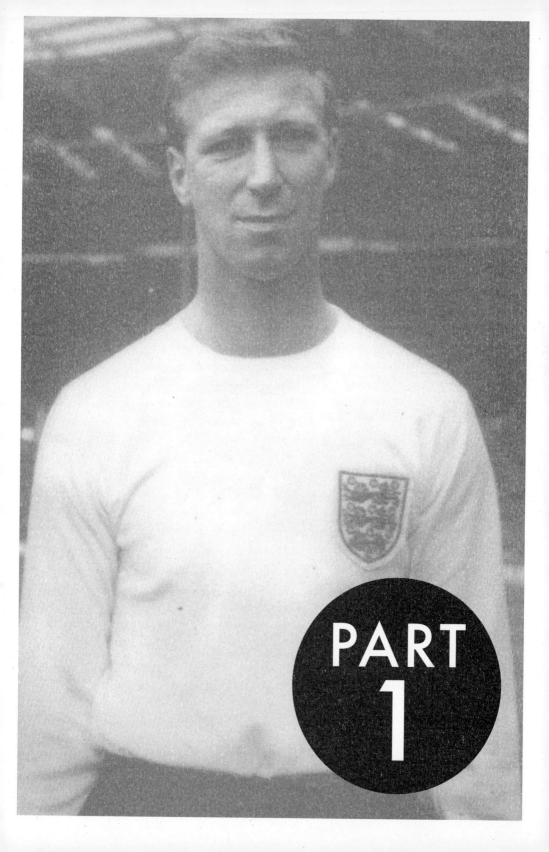

PART
1

LEEDS UNITED

JACK CHARLTON could have been a policeman rather than Leeds United's appearance record holder. On the same weekend he had to travel to Elland Road for a trial with Leeds, Jack also had an interview in Morpeth with the Northumbria Police Board.

After turning his back on the pit to avoid a lifetime of bending over underground, he felt his height made him perfect for the police force and at the age of 15 he applied to become a police cadet. His interview was on the Friday.

As a young lad Jack never really thought he would make it as a footballer. He lacked his brother Bobby's natural skill and finesse. He loved the game, but he had other interests in his outdoor pursuits. Unlike his sibling, he had never really pursued any ambition to become a professional footballer.

It was always in his mind to follow his dad down the mines and signing up for his apprenticeship at Ashington colliery. In truth, he was scared of failure, and of returning to the town in disgrace and embarrassment. He really didn't think he was good enough which was why he'd applied to join the police force, but didn't turn up for his interview. Jack's uncles Jack and Jimmy were on the Leeds playing staff, and had tipped off their local scout. He had seen him play and persisted with his interest. He liked the rugged, no-nonsense defender in him, and he could see Jack could play a bit. Jack was asked to report for a trial match in Leeds against Newcastle's youth team on the Saturday.

The train was the only travel option for the Charlton family in those days, so he could not do both. With Cissie's full blessing, he decided to go to Leeds. Using some money from her emergency fund, she bought him a Burberry overcoat and blue pinstripe suit, Jack's first pair of long trousers. She wanted him to look his best and gave him three pounds spending money as well.

After the game, one of the coaches told Jack he had done enough to join the ground staff. He was to report for work at Elland Road on Monday morning when he would meet the manager, Major Frank Buckley for the first time.

MAJOR BUCKLEY was an uncompromising, no-nonsense manager who had played for England and managed Wolves just before the Second World War. He had earned his rank fighting in both the Boer War and the First World War. Although his controlling powers were starting to wane when Jack joined Leeds United in 1950, he was still an imposing figure. He would sit in the old stand at Elland Road during training, shouting instructions to his players via a megaphone. Eventually the nearby residents complained about Buckley's foul-mouthed outbursts and the club had to confiscate the megaphone.

The Major did have a softer side, and when he saw his new recruit walking into Elland Road one morning with a scuffed pair of shoes he took pity on him and bought Jack a second pair the following morning. The shoes lasted for several years. But Jack also had an early run-in with the Major.

When Buckley saw Jack and a youth teammate removing weeds from the Elland Road pitch and replacing them with grass seed, he walked up to them and offered them five shillings for every bucket they filled with weeds. Task completed, Jack walked straight up to the Major's office. He had filled six buckets and wanted his 30 shillings. He was sent packing with nothing more than an earful for his sheer impertinence. Such menial tasks were commonplace. The apprentices were expected to sweep the terraces, paint and oil the turnstiles, scrub and polish the pros' boots, clean out the toilets and keep all the balls pumped up.

Despite having relatives at the club, Jack lived in a boarding house near Elland Road, which was run by Mary Crowther and her spinster daughter Laura. Although later in life he was to enjoy nothing more than a pint and a cigarette in the local, in those early days he shunned the bright lights of Leeds. During his first two years as an apprentice he went into the city centre just twice, preferring to socialise with a small circle of friends in Beeston. He sent £1 of his weekly £4.10 shillings wage home to Cissie and Bob. He lived with Mrs Crowther for seven years and concentrated on becoming a professional footballer, driven by that fear of failure.

'There was shame for the lads who were rejected,' he revealed in his autobiography *Jack Charlton*, co-written by Peter Byrne and published by Corgi in 1996. 'That was the fear that drove me during my first two years at Leeds. I did not regard myself as anything special when it came to playing football, otherwise I would have jumped at the first offer from Leeds and never gone near the mines.

'But now I had been given a second chance I was determined that, come hell or high water, I'd take it.'

HE KNUCKLED down to life as a member of the ground staff at Leeds. He trained five days a week and played for the youth and third teams; sometimes for both on the same day. Jack always said playing for the thirds, who competed in the Yorkshire League, was the making of him. 'I was just 16, playing against hard, fully mature men, big strong buggers who clattered into you with no quarter asked or given.'

In his second year, with Major Buckley retired and Raich Carter now in charge, he was promoted to the reserve team and impressed when marking the legendary John Charles in a practice game. By the time of this 17th birthday, deadline day according to FA rules, Carter had still not announced his decision on Jack's future and whether he would be taken on as a professional.

So Jack walked into the office of Leeds United secretary Arthur Crowther on May 8, 1952. He demanded to know whether he was to be signed, or should he make plans to return to Ashington?

Crowther, unfortunately, had no idea. Carter was away with the first team in Holland and had left no instructions. After a sleepless night, Jack returned to Elland Road the following morning and went straight to see Crowther again. Carter, in the meantime, had told the club secretary to offer Jack professional terms. He received a £10 signing on fee and £14 a week, the maximum wage, and more than three times what he'd been earning as a trainee. He was the highest paid of all the young pros at Leeds United. If there was any uncertainty that he had a future in the game, he received reassurance in the unlikely guise of Jim Johnson, the newsagent opposite the ground, when he called in for his *Daily Mirror*.

Jack told him he had just signed pro forms.

'Thank God for that!' Jim exclaimed. 'I've had half the scouts in the Football League in here this morning... wanting to know what you were doing? There must have been a dozen of the buggers, all wanting a word.' In that moment, for the very first time in his 17 years, Jack realised that he might have a real future in the game. 'Within hours, I was on a train back to Ashington, to give the good news to my mother and father.'

He made his first team debut for Leeds United on April 25, 1953.

He had received no indication from Raich Carter that he would be selected. The first he knew of his elevation was when he made the weekly check on the team sheets pinned up on the back of the first team dressing room door after Friday training. Jack was not on the list for the reserves or thirds, as was usually the case.

He was down to play for the first team at Doncaster Rovers, the first of 629 appearances for Leeds United.

THAT DAY and indeed in the build up to the game Carter barely spoke to him, and his teammates were the same. One of the few who did, experienced first-teamer Eric Kerfoot put him at ease and told Jack he had to be good enough, otherwise he would not have been selected. His task was to mark Eddie McMorran, a big uncompromising Irish striker. McMorran went easy on the new kid and Carter and the local papers felt that Jack had not let Leeds down in a 1-1 draw. But soon afterwards his football career was to be put on hold because his country needed him.

Jack was called up for two years National Service.

He spent his time in the army, in Windsor. 'The Duke of Edinburgh came in one day when I was on guard,' he told the BBC's *Alfie's Boys* that detailed England winning the World Cup in 1966. 'I was standing next to the gate as I had to let people go through. He was walking up towards the gate and I pointed my gun.

'"Halt! Who goes there?" I shouted.

'"The King!" he says.

'And I said, "Pass. All is well."'

He made an inauspicious start to army life, and that was thanks to football. After a 16-weeks training programme in Carlisle, followed by seven days' leave in Ashington, he had travelled to Windsor to join his regiment, the Royal Horse Guards. But when he arrived for his first tour of duty, he was put in solitary confinement immediately for most of the day as punishment for going absent without leave. He was supposed to have reported to Catterick first to play football for Northern Command but had not received the message.

But once he settled into life in the military, Jack loved it. He has often said that his two years of National Service were among the happiest days of his life. It was certainly the first indication that he had the capabilities and ambitions to be a football manager. He was made captain of the army football team, the first private to be given the honour, and throughout his two-year stint he organised training and matches for the team. He also looked after his teammates, making sure they were given 'cushy jobs', late breakfasts and days off that coincided with training or games.

The Royal Horse Guards were not required for foreign tours of duty, so Jack's only overseas trips were to play football. They travelled to Germany and won the Cavalry Cup in Hanover. It was the military equivalent of winning the FA Cup and hundreds of soldiers travelled from England to watch the final.

Jack devised a system to use his 48-hour leaves to return to Leeds occasionally and play for the club's reserves. He even managed a first team appearance against Lincoln City in his second year of service. As much as he was frustrated that his time in the army hindered his football development and career, it had a profound and galvanizing effect on him.

Mindful perhaps that he would have to concentrate on his playing career on his return to Yorkshire, Jack took full advantage of the social options in London and Windsor, frequenting dances and the local boozers. He also started to smoke for the first time, and was a regular smoker for most of his life thereafter.

When his two years were up, Jack was ready to return and stake his claim at Leeds United. While others might have been happy to be in contention for reserve team football, Jack set off from Windsor with a first team place in his sights.

But he was immediately frustrated by the lack of coaching under Raich Carter and was not afraid to say so. He quickly fell out with his manager and his teammates.

'Maybe I was a bit too full of myself,' he wrote in his autobiography. 'I remember one run-in I had with John Charles, of all people, when he came back for a corner against us and started telling me where to go, sort of saying, "You go over there and I'll go here". I soon told him where to go, in the way that he couldn't have misunderstood.

'After the game he put me up against the wall and pointed a finger at me.

'"Don't ever speak to me like that again!" he said.

'I took his advice to heart.

'John was a team unto himself. People often say to me, "Who was the best player you ever saw in your life?" and I answer, probably Eusebio, Di Stefano, Cruyff, Pele or our Bob… but the most effective player I ever saw, the one who made the most difference to the performance of the whole team was, without question, John Charles.'

Charles was the complete footballer in Jack's eyes, and he marvelled at how he could defend, compete in midfield with everyone, and prove so formidable up front. Charles also had pace, and that also impressed Jack who was no Olympic sprinter himself and relied on that long stride to beat his man to a ball.

John Charles was also the greatest header of the ball Jack ever saw.

'His power in the air was phenomenal,' Jack recalled in his memoir. 'Normally when a player heads the ball his eyes close automatically, but John's didn't, they stayed open. If you tried to challenge John in the air, he'd always jump a fraction of a second earlier, and he seemed to be able to hang in the air.'

Heading a football in those days was a bit like taking your life in your hands, if it was raining and the pitch was soaked. A football in the 1960s and 70s was a whole different proposition to a football nowadays. Footballs no longer absorb water. But in Jack's day they soaked up moisture like a willing sponge.

'If you headed it wrong, you sort of stood there groggy for five or six minutes before you recovered,' Jack recalled.

'I learned loads of things from John. I remember him saying to me, "When the centre forward's got the ball and he's coming at you, just turn sideways on slightly… just slightly… make a little dart towards him as if you're going to tackle him… and he'll push it the other way. Then check, turn and go the way he is running. You will have a yard or two start on him anyway, so you'll get to the ball first."

'That was one of the great lessons I learned in my early 20s.

'I picked up something else from John, which has become a bit of a joke with me, and that is the habit of cadging cigarettes from other people.

'On a lot of occasions I don't carry any, on the basis that if I don't have any with me I won't smoke them, but then I weaken when I see somebody I know smoking and I say to them… "Go on, give us a fag".

'It is a good way of introducing yourself and joining in the conversation.'

JACK RETURNED to the Leeds United side in late September, 1955 and didn't miss another game that season. With John Charles scoring 29 goals in 42 appearances, Leeds established a home record of 34 games without defeat and finished second to Sheffield Wednesday to win promotion and return to the First Division after an eight-year absence.

Carter had to sell Charles to Juventus for a world record £65,000 in April, 1957 a year after winning promotion. Charles went on to win three Scudettos and European Footballer of the Year, eventually returning to Elland Road five years later, but playing less than a dozen games. His original transfer to Turin also meant Jack took up his position in the Leeds United defence from the 1955-56 season onwards.

He'd also met Pat Kemp at this stage, and after a short courtship they were married. This stability in his home life undoubtedly coincided with a desire to act more responsibly on and off the field.

PAT CHARLTON

I was at a dance with my mother and a friend, when Jack came upstairs to the dance hall because there was a late bar. I had only gone because my mother wanted to go.

There was no way my dad would go, so she had insisted I went with her and I took my friend. I had no idea who he was or that he was a footballer. He said he was a player for Leeds United, but I didn't believe him.

They used to do spot–dances in there and we were dancing and they said, 'We are delighted to say Jack Charlton is here with us tonight' and he had to go up on to the stage and pick the spot. I turned to him and said, 'Well, if you are him, you'd better get up there', because I was sure he was having me on.

Then he did, with this big beam on his face. He was very tall obviously; he had blond hair and blue eyes and he was quite good looking.

He didn't really ask me out; we just started courting and it evolved. Jack lived in digs at Mary Crowther's house. Mary was an old lady, 80 odd, and she lived with her daughter Laura who was about 60, a spinster.

It took her years to get a television. She didn't want one in the house but Laura made her get one. She used to enjoy a glass of stout every night.

Jack came in one night and Laura was sat there, drinking her stout from a cup and saucer. Jack asked her why she wasn't drinking from a glass, and she said it was so the people on the television wouldn't see her.

He didn't really propose.

He just said, 'Shall we get married then?'

PAT AND JACK Charlton were married on January 6, 1958 at St Peter's Church, Bramley, near Leeds. Bobby Charlton was Best Man and his Manchester United teammates Tommy Taylor and David Pegg also attended. Both lost their lives in the Munich Air Disaster a month later.

THE PROBLEM for Raich Carter was that he was not given the Charles transfer money to strengthen his squad and Leeds therefore struggled in the top flight of English football. For his part, Jack continued to be infuriated by the lack of proper coaching under Carter. The former Hull City and Sunderland legend's idea of a training session was a run up the pitch, a walk across it, and a run back down again. If they were lucky, the players had a game of seven-a-side in the car park.

Carter was sacked in December, 1958 and replaced by Bill Lambton, who was an ex-Army one-time journeyman footballer with even less authority than Carter. However, he made two particularly significant signings in 17 year-old Billy Bremner and veteran defender Don Revie, but he too was not a coach. Not surprisingly, Jack was disillusioned by the appointment. And so were the rest of the squad. Within a few weeks, the Leeds players were asked by the Board if they wanted Lambton to leave. They all said yes and he was sacked later that day.

Leeds appointed Jack Taylor as their next manager and he brought along his brother Frank. And he was a proper coach, the first Jack had really encountered. He taught him how to kick a ball properly; for hours on end he placed one between two bricks and ordered him to kick the thing at full pelt. 'You soon learned to keep your eye on the ball!' Jack recalled.

With the encouragement of the Taylors, and buoyed by their regular chats about football, he continued to develop his interest in coaching. Jack had made a friend in former Leeds player George Ainsley, who coached in local schools and invited Jack along to help. He encouraged Jack to take his FA preliminary coaching badge and enlist in summer courses at Lilleshall. Bobby Robson, Malcolm Allison, Dave Sexton, Lawrie McMenemy and future adversary Billy Bingham were among the players attending. When he was fully qualified, he started coaching in schools around Leeds and Castleford, nearly doubling his wages with payments for his time from the FA, and often holding early morning sessions near Elland Road before he rushed to the ground for training.

His first visit to Lilleshall was to make a lasting impression.

Walter Winterbottom was in charge, before being followed by Alan Wade. 'I remember Alan introducing a guy from college one day. This counsellor spent all afternoon giving us advice about how to handle players, and I have to say it was pretty boring. Then he said, "We're going play a game." We divided into two teams and trooped off to the dressing room to change.

'Before we went out to play, this counsellor came round to see each of us individually; he just sat down with us quietly and said, "I am going to give you a word to remember, and at half-time I am going to come and ask you what it is?" Then we went out to play football.

'At half time he came around to each of us in the dressing room again. Not one of us could remember the word he had given us.

'"Ok," he said, "I will give you the word again. But this time, try to remember it." So he repeated the word, and then we went out to play the second half.

'At the end of the game, he came back... and again, no one could remember their word!

'We couldn't really understand the point the guy was trying to make until he got us all together again. Then he explained. "The game of football wipes everything from your mind; you are so engrossed that you think of nothing else. So don't tell your players, "I want you to do this," or "I want you to do that," and expect them to remember what you say, because they won't.

'"Players react to situations automatically. Unless you programme them differently, they'll do things the way they have always done them. You have to be prepared to work with them for weeks and months to get an idea to stick."'

The lesson remained with Jack throughout his managerial life. The bottom line was to keep the game plan as simple and direct as possible. 'The point has stayed with me throughout my life,' he wrote, '... that you must programme players in what you want them to do until it becomes second nature to them. And the best thing is to keep it very simple.

'The less choice you give a player, the more likely he is to make the right decision. If you keep it very simple, each player will know what he has to do, and will know what the other players are going to do and the positions they will take up.'

LEEDS WERE relegated to the Second Division in 1960, and a year later were struggling to stay out of the Third. Jack Taylor resigned and Leeds appointed Don Revie as player-manager.

'Don was very single-minded; his attention to detail was terrific, as was his honesty and the care of players,' Jack recalled in a BBC *Football Focus* interview in 1988. 'They were always the most important people. They are the ones you look after and we always travelled in the best way, stayed in the best hotels. He was also very open-minded; he was open to ideas from other players.

'The idea of me standing on the goal line and playing the in-swinging corner to the near post, actually was because I told him about it. Les Cocker had practiced it in London against our kid and Jimmy Greaves in goal, just messing about. And we came up with the idea. And as soon as we said it to Don, he was prepared to try it and prepared to give it a go.'

It was an appointment that changed the course of Leeds United's history and it had a significant impact on Jack's life. But it was tempestuous in the early days, to say the least. Revie didn't like Jack when he played in the same team as him, and he didn't hide it. And when Revie took over there were inevitably fireworks between the pair that almost cost Jack his Leeds career.

Revie thought that Jack had a 'chip on his shoulder' and he did not shirk in letting him know about it. 'Maybe I had a bit of a chip. Maybe I just needed some discipline... I don't know. I remember what Don told me during one practice match. I used to go charging up the field for corner kicks and I ran about all over the park during the play.

'The crowd liked it when I ran with the ball, although half the time - no, 90 per cent of the time – I'd overrun the bloody thing... totally unprofessional. Anyway, I'd gone charging up the field with the ball and Don said to me afterwards, "If I was manager, I wouldn't play you... you're always messing about".

'"Well, you're not the manager," I said, "... so what the hell?" And then... lo and behold, Don became manager!'

ONE OF Revie's first moves was to play Jack as centre forward.

Although he actually scored 12 goals in 21 games as the No. 9, he hated it, and complained to Revie that he had no idea what he was doing.

The relationship continued to deteriorate.

As Revie was giving out to him after one particular game, Jack threw a teacup at the wall, narrowly missing his manager. Revie walked out in silence and then after the game announced any grievances he or the players had in a game would now be discussed on a Monday morning.

The following season Revie bought Freddie Goodwin from Manchester United to take his place at the back and made a second attempt to convert Jack to centre forward. 'We had a bloody awful spell and went quickly down the league.' Leeds finished 19th, avoiding relegation to the Third Division with a last day 3-0 win over Newcastle.

Jack was called into the manager's office and was told that he was being let go. He was taken aback.

'Wait a minute,' he replied furiously. '… are you letting me go as a centre forward or a centre half, 'cos I've been playing for you for fifteen games or whatever as centre forward, which is not my position! But I've been doing it because you asked me… when really I should be coming back to my own position if I'm in the side.'

Jack found himself in the reserves, though interestingly, Don Revie never did place him on the transfer list. That did not stop Bill Shankly telephoning Jack and telling him that he wanted him to come to Anfield, although Shankly explained that Leeds were making any agreement difficult.

Shankly was offering £28,500.

Leeds wanted £30,000. 'I'm not going to be held to ransom…' the Liverpool boss informed him. 'So… the deal's off… for the time being.

'I'm sorry son, but that's the way it is.'

Manchester United were also interested. The word was that they were going to make a bid at the end of the summer, when they had completed a tour of the United States. Jack held out on signing a new contract with Leeds, but his attitude was beginning to ruffle feathers. 'Syd Owen took me by the arm and asked me what the problem was, but I told him to shove off,' Jack remembered. 'Then I got a message to go over to see Matt Busby.

'We sat talking in his office, and he explained that while they were in America they had played a young lad at centre back, someone who had just come into the side, and Matt wanted to wait until the new season started so that they could have a look at this lad before giving me a decision.

'I couldn't believe what he was telling me.

'"I have caused ructions at Elland Road… I have refused to sign a contract, nobody there is speaking to me," I said. "I have caused bloody havoc in the club; I have been offered a deal and turned it down… and now you are telling me I have got to wait until the beginning of the new season, until you have had a look at someone else?

"'No," I said, "I am not going to do that…

"'I am going back to Elland Road, and I am going to apologise for what I have done. I am going to sign a new contract with the club and I am not bloody well coming here"'

He was upset as he walked out of Busby's office. Back in Leeds he sought out Revie without delay. 'Have you got a contract you want me to sign?' he asked.

Revie said he had. 'I have caused you enough problems at this club,' he courageously admitted. Jack signed on the dotted line.

He made 629 League appearances for Leeds United, winning a League Championship, Second Division Championship, FA Cup, League Cup, and two European Fairs Cups. He was the Football Writers Footballer of the Year in 1967.

JOHN CHARLTON

Don Revie brought in pre-match meals, mid-season getaways and the team stayed in the best hotels. He brought in his ideas from being a player at Manchester City and Leeds, and changed the whole philosophy of the club and the players he inherited.

Billy Bremner lived not far from us and he would occasionally call in.

My dad and Billy used to go for a drink on a Friday night, for a couple of pints at The Woodman nearby. Somebody reported them. Don Revie called them in and my father said, 'What do you want us to do? We just go for a game of dominoes with the old fellas… a couple of pints and we chill out, then we go home about ten o'clock… get into bed and sleep like a baby.'

And Revie said, 'Just make sure it's only a couple of pints and you're out of there by ten', and he let them get on with it.

We used to live in a house on a street opposite Elland Road.

People like Ray Illingworth, the England and Yorkshire cricketer, and Paul Lutey, who was a wrestler, used to come and park their cars in our drive; call in for a cup of tea with my mam and head down to the ground for the game. Then after the game, I'd get back to our house before the final scores came on the telly… and they'd call in again before they headed home, and ask me what the scores were?

To me, around about 11, 12 years of age, Elland Road was like a playground to me. I had the freedom of the ground, every day, not just match days. But I didn't know any different. That's how I was brought up and it was the norm for me.

I'd walk out of the house, round a horseshoe, couple of hundred yards and the ground was in front of me. On a match day I never had a ticket, never had a pass. They'd let me in; I'd go to a refreshment bar in the ground where this woman used to always give me a hot drink, like a combination of oxtail soup and Bovril which I can still taste now.

There was a big fat ex-policeman called Eric, who still used to be in his uniform, always on duty. And he was the laundry man as well and he would take off his tunic, and be stood there in his white shirt cleaning the players' strips. Then he'd hang the shirts on coat-hangers on these rails across the walls in this boiling hot room to dry them off. And there was a boot-room with all the players' boots on pegs, and there were big boxes, just full of studs for replacements.

I'd spend most days during the school holidays at the ground and I could go anywhere I wanted. At one point they built a sauna at the back of the dressing room, and me and my dad used to going in there after training, then have a shower or a bath and head home.

There was a standing area just to the right of the tunnel where all the apprentices stood and watched the game, so I'd lean on these steps with them and watch the matches. As soon as it was half time I'd go into the tunnel, and then go back on the steps to watch the second half.

The only place that was out of bounds was the dressing room, just before kick off, half time or immediately after the game. Other than that, I could go anywhere.

They all knew me, and they'd all talk to me but there were always players that took more of an interest in you than others. Billy Bremner, Norman Hunter, Eddie Gray and Johnny Giles… who had a son Michael about the same age as me.

REVIE WAS convinced that Jack could play for England and he told him so. He also made him his first choice at the back and started to build his new Leeds team around him and the young Scot Billy Bremner.

In March, 1962 Revie signed former Scotland international Bobby Collins from Everton. Although he frequently clashed with him, Collins' determination to win and his professionalism came into Jack's life at the right time. The move to Elland Road didn't do Collins any harm either. He was recalled to the Scotland squad and won Footballer of the Year within two years.

Collins was a major influence on the younger players, particularly Bremner, but he and Jack had their moments. During one pre-season tour in Italy, the pair came to blows in the showers after a match against AS Roma, and had to be separated by Revie in his suit. And during a stay in a Harrogate Hotel in March, 1965 Jack threw a jug of water over Collins and in his desperation to catch his teammate and teach him a lesson the Scot put his arm through a glass door and needed 16 stitches.

Revie was furious. But Collins told him, 'I'll be playing tomorrow and I'll be the best player on the park'. And of course, he was.

Not everything about Revie's philosophy pleased Jack. Leeds soon became notorious as an uncompromising side that intimidated teams. The Leeds fans loved it but opposing teams, and many gentlemen in the media didn't. And Jack wasn't always a fan of that particular style of play either. But he remained a Revie convert, even adopting some of his manager's quirky pre-match superstitions. He admitted it could sometimes take an hour to be fully prepared.

'I would always put on my left boot first, followed by my right boot, my jock strap and my shorts. Then I would take a programme and go and sit on the toilet for three or four minutes. I'd always leave the programme on the left hand side of the toilet before I went back to the dressing room. I wouldn't put my shirt on 'til I was ready to go out on the field. And I liked to be the last out.' And he always had to score a goal past Gary Sprake in the pre-match kickabout.

Ultimately, all that fuss in the dressing room was to cost him the Leeds captaincy. When Collins suffered a serious injury, four years after signing, Revie handed the armband to Jack. But how could the man who insisted on being last out of the tunnel also lead the team out? Superstition won in the end. Bremner became the Leeds captain and Jack remained the 11th man on to the pitch. Revie promoted players from the youth team and started to assert his methods with them. And it worked almost immediately.

'There was a game against Swansea in September, 1962 that marked a turning point in my life. Don had left a lot of senior players out of the side, a very brave thing to do at the time, and he brought in a lot of new, young players he'd just signed – Gary Sprake in goal, Norman Hunter, Paul Reaney, and a fellow called Rod Johnson.

'I said to Don, "Well. I'm not going to play the way you've been playing with Fred (Goodwin); I don't want to play man-to-man marking, I want to play a zonal system where you pick up people in your area.

'"I'll sort out the back four for you the way I want them to play."

'And Don said okay.

'That, for me, was the moment when I stopped being one of the awkward squad and came on board the Leeds United ship. It was a sign that I would be one of the key players in the new team Don was building. I was sort of the organiser at the back; I was the pusher, I was the one who told the young lads where to go, when to cover, and how to pick up positions.'

After avoiding relegation to the Third Division in 1962, Leeds finished fifth the following year and won promotion 12 months after that. Jack missed only 14 games in four years until a three month lay-off with his first serious injury in 1963.

His partnership with a young Norman Hunter was the cornerstone of the Revie Plan, with Bremner and Johnny Giles, a new signing from Manchester United, leading the fight and pulling the strings in midfield. Jack loved Hunter, his central defensive partner in crime, and was never comfortable with Hunter's infamous "Bite Yer Legs" monicker.

'The centre half is meant to win the ball and if he starts giving fouls away around the penalty area he'll soon have the manager on his back. Norman was a great tackler, but occasionally he would mistime one. People laugh when I say that and think it's a joke, but nobody should have picked on Norman.

'We were both Geordie lads and they always teach you how to tackle right up there. We were a good partnership. My strength was in the air and Norman's was on the floor. We got on well enough and played for a few years, and then he came to me one day and said, "I'm sick of listening to you telling me what to do all the bloody time".

'I said, "Good lad… you'll be all right now, then."'

NORMAN HUNTER

Coming into that team as a young lad was perfect for me because Jack would tell us what to do. There was Gary Sprake… young lad, Paul Reaney… young lad, Willie Bell, and myself… young lad. He was the one who controlled the middle. We always said he was like the policeman on duty and we were the ones that ran around him.

He was always the boss, always the one that was in charge and of course, looking back, he was never wrong and it was never his fault but we learned a lot from him because he was the linchpin.

Being involved in the England squad in 1966, I got to watch those game very closely and in that series of games, Big Jack Charlton was absolutely brilliant; he couldn't have played any better. He won a World Cup medal and he was awesome in the final, but he hardly gets a mention. Bobby Moore, Bobby Charlton and Geoff Hurst get all the plaudits, but if you look at the team that day, Jack Charlton was absolutely brilliant.

When he really and truly put his mind to it, 100 per cent, I don't think there was a better centre half around at that time. But getting him to put his mind on the job all the time was difficult. I used to like it when a centre forward bashed him or battered him in the first five minutes because then he got angry and he would be superb.

I was a bit younger than Jack and his big mate was Billy Bremner, and the younger lads like myself, Terry Cooper, Paul Madeley and Mick Jones used to love winding Jack up. And it never did take much really but you knew, when the bottom lip started to quiver, then it was time to get out of the road because he was going to blow.

Jack and Gary Sprake had a love/hate relationship. There was a mutual respect but they were always very close to exploding. I remember Sprakey coming out for a ball once, and he shouted 'MINE... JACK' and then 'JACK... YOURS' and when he came out, he punched Jack and the ball.

*Jack fell on the ground. I went over, Jack had broken his nose and there was blood everywhere. He said to me, 'Why doesn't that stupid **** shout for the ball?' He played for six weeks with a broken nose and I remember to this day the gaffer said, 'You'll be all right Jack,' and we'd say, 'Go on big man... head that one... head this one' and he did. And if he didn't head it with his forehead, it would invariably hit him on the nose and you'd hear him swearing.*

We're not bosom buddies but, because of Leeds United, 1966, Mexico and our families, we have that bond. Susanne and I have been very fortunate to get to know Jack and Pat very well, and we saw them in London recently for the reunion for the '66 squad.

Pat still keeps him right. She is very strong but also a very, very nice lady and she can sort him out in her own way, very quietly and efficiently.

LEEDS TOOK the First Division by storm in the 1964-65 season.

They went 25 games unbeaten and were top for most of the season, until Manchester United beat them at Elland Road. When they met United, and Bobby Charlton, in the FA Cup Semi Final at Hillsborough in April, they were both in contention for the double. Manchester United won the title on the last night on goal difference. Leeds blew it by drawing with Birmingham, after going two-down before half time. Jack scored the equaliser with four minutes remaining but they could not get the winner to snatch the title from United.

It was the start of their "Chokers Leeds" phase.

Leeds did get their revenge over Manchester United in the FA Cup. The first semi-final between the sides was a bad tempered affair that ended in a goalless draw. It was during this game that Jack, pulling at Denis Law, ripped a hole in his opponent's shirt; a famous image from the era that portrays Jack in an unfavourable yet characteristic light in many a football history book.

He has no problem with that. 'You had to hang on to Denis, because he was so sharp and so good in the air. I used to hate playing against him, though I've always regarded him as a good pal of mine.'

Leeds won the replay 1-0 thanks to Bremner's winner two minutes from time. But Leeds froze against Liverpool in their first ever FA Cup final at Wembley Stadium. Roger Hunt put Bill Shankly's men in front three minutes into extra time after Leeds scraped through a goalless 90 minutes dubbed the "Bore of the Roses".

Jack went up front and headed a pass from Hunter into the path of Bremner to equalise. But with nine minutes of added time remaining, Ian St John headed an Ian Callaghan cross past Gary Sprake. Leeds had choked again.

DAVID WALKER

Jack was unique as a manager. Just when the football PR men were arriving to guide and control what a manager had to say, Big Jack was at his irrepressible best.

It was the FAI (Football Association of Ireland) sponsors Opel who organised the sing for your supper evenings. This involved Opel, with some help from John Givens and Trevor O'Rourke, booking a private room in a restaurant wherever Ireland were about to play. It might be Budapest before a qualifier against Hungary. It might be Palermo, Sicily during the Italia 90 campaign.

But the booking was made and the rules of the evening were simple. Every member of the travelling press corps was invited and when called upon would have to deliver a song, joke or story.

Jack needed little encouragement. Up he stood to deliver a song from his childhood days in Ashington. Blaydon Races *would be delivered with Jack insisting the assembled throng join in with the chorus. Or, as Jack would say, 'Come you boogers… sing up!'*

Jack's relationship with the media who covered Ireland during his reign was unique. As one of the Brits covering Ireland I remember reflecting on the juxtaposition of Jack singing with the press in Sicily while his friend and counterpart Bobby Robson was hiding from many of the England press corps in his hotel bunker.

Jack was always opinionated and willing to be quoted. A journalist's dream. He was also brilliant towards the British journalists covering the Republic. Before any away game, with the team scheduled to travel on the Monday, he'd invite us to join him for a few pints at the team's Dublin airport hotel on the Sunday night.

In these moments Jack would hold court and share some of the information he'd gleaned since we'd last met.

'Lads… did you know Vinnie Jones thinks he qualifies for Ireland?'

That was one of the nuggets he teed up when the Wimbledon and Leeds star was a massive presence in the media. As we now know, Vinnie was wrong. He was Welsh!

That's not to say Jack was always laid-back and relaxed when having a beer with his media mates. I realise the late, great Billy Bremner still divides opinion among some fans but, even though I didn't grow up as a Leeds fan, I admired his skills, tenacity and ability to score match winning goals in vital games.

Anyway, on this occasion we were sitting in a bar when the late and much missed PA correspondent Rob King decided to offer his opinion to Jack on his old club roommate Bremner.

'Jack… don't you think that Billy Bremner wasn't much more than a kicker?' opined Rob. The next few minutes were spectacular. Jack erupted with fury.

They say blood runs thicker than water and nobody should underestimate what wee Billy meant to Big Jack. He was livid and let Rob know.

Jack managed to stop short of inviting Rob out for a fight but he spelled out the virtues of Bremner as a player, a captain and as a man. Jack ended, and I literally mean ended the debate, because Rob didn't come back with any reply, with the words, 'Billy Bremner was a truly great player and Billy was my mate'.

One of my personal favourite memories of Jack came at the World Cup finals in the United States in 1994. By some ludicrous quirk, the Daily Mail *had booked me a hire car that was a flame red Pontiac Firebird convertible. It was a two-seater with a shelf for a back seat.*

On one rest day I ventured in the flame red Pontiac to a shopping mall near the Orlando North Hilton where we were staying with the team. This was the hotel where Jack was supplied with a barrel of the best Guinness in his suite and would invite the media to join him.

Well, as I looked around the shops I bumped into Jack and his wife Pat. Jack asked for a lift back to the hotel, which I was happy to do, until I remembered my car only had two seats. It's at this point I really wished I'd had a camera with me – or we'd been spotted by the paparazzi who arrived on the scene a few years later.

I dropped the roof on the convertible, invited Pat into the front seat, and lanky Jack climbed onto the bench. I'm sure we were breaking local road traffic laws but we headed back with the manager of the Republic of Ireland perched on the back shelf, his knees tucked under his chin and no seat belt to be seen.

I'm not sure any other competing manager at the World Cup would have been seen in a similar position. But Jack was typically oblivious to the situation.

'Thanks bonnie lad,' he said. 'Cheaper than a taxi!'

A few years later I was one of the guests at the memorial service for Lord Harewood, the Queen's first cousin. The service took place in the private chapel at Harewood House, the family home between Leeds and Harrogate. I got to know Lord Harewood, or as he always said, 'Call me George', during my time as a director at Leeds United. His passing was a great loss to football and particularly Leeds United. At his memorial service one of the eulogies was delivered by Jack. He talked about how the two become friends through football. Yes, the Queen's first cousin was a friend of rough, tough Jack, son of the Ashington coalfields. They met through football and they used to go shooting together.

At the end of Jack's tribute to his deceased friend he delivered this succinct sentence, 'George was a fine man and George was my mate'.

Well, to scores of journalists who worked alongside Jack at his clubs in England and with Ireland we all felt the same way.

Jack was our mate. A great man.

JACK MADE his England debut against Scotland at Wembley on April 10, 1965 a month before his 30th birthday. He became an England regular in the build up to the 1966 World Cup as Leeds finished second again in the title race, this time to Liverpool.

The 1965-66 season also saw Leeds' first foray into Europe, and some memorable matches for Jack.

'We'd qualified for the old Inter Cities Fairs Cup. Bobby Collins broke his thigh bone in the opening match in Turin. I remember it very vividly – Bobby was lying there, the referee wanted to move him off the park, and the Torino players were trying to bundle him off.

'I wouldn't let them move him; I knew that if Bobby Collins wouldn't get up, he must have something broken. I stood over him, whacking one Italian and punching another to keep them back, until eventually the referee realised that Bobby must be seriously hurt and called for a stretcher. We won the game 1-0, but Bobby was never the same player for Leeds again.

'In the third round we were drawn against Valencia. The first leg at Elland Road ended in a bit of a barney between myself and their defender Francisco Vidagany. I'd come up for a corner kick, like I always did at the time, and as the ball was cleared he just kicked me across the ankles.

'I stumbled and fell, and then I got up and went after him. He ran towards the goal and hid behind the net, with three or four Spanish players blocking my path. I was trying to get past them when the goalkeeper punched me in the mouth, so I went after him instead.

'The keeper backed away, kicking to keep me off – and then a policeman brought me down. The referee took us all off the park, and then he came into the dressing room and told me that I would not be coming back when play resumed. Vidagany didn't come back either.

'The press lads had a real go at us afterwards. There was an FA inquiry. Don defended me, saying that I'd been provoked by being constantly kicked. The referee, a Dutchman called Leo Horn, flew into London and gave evidence. To his great credit he took some of the blame. "I actually saw the player kick Mr Charlton and I didn't do anything about it," he said. "Then I looked back and I saw that Mr Charlton was chasing that man with madness in his eyes." The FA fined me twenty pounds.'

JOHN HELM

One of their ploys was to send Jack up for corners to make a nuisance of himself with such unsaintly acts as standing on the goalkeeper's toes. Perhaps, not surprisingly, on this occasion Senor Nito, the Valencia No. 1 took exception to Jack's size 15's and promptly spat in the big man's face. Well, Jack was incandescent with rage and set off like a giraffe that had just been stung by a wasp in pursuit of the enemy. Nito got to the corner flag, decided against leaping over the wall into the fans, and turned around to be met by a giant fist, not once, but twice. I was working for the Yorkshire Evening Post *at the time, though had witnessed that hilarious incident not from the press box but from behind the goal, standing with the fans.*

THE SECOND leg in Spain was naturally billed as a potential blood bath, but the game passed off peacefully, even when Jack scored the winner. Leeds beat Hungarian side, Ujpest Dozsa to set up a semi-final with Real Zaragoza and drew 2-2. Because the Fairs Cup was not under the auspices of UEFA, there was no away goals rule, so a replay was required. Jack correctly called the toss to decide the venue but Leeds lost the replay 3-1 at Elland Road.

After the euphoria of the 1966 World Cup win, the following season was one of frustration for Jack and Leeds, who finished fourth in the table and lost the FA Cup semi-final to Chelsea. Jack won the Football Writers' Footballer of the Year. Normally the winner said a few 'thank-yous' and sat down, but Jack entertained the journalists and their guests for quarter of an hour, cracking jokes and telling stories. He received a standing ovation.

The invitations started to come in from golf clubs and sporting associations for Jack's services and at one such event he was on the bill with famed England and Yorkshire cricketer, Fred Truman, an equally blunt and opinionated sports star of the 1960s and 70s. When Jack told him he was on fifty pounds for the gig in Burnley, Truman gave him some advice.

'You have to get more than that. You are a star now. I tell you what I do. When they phone me up to do a dinner, I say, "How many people will be there?" When they say 200, I say, "OK, add an extra pound on the tickets and pay me 200 quid". Jack took this advice and handsomely topped up his wages for many years.

The 1967-68 season opened with a two-legged defeat to Dinamo Zagreb in the Inter Cities Fairs Cup final, which was held over from the previous season. But the year improved and, when they met Newcastle, Jack broke Ernie Hart's club record of 477 league games for Leeds.

ALTHOUGH THEY were knocked out of the FA Cup in the semi-finals again, this time by Everton, Leeds won their first ever League Cup with a 1-0 win over Arsenal. They also registered their first European triumph, beating Ferencvaros in a Fairs Cup final that was also held over to the following season. They beat the Hungarian side 1-0 at Elland Road and held out for a 0-0 draw in Budapest.

Leeds appeared to have shaken off their "chokers" label in 1968-69. They lost just two league games all season and won the title in late April with a goalless draw on a dramatic night in front of an attendance of 53,750 at Anfield against nearest rivals Liverpool. Jack was imperious in a game with few chances, although young striker Alun Evans was to rue two early misses. Leeds came closest to breaking the deadlock through Bremner before referee Arthur Dimond blew the final whistle, sparking wild celebrations among the Leeds players, coaching staff and supporters.

Before the game, Revie had told his captain that if Leeds won the point required he should take the team to the Kop end. Amid the celebrations Revie reminded Bremner of their conversation and nodded towards the seething sea of red to their right. Reluctantly, Bremner did as he was told and set off towards the Kop.

At first, there was an eerie silence before the Liverpool crowd broke into a chant of 'CHAMPIONS… CHAMPIONS… CHAMPIONS…'

It was an unforgettable moment, and Leeds basked in it for nearly half an hour. Once the Leeds players had returned to the dressing room, Bill Shankly appeared. The Liverpool manager had cranked up the pressure in the build up, telling the press if Leeds didn't win the title that year, they never would.

But it was harmless mind games. Revie was an old friend. The Leeds manager called for quiet when the Scot walked in. Shankly stepped forward.

'We have not lost the title,' he told them, '… you have won it… and you're the best team in the country.'

'You've got to remember that Liverpool were THE big team of the time,' Jack insisted, 'and they were pressing us hard in the championship even though we had built up a record number of points.

'I have to admit it surprised me that the Liverpool fans reacted the way they did that night; I hadn't expected them to be so generous. They called me a "Dirty Big Giraffe" – but it was affectionate, and Anfield became my favourite away ground after that.' Anfield was to be the venue for Jack's last game as Ireland manager in December, 1995. He was to stand in the centre circle in tears as the Irish fans serenaded him for the last time.

JOHN HELM

I was standing with them again on the famous Anfield Kop when Leeds clinched their first ever Championship title in 1969. The idea was I should capture the mood of the night by standing shoulder to shoulder with the Liverpool fans whose own team missed out because of Leeds securing a 0-0 draw that clinched the title.

You can imagine my nervousness about being behind enemy lines, but when Don Revie told Billy Bremner to take the Leeds players to that end of the ground the Kop applauded in recognition of a great side.

It was a moving tribute, and my night was complete when Big Jack spotted me and I was invited into the jubilant Leeds dressing room to share in the celebrations.

I still have a picture of Jack enjoying a huge cigar and a glass of champagne, though I suspect he'd have preferred a pint of bitter.

Mention of Don Revie reminds me that when he became manager he told the players to call him 'gaffer' or 'boss', and that his surname should be pronounced 'Reevie'. Typically, Jack who had played alongside his new leader defied the order and much to Don's annoyance insisted on referring to him as 'Revvie' – something he does to this day.

By the time Jack was hanging up his boots as a player I'd moved to BBC Radio Leeds and one day at Elland Road he came up to me and said, 'I've got a good idea for a programme'.

That idea turned into Jack's Track, a weekly show not only fronted, but also edited, by you know who! Jack was determined to do it right so he came into the studios and I taught him all the broadcasting controls; showed him how to edit tapes, and how to get himself on and off air. He was brilliant. What really appealed to me was that he didn't just want the show to be about football. He went out to a glass-blowing factory, to Rowntree's in York to interview the workers; he went to an abattoir, and he even went poaching one night. And do you know what affected him most?

The sound of pigs squealing one minute… then deathly silence the next. 'That sent a shudder down my spine… the finality of it all was chilling,' he told his listeners.

When I joined Yorkshire Television in 1981 I was dead lucky that Jack was managing Sheffield Wednesday, one of the major clubs in our region. I'll never forget after one midweek game he invited me down to the boot room and we set off immediately for the pub just up the road from Hillsborough. We were walking with the fans who were peppering him with questions, and about 20 minutes after the end of the game we were propping up a bar – mind you I don't think we ever had to buy a drink. I'm not sure Jack had even bothered to say well done to the players who'd won the game.

He left that to Maurice Setters, his trusted assistant.

Both coming from the north of England, we would travel together on British Rail to

London for Mid-Week Sports Special. Despite ITV offering first class travel, Jack always insisted on going in carriages with economy tickets, because he loved swapping yarns with folk. He loves people and is fascinated by their lives, not his own. Though, of course, his propensity for getting names wrong is legendary.

During the 1982 World Cup in Spain we fell about as he talked about Peel (Pele), Socrates and Psycho (Zico). During the 1994 World Cup in the United States, after Ireland had been knocked out, Jack joined the ITV team based in Dallas, and one afternoon he and I and Matt Lorenzo had a day out in Fort Worth… a setting for many of John Wayne's biggest movies. Jack was a huge fan of westerns, and on arriving in Fort Worth we were not sure where to start our sightseeing. Jack leapt from the car.

'Is this where the gunfight at the O.K. Canal took place?' he asked one startled young man. That's Big Jack. I love the Big Man to bits and there'll never be another like him.

LEEDS HAD the opportunity to underline their winners' credentials the following season when a unique treble looked on. Jack got the winner in the Charity Shield win over Manchester City and notched his 500th appearance against Manchester United in March. Playing more open, entertaining football, Revie's side challenged Everton for top spot and reached the European Cup and FA Cup semis. But Leeds were to pay the penalty for England's preparations for a World Cup defence.

The FA brought the end of the season forward by three weeks to allow manager Sir Alf Ramsey to take his squad, including Jack, to South America to acclimatize to high altitude for the Mexico finals. However, with Leeds chasing three trophies, they were left with a severe backlog of fixtures and an FA that refused to change its dates and arrangements.

To emphasize the association's stubbornness, they fined Revie and Leeds £5,000 when the manager fielded a weakened side against Derby County on Easter Monday. Leeds were out of title contention and Revie wanted to save his players for the two remaining competitions.

They came through three gruelling battles with Manchester United in the FA Cup semi-finals before a Billy Bremner goal finally won the tie. It was their eighth game in 15 days. Halfway through the marathon, Jack told Pat that he and Billy were booking into the Oxford Road Hotel because they were going to get very drunk. She left them to it.

Everton clinched the league on the night Celtic won a scrappy European Cup first leg game 1-0 at Elland Road. The FA Cup final against Chelsea was five days before the second leg in Glasgow.

'We should have won, because we dominated the game from start to finish. I headed the first goal from a corner kick, but then Chelsea equalised after Gary Sprake dived over the ball. Then, only seven minutes from the end, Clarkey's shot hit the post and Mick Jones scored on the rebound.

'We thought we had it won, but then they got a free kick, the ball got played in, and Ian Hutchinson suddenly appeared at the near post to make it 2-2.

'The replay took place at Old Trafford. At Wembley, Eddie Gray had run "Chopper" Harris to bits, but in the first few minutes of the replay "Chopper" gave Eddie a beauty. Eddie stayed on the field, but he was virtually a spectator after that.

'Clarkey went on a brilliant run before setting up Mick Jones to score the opening goal. But twelve minutes before time, Chelsea equalised through a Peter Osgood header. I blame myself for that goal. I'd been waiting on their goal line for a corner kick when one of the Chelsea players whacked me in the thigh with his knee. After the corner was cleared I started to chase him... way over to the right. Then the ball was knocked in long to our box and I started to run back, but I was still hobbling after the whack in the thigh and I couldn't get there in time to stop Peter Osgood heading the goal.

'So we were again in for extra time. Ian Hutchinson did one of his long throw-ins, and I remember jumping and heading the bloody thing. Then John Dempsey climbed on top of Terry Cooper to flick the ball on, and somehow it finished at the far post for Dave Webb to nod the ball in. It was the first time they'd been ahead in 224 minutes play, but that was how it stayed.

'The disappointment was incredible. I went straight to the dressing room and kicked open the door. I've never been more upset over losing a game, maybe because it was partly my fault. Nobody else came into the dressing room, and I just sat there and sat there for ages, before all of a sudden the lads started to drift in with their losers' medals. It was only then I realised I hadn't collected my own medal. To this day I'm not sure if I ever got it – though I suppose I must have done.'

FRED DINENAGE

I was lucky enough to be senior sports presenter at Yorkshire Television, in Leeds, from the late 1960s – when the company was founded – until the early 80s.

In that time I met and interviewed Big Jack on many occasions; as a player at Leeds, and in his management roles at Middlesbrough and Sheffield Wednesday.

I suppose our most famous – or infamous – interview was the 'little black book' incident in 1970. It happened in a pilot programme for Tyne Tees Television, *in Newcastle, in 1970. It was supposed to be a recorded trial programme for a new chat show they were hoping to produce. It was never intended for transmission.*

I was interviewing Jack in a spot on the programme called "The Big Interview". His mum was in the audience as well as other family members. I was speaking to Jack about how he was feeling as his playing career was drawing to a close. He surprised me by saying he had a little black book in which he'd written the names of players who'd tried to hurt him in past encounters, and whom he was intending 'to get' before his playing days were over.

The audience laughed, but Jack seemed quite serious! I told him, 'Be careful, Jack… or you'll get yourself banned!' After the recording I remember saying to Jack, 'That was controversial. Tyne Tees *are bound to ask you if they can transmit that interview.*

'If I was you, I'd say no,' I advised him.

But Jack being Jack, he said, 'yes'.

And transmit it they did. What followed, of course, were front-page headlines in several national newspapers. Jack was called to an FA hearing with Don Revie, who was to show compassion and support for Jack at a time of great stress, which he would never forget. A precedent was set at his disciplinary hearing when TV evidence was used for the first time. The Leeds duo insisted the FA Board watch the film of his interview. At that stage they had not and were basing their case on the numerous newspaper articles piled in front of FA secretary Dennis Follows when they walked in the room. After they'd watched the interview, Jack was not fined or banned. But he was asked to apologise, issuing a statement that included the immortal line, 'I apologise for the fact that through me, the press was given an opportunity to knock football'.

I interviewed him at YTV a few weeks later and the big fella apologised to me, 'for any trouble I might have caused you' – though, in actual fact, he'd given my own career a bit of a boost!

My lasting memory of Jack came at Hillsborough in 1980 when, as manager of Sheffield Wednesday, he'd taken them out of the Third Division. As promotion was achieved the crowd went mad and the players did a lap of honour. But there was no sign of Jack himself. I finally found him sitting alone in the Wednesday dressing room quietly reflecting and smoking a cigarette.

'Jack,' I said, 'why aren't you out there with the players?'

'Well, Fred,' he replied, 'don't think I'm getting big-time. But, after you've won the World Cup... everything else is a bit of an anti-climax. This is a time for the players and the fans...

'... I've done my bit.' Typical of the man. A footballing giant. But, deep down, a quiet, modest and unassuming man.

The last time we worked together was in a celebrity fishing competition at a lake owned by rock star Roger Daltrey in Kent. Jack was taking part; so was Roger and others, including Chris Tarrant and singer, Frankie Vaughan. We were filming the event for Television South, and it was serious and quite competitive.

Jack loved it. And, of course, he won!

I was delighted when, in 2006, he was voted by Leeds United supporters into the club's "Greatest Ever XI". Well deserved. As the late, great Don Revie once told me on air... 'Jack Charlton was the rock on which I built a great football team'.

These days at ITV Meridian in the south of England I'm working alongside one of Jack's granddaughters Emma. Like her grandfather; modest, talented and destined for the top. And, unsurprisingly, incredibly proud of the man she calls, 'Grandpop'.

JACK ONLY made one appearance in Mexico in the World Cup, his 35th and final cap, in England's group win over Czechoslovakia. He'd lost his regular place alongside Bobby Moore to Everton's Brian Labone as England were knocked out by eventual winners Brazil.

Leeds were to finish second again in 1971.

They suffered one infamous defeat to West Bromwich Albion, that resulted in a pitch invasion and Leeds kicking off the next season with Elland Road closed by the FA as a result. But as Barry Davies had rightly called in his *Match of the Day* commentary, following Jeff Astle's controversial winner, 'Leeds will go mad. And they have every justification for going mad'.

The name that lives long in the memory of Leeds United fans is referee Ray Tinkler. With the game goalless after half time, and Leeds patiently trying to break down their opponents to get a decisive score, Tony Brown blocked a Norman Hunter pass and it flew into the Leeds half and in the direction of Colin Suggett, who was sauntering back but clearly offside. There was no 'interfering with play' interpretation in 1971. The linesman flagged and Brown, who had initially stopped, along with the entire Leeds defence, spotted Tinkler waving play on and sprinted to the ball before squaring for Astle to tap into an empty net.

Tinkler gave the goal. The Leeds players went ballistic and immediately surrounded the referee. Revie even went on to the pitch to plead their case, and several supporters tried to get to Tinkler too. But he remained defiant and gave the goal which was to ultimately cost Leeds the title.

They were pipped on the final day by Arsenal and finished second with 64 points, a league record for First Division runners-up until the points for a win were changed from two to three. The title was briefly in their grasp after Jack's winner beat the Gunners in the penultimate game at Elland Road. But Arsenal beat Tottenham Hotspur in the final game of the season to clinch the league, and eventually achieved the double with a 2-1 win over Liverpool. Leeds' FA Cup challenge had ended with an embarrassing defeat at Colchester United.

But they were still left with a two-legged Fairs Cup final against Juventus. They drew 2-2 in Turin and held on for a 1-1 draw at Elland Road to win their second European trophy.

DUNCAN REVIE

It's neither here nor there, but the correct pronunciation of our surname is 'Ree-vie', and for some reason, Jack always insisted on saying 'Rev-vie'. But then he didn't know the names of half the players in the Ireland team, so I guess we were lucky he remembered!

I'm only speaking anecdotally but they had two major conversations. The first when my dad was playing alongside Jack and told him if he was manager, he wouldn't play Jack because he didn't take his football seriously enough.

The second was after my dad had taken over, and he sat him down in his office and said, 'Listen, you silly bugger, if you play the game properly, you could play for England'. Jack didn't really believe him when he said it. After the '66 final, my dad went into his office, and Jack's medal was on the table. Jack had left a note.

'That's for you boss.'

They had a few toe-to-toe, up-against-the-wall moments. I was a teenager, growing up, so my dad would sometimes tell me the tales and I think Jack struck a chord with him because he was direct and always thought he was right. He once told us about the time Jack fell asleep during a team meeting. They had come in after training and my dad was going through the scouts' notes on the opposition, and Jack was asleep at the back.

My dad stopped the meeting, tapped Jack in the chest and told him to follow him to his office. Billy Bremner and Allan Clarke took their boots off and tiptoed down the corridor to listen to the conversation, which was very one-way.

My dad had a huge admiration for the way Jack played.

He was very under-rated as a footballer, but my dad told him just to get the ball and give it Billy Bremner and John Giles. If you look at the videos, he did worry when Jack went on one of his runs. There was no striker anywhere in the world who relished the prospect of being marked by Jack and Norman Hunter; they were a great partnership.

When my dad became ill with Motor Neuron Disease, they moved to Kinross and Jack often called in with a whole salmon he'd caught on one of his fishing trips to Scotland. He made frequent trips to see him until my dad decided he didn't want visitors. I know it was very much appreciated.

KIM REVIE

I was eight or nine when I was first allowed on the Leeds United bus and my memory is of such a happy family. Jack and Billy in particular were so friendly and they used to encourage me to start the community singing on the bus journey home if they'd won. Always the same three songs… Glory, glory, Leeds United…: *It's a Grand Old Club to Play For… and* Bye Bye Blackbird.

And then Jack would always give a rendition of Blaydon Races.

REVIE'S EUROPEAN successes were no accident. He was an expert at playing European teams at their own game.

And Jack clearly took note. 'Don made us very aware of the importance of not giving goals away at home. You've got to be patient, you can't go charging off trying to score at the other end. You've got to keep your shape and fill the midfield.

'The main thing is not to over-commit yourselves, because they'll draw you in and then they'll beat you on the break. If you're patient, the chances will come.

'Nobody fancied playing Leeds – it was very difficult to get a result against us.'

The trip to Turin also opened Jack's eyes to the difficulties of spouses travelling with the team for European games. The original game was abandoned halfway through due to a waterlogged pitch but the Leeds squad stayed on for three days and some had brought their wives.

It was the only time Jack remembers Don Revie threatening to resign. 'Don didn't like players mixing with their wives before a game.

'Whenever we went away, he always insisted that the wives travelled on a different flight and stayed in a different hotel. They were looked after properly, they were taken on a bus to the ground, but they were kept away.

'We had a meeting after the abandoned game and several of the players insisted that their wives should come and stay with them in the hotel. But Don was adamant, and he threatened to resign if he didn't get his way.

'I didn't mind myself, because I'd been married long enough to know that Pat wouldn't worry whether we were together or not for a couple of nights. Some of the younger players were very unhappy about it.

'I agreed with him, actually. There's a place for men and there's a place for women – but certainly not a place for women on the night before you play a big game.'

JOHN CHARLTON

He was never one to come home and kick the dog, or take it out on us; not that I can ever remember. Apart from anything, with the number of games and the fact that there were no 25-man squads in those days, there was no time to mope about and think about defeats.

And that was very much the mentality at Leeds during his time. And even with Ireland, his attitude after a game, win, lose or draw, was, 'Right lads… let's go get lashed'.

He was obviously a hard player and he had his fair share of bust-ups.

There was the time he was involved in a little altercation with Terry Paine, and he had played with Terry for England.

*Terry Paine did him, snapping his shin pad in two, taking the skin off from below the knee to his ankle. My dad thought he'd broken his leg. He hobbled after Terry, hit him on the head, grabbed him by the throat and sat on him. And the referee Jim Finney grabbed dad and pulled him away, and said, 'You, you big sod… I should send you off for that'. Then the ref pointed at Terry Paine and said, 'But that little b*****d got exactly what he deserved'. My Dad always said that's what you call an understanding referee!*

LEEDS GAINED some revenge over Arsenal when they won the Centenary FA Cup final in 1971, on Jack's 37th birthday, thanks to Allan Clarke's winner.

Mick Jones dislocated his shoulder in a fall, and Bremner delayed the cup presentation from the Queen until their stricken striker, his shoulder heavily bandaged, was rescued from the treatment room by Norman Hunter and went up first to collect his medal in absolute agony. He was taken straight to hospital while Bremner was held aloft as Leeds' first cup-winning captain.

However, the double was to elude them once again.

In the dressing room, Revie rationed his players to one plastic cup of champagne and a sip from the cup, which was taken back to Elland Road by secretary Keith Archer. The celebrations continued with a cup of tea and a sandwich at a service station on the way to the Midlands to prepare for the final game against Wolves. Brian Clough's Derby had finished their season on 58 points. Leeds needed a draw, while Liverpool, who were playing their last game at Arsenal the same evening, needed a win.

Leeds, without Jones of course, were exhausted and carrying at least three injured players. Wolves went ahead just before half time through Derek Dougan, and made it 2-0 in the 65th minute. Billy Bremner pulled one back, and they desperately pressed for an equaliser, with referee Bill Gow turning down three penalty appeals. Meanwhile at Highbury, Liverpool were denied a winner two minutes from time against Arsenal when John Toshack's goal was ruled offside. Derby County were crowned champions. Leeds United were runners-up, again.

Although approaching his 37th birthday, Jack kept his place in the side alongside Hunter that season. Revie signed cover in Roy Ellam and John Faulkner, but not until he brought in a young Gordon McQueen did the boss feel he'd found a long-term replacement for Jack. Jack's appearances, by now over 600, were to be curtailed in his final season and he missed the 1973 FA Cup final defeat to Sunderland through injury.

'We had a great run in the League in 1971, with some famous victories: most famous of all, 7-0 over Southampton on the 4th of March. We absolutely murdered them that day. The movement, the pattern - everything seemed to go right. Some of the moves included 24 or 25 passes. Seven of us scored, including me.

'The game was shown on *Match of the Day*, and people started to look at us in a different way. They started calling us "Super Leeds" and comparing us to Real Madrid. I reckon that was the game when people took a look at us and finally said, "Yeah, this is a good team."'

What's interesting about that story, and something Jack failed to mention in his autobiography, is that the only outfield player who did not touch the ball in that famous clip of Leeds playing "OLE... OLE... OLE..." football, is Jack.

LEEDS OFFERED Jack another contract extension that would have taken him beyond his 40th birthday, and a coaching role. But Jack had his eye on a managerial role elsewhere and he knew his playing days at the top level were numbered. Leeds granted him a testimonial against Celtic. The club bagged £12,000.

Jack was given £28,000, which he put in a trust fund for his children. Not bad for a man who had never earned more than £125 a week in his 23 years, but he resented the money kept back by Leeds, who had arranged an additional friendly at Parkhead without him. He played a record total of 773 games, one more than Billy Bremner, and scored 96 goals which is still the ninth highest in Leeds United history. Arch critic Brian Clough, who took over from Revie, took home £100,000 when he was sacked after just 44 days less than a year later.

'We didn't get paid that well,' Jack admitted. 'And when teams came to play at Elland Road, before the match I would go to the hotel and say to the lads, "I have got some fantastic cloth, tell me what you want and I'll get them made up". And the lads would get two pairs of trousers... a jacket, a suit. And it worked, it did.' Amongst his returning customers was future England manager, Terry Venables.

PAT CHARLTON

Leeds United had tried to run a football shop but they were not very successful. So Jack and I just had this idea to start a club shop. To begin with it was a shed with a drop down window; we sold hats, scarves, little photos, socks and shirts, etc.

I used to work before every match until about five minutes after kick-off, then I would pack up and the put the wooden window back up.

Then, I'd just come back out five minutes before the end of the game, and start selling again. It just got bigger and bigger and more and more popular, and in the end we had three shops. When they took off, Leeds wanted to take them off us and start running them, but Don Revie said no. He said it was Jack's business and he should be allowed to continue. For all the time Jack was playing for Leeds, we ran the club shops and when Jack left we sold them to the club.

We ran a café and a menswear shop near the family home too and when Jack joined Middlesbrough I helped them with a club shop at Ayresome Park.

ENGLAND 66

JACK CHARLTON made his England debut less than a month shy of his 30th birthday, on April 10, 1965.

He discovered he had received his first call up from England manager Sir Alf Ramsey after Leeds United had defeated Manchester United in the FA Cup replay earlier that month. It was the culmination of a three game cup marathon between the two great rival teams. Jack was of course delighted. And he couldn't wait to share the news with brother Bobby.

'I didn't think,' he admitted in his autobiography.

'I just had to tell our kid. I went straight round to the Manchester United dressing room and said, "Hey, I have been selected to play for England!"

'I'm smiling all over my face, and there's all the Manchester United team sitting round looking miserable. There was a bit of a pause, and then Bobby went, "Ah, yeah, well, congratulations, great".

'"Now f**k off out of here," said someone else. And, suddenly, I realise what I'm doing.

'"Excuse me," I said, and left. That's the tact I'm famous for.'

Jack played in the same England team as Bobby for the first time against Scotland at Wembley on April 10, 1965. They were the first siblings to play together for their country in the 20th century. Their mother Cissie Charlton was ecstatic, as she recounted on the BBC's *Alfie's Boys*.

CISSIE CHARLTON

One son who is the star and the other who is hard and coming up the hard way, you know… like Jackie had to. And then you see them walking out of the tunnel playing for England. That was the happiest day of me life. One had reached the other then.

CISSIE QUICKLY became a media darling. She had befriended a journalist from the *Daily Sketch*, who asked her to write a match report of that first game against Scotland in which her two boys played together.

She and Bob travelled to Wembley by train; photographers catching the pair as they left Central Station in Newcastle. They stayed at the Waldorf Hotel. The newspaper, keen to keep their star signing from its rivals, treated the couple to a guided tour of London and tickets for a West End musical. After a post-match walk down the Thames, Cissie travelled to Fleet Street to write her *Daily Sketch* match report.

CISSIE CHARLTON

No guest sportswriter can ever have sat down to describe a game with such a red face as I have this morning. Because it is just impossible for me to describe Saturday's international at Wembley without naming my son Bobby as man of the match.

That first great goal, his perfect pass to Jimmy Greaves for the second, and the unique experience of seeing him play so brilliantly in both attack and defence puts Bobby among the greats in my mind.

And if you call me big-headed I can only tell you that when I kissed my son after the game and told him how well he had played, he replied, 'I have waited 12 years to hear you say that Mam'.

But I wasn't only proud of my sons yesterday. (I am sorry but I shall have a word to say about Jackie too, later) I was so proud to be English I thought I'd burst.

For sheer guts and fighting spirit I can never remember seeing a game like it, and if we hadn't lost two men we would have routed Scotland. I can't remember such a personally emotional day in a lifetime spent watching football.

In the morning I was all butterflies; unusual for me. But I worried myself sick about Jackie. After all, it might have been his brother's 57th cap but it was Jackie's first and I passionately wanted him to show that Wembley lot what he was made of.

My worries were eased within minutes of the kick-off because Jackie seemed so cool and relaxed. And after 25 minutes my secret dream came true.

That wonderful telepathy which my boys have always had between each other since they were little lads went into action... and so did my new white hat, flying into the air as I shouted in that Charlton goal, scored by Bobby from Jackie's pass.

People say daft things at such moments, but when my husband Bob reminded me that the doctor said excitement was bad for my heart I said, 'Oh, shut up'. All I knew was that Jackie had shown the world he knew what this game of football was all about, and I was glad his wife had made the decision not to tell him before the match that their little boy John had had an accident which meant six stitches being put in his head.

Back to the match... I admit I called Gordon Banks a few Geordie names when he seemed to help that Denis Law goal over the line. But I took them all back when he made so many brilliant saves after that. But that was nothing to the name Jackie called me after the game.

'How could you?' he said when he looked at me...and I realised that my new navy-and-white outfit was in Scotland's colours. Saturday was the kind of day every mother dreams of when she's skinning her knuckles getting the mud off her lad's shirt, or diddling the housekeeping for a new pair of football boots.

When the family and I celebrated over champagne in the Blue Angel nightclub, and every member of the Charlton family was mentioned in a wonderful calypso, I couldn't help saying to myself, 'Cis, for a colliery family we have come a long way'.

JOHN CHARLTON

She was brilliant fun, very much like my father, headstrong, always right. I was back from Australia once. I'd gone there to play for two years; stayed for 14. Two of the lads I went with from Middlesbrough, Peter Bryan and Ian Parker, are still there.

You couldn't get Roy "Chubby" Brown CDs Down Under back then, so I got a few from Chubby's manager in Newcastle. I'd left them in my grandma's room. I went to see her one day and I could hear this... 'Eeee lad... eeee,' ... because that was how she laughed. 'Eeee... eeee'. She was only listening to Chubby! And this was him at his bluest, rudest and not being very politically correct, to say the least. I went over to switch it off. 'Don't you dare,' she said, '... funniest thing I've ever heard.'

A KEEN student of the game and a qualified coach at the time of that first call up, Jack was fascinated by his inclusion in the England squad at such a late stage of his career, and with the World Cup pending.

He knew he could play, and defend, and Don Revie had told Jack he believed he was good enough to play for England. But he was still intrigued by Ramsey's thinking. Ramsey had vowed England would win the World Cup when he had taken over as the country's first professional manager and Jack was clearly part of the brilliant tactician's masterplan. Jack wanted to know why?

So in a hotel bar one night, during one of their many pre-World Cup preparation camps, he quizzed the England manager on his selection.

'Well, Jack,' replied Ramsey, 'I have a pattern of play in mind… and I pick the best players to fit the pattern. I don't necessarily always pick the best players, Jack.'

That response became one of Jack's favourite one-liners in his after-dinner act. It was true, and it was guaranteed to get a laugh every single night, especially when he attempted to deliver the killer line in Sir Alf's clipped tones, with just a hint of Geordie.

At the time, it was also the source of relentless mickey-taking by his England teammates who, if they didn't really overhear it, as some have claimed, certainly became aware of it very quickly.

RAY WILSON

I don't know if Jack was looking for a pat on the back, but he got a slap in the face on that occasion. He was crestfallen.

JIMMY GREAVES

I believe it was Alf's way of putting Jack down at the time because Jack could be a bit lively. I think that was his way of saying… 'You are not the best footballer in the world, Jack. Shut up'.

RAMSEY WAS a completely different manager to Don Revie.

He was a stickler for time; he was strict, like a schoolmaster, and he didn't shout at his players or have arguments. When Jack and Jimmy Armfield fell out on the training ground once, Ramsey marched over angrily and told the pair to 'sort it out between them'. Revie, said Jack, would have insisted on working on the issue until he and the players concerned were happy. Ramsey simply expected his players to come up with their own solutions and get on with it.

There was one practice match bust-up involving Jack and Nobby Stiles that Ramsey was happy to leave alone. The pair were arguing with each other throughout the first half of the game.

It was relentless. 'We were really slanging one another. We were at it like five year-old schoolboys. It was a good job we didn't come to blows because I would have dropped him... if I'd had a stepladder to reach him,' said Stiles.

The row escalated at half time, and eventually Stiles started to move towards Jack, his fists preparing to settle the argument. Jack, sensing danger, legged it.

GEOFF HURST

They didn't mince words. I remember Jack being very cutting about Nobby's performance when Partizan Belgrade beat United in the European Cup. Nobby, in turn, probed open an old wound by vividly describing Jack's performance for Leeds against Zaragoza. It really was pretty brutal stuff. But I was delighted. I realised then that if we had players who felt that they knew each other well enough to tear strips off each other's carcass, then we certainly knew each other well enough to act together. It certainly worked out that way.

Players got into the habit of telling each other exactly what they thought.

JACK REMAINED fascinated by Ramsey's methods, however, which had proved so successful in taking his Ipswich Town team from the Fourth Division to the First Division League title.

There were aspects of his anti-square-pegs-in-round-holes philosophy that was to help England win the World Cup. And it didn't do Jack any harm when he eventually moved into international coaching and management.

As well as providing the perfect punchline to those golf club stories later in Jack's life, Ramsey had expanded on his theories in subsequent discussions between the pair. Neither man could know it, but Alf was planting a significant seed in Jack's mind.

Later, Alf explained himself a bit further. 'I've watched you play... Jack,' he said, '...and you're quite good. You're a good tackler and you're good in the air, and I need those things. And I know you won't trust Bobby Moore.

'You and he are different. If Gordon Banks gives you the ball on the edge of the box, you'll give the ball back to him and say, "Keep the bloody thing", but if Gordon gives the ball to Bobby, he will play through the midfield, all the way to a forward position if he has to.

'I've watched you play and I know that as soon as Bobby goes, you'll always fill in behind him. That way, if Bobby makes a mistake, you're there to cover it.'

Jack never believed that Alf liked him all that much. 'But I learned a lot from him,' he happily admitted. 'Alf always picked his teams to fit the way he would play them. I have been a method man ever since; I have always tried to design my teams to cause the opposition the maximum problems.'

'He'd developed the 4-4-2 system when he was manager of Ipswich. Most of the teams at the time played the old 'WM' formation, with one centre back and the full backs covering him. Then, all of a sudden, Ipswich wingers weren't wingers anymore, they were midfielders, and they had another centre forward up front, so the other team's centre half was now marking two players.

'When teams first came up against Alf's system they didn't know what to do – and they panicked.

'If Alf was disappointed with the way you played, he just wouldn't speak to you – and if he came over and smiled, you knew you'd done all right. He didn't give much away either. No matter what you asked him, he'd never answer immediately. He'd look at you with a little smile, and then just say yes or no. You knew then it was a waste of time trying to carry on the conversation.

'Maybe because I was a coach, I would try to draw him out, but I wasn't very successful.' But the icy relationship between manager and centre half didn't matter. It was the same with all 22 players Alf Ramsey selected for the finals, and the many he discarded along the way. Jack was in Ramsey's England side; that was all that mattered.

And he made the most of his inclusion as Ramsey plotted England's attempt to win the world crown, and make the most of playing on home soil.

England beat Hungary in Jack's second game, going some way to burying the memory of the catastrophic 6-3 defeat inflicted by Ferenc Puskas et al at Wembley 12 years earlier, and the even more humiliating, but often forgotten, 7-1 thrashing England suffered in Budapest six months later.

The English FA then arranged a short European tour and Ramsey expanded the number of players he wanted to experiment with, bringing in Alan Ball for his debut in a 1-1 draw against Yugoslavia in Belgrade. He partnered Nobby Stiles, who had made his debut on the same night as Jack against Scotland. The team as millions would soon know it was beginning to take shape.

They beat West Germany 1-0 in Nuremberg, and then Sweden 2-1 in Gothenburg four days later. After a draw against Wales at Cardiff Arms Park, and just eight months before the World Cup kick-off, England suffered the first of only two defeats in Jack's 35 games for his country, a 3-2 reversal to Austria at Wembley. Normal service was resumed with a win over Northern Ireland at the same ground. And then came an excellent 2-0 victory over Spain on a freezing cold night in The Bernabeu in December, 1965.

The Spaniards were bewildered by the English tactics, their two full backs waiting for the customary attacks down the flanks that failed to materialise. It was the first time England were labelled "Alf's wingless wonders" and his plans were starting to take shape, literally. There was one dissenter in the camp, though.

Jack remained the only player who actively disagreed and opposed Ramsey's methods. 'That was Jack Charlton, the rebel,' Ramsey later reflected. 'He argued against it, queried it and left me in no doubt that he was not in favour.

'He didn't take kindly to changes and I had to tell him, "Do it my way… or else."

'"Or else what?" he said.

'"You are out," I replied.

'It was necessary to let him know who was boss, that I felt the system was successful and that our World Cup hopes might well depend upon it. Jack used to enjoy moaning; if he could make things difficult for me, he would. But once he saw that the tactics worked, he held up his hands and admitted defeat.

'Jack was basically an uncompromising man, shrewd and calculating. He knew the game, that's why he tried to cross swords with me.'

In January, 1966 Jack won his 11th cap as England drew 1-1 at Goodison Park in their first ever meeting with Poland. Geoff Hurst made his full debut a month later against West Germany. Within six months he would score the hat trick that would change his life forever and help win the World Cup for his country. But he had a quiet first start as Jimmy Greaves' partner when England beat the West Germans 1-0 for the second successive time.

ENGLAND WON their last pre-tournament friendly at Wembley, 2-0 against Yugoslavia, with Martin Peters making his debut before Ramsey gave his squad three weeks' holidays.

While brother Bobby and his wife Norma went to Majorca, Jack took a heavily pregnant Pat and John and Debbie to stay with his former Leeds teammate Bobby Forrest in Weymouth. He ran every day on the beach to keep in shape and also became a popular regular in Forrest's local pub.

The squad reconvened at Lilleshall, base camp for nearly a month as the Ramsey preparations intensified and before they moved to Hendon Hall for the tournament. Lilleshall was, in the words of Jimmy Greaves, a 'fitness fanatics' paradise' and the England players were put through a tough programme of exercise, practice matches and training films, often from nine o'clock in the morning until nine o'clock at night. It felt like prison to Jack.

'Lilleshall was hard to take... training and preparation all day, and nothing to do in the evenings, because we were confined to the hotel grounds,' Jack reflected. 'I used to walk down the drive leading to the main road with Nobby and Bally and a few others. It was a couple of miles or so to the gate, and we just had to stand there and watch the traffic going past. I remember sticking my arms through the wires once and shouting, "Let us out... let us out!"

'A few of the lads used to nip over to the golf clubhouse for a pint. You could get there by going across the playing fields, over a fence, over a wall and then across the golf course. I wasn't brave enough to go myself.

'Inevitably, Alf found out and called a meeting, where he said that if anybody else did it again, they'd be out the door immediately. Nobody went back after that.'

The boredom was relieved when the squad travelled to Scandinavia and Eastern Europe where they won all three games. Jack scored his first England goal in a 3-0 win in Finland, and then netted again a week later against Denmark.

But the euphoria surrounding those healthy wins was soon deflated in England's dismal opening game in the World Cup against Uruguay. The hosts could not break down the South Americans who had clearly come for a goalless draw, and got one. Ramsey was content that his side had not lost their opening game but the result was a setback and the press turned on the team and manager for the first time.

Jack had an additional concern after the Uruguay game as he and Bobby Moore were selected for the random drugs test. He was actually selected for nearly every game of the competition, much to his chagrin. 'Before the tournament ended we presented him with a potty and named him "England's Jimmy Riddle champion",' said Gordon Banks.

Five days after the goalless opener, England's campaign was back on track with a 2-0 win over Mexico; Bobby Charlton scoring one of the greatest of his 49 England goals and Roger Hunt adding the second. Another 2-0 win over France followed, with Hunt this time scoring both. Jimmy Greaves, who had not scored in the three games, was badly injured and was forced to watch Hurst take his chance in his absence. England had reached the last eight without conceding a goal as Jack and Bobby Moore established a central defensive understanding that has remained unrivalled in the English game since.

GORDON BANKS

Jack was strong and commanding in the middle. We used to get on at each other during matches, but this was purely to keep each other on the alert. The sometimes rude and brutal things we yelled in the heat of the battle were always quickly forgotten once the final whistle had blown.

RAY WILSON

Me and Big Jack were mouthy players and it's very important that people talk. We never used to break, we tried to keep the back four solid, we never tackled until they got round the penalty area and the other lads put them under pressure; so they couldn't squeeze the ball through.

THE QUARTER-FINAL showdown against Argentina was, in Jack's words, 'a strange game'. Argentine skipper Antonio Rattin was sent off in the 35th minute for continual back-chat to the referee. The game was held up for seven minutes because Rattin refused to leave the pitch, even after the intervention of the police. He continued arguing, ranting and gesticulating as he headed down the tunnel.

'I thought it was stupid and unnecessary, but at the same time we were delighted to see him go, because he was a bloody good player,' Jack admitted.

Down to ten men, Argentina made no attempt to play, or make English friends on and off the pitch; but their brutality was undone by Geoff Hurst's headed winner.

Ramsey, who had told his players not to retaliate to any provocation, was furious with their opponents' behaviour. He stormed on to the pitch, refusing to allow his players to swap shirts.

The English manager called the Argentinians 'animals'.

The win set up a classic semi-final with Portugal, and star player Eusebio. Bob Charlton did not get to see the semi-final, insisting he could not miss his shift at Ashington pit. But Cissie was there, of course.

She travelled down from the North East for every game, although her visits were not without incident. By displaying a stubbornness that Jack could only admire, she had passed up the opportunity to stay at a London hotel for the duration of the finals. The city hotels were full but Jack told her to contact a friend of his, also called Jack, at the Great Northern Hotel.

She asked for him at the hotel reception but was told it was his day off.

CISSIE CHARLTON

'Just my luck,' I thought and asked the girl if there was a room available. She was sorry but they didn't have one room left. I said, 'All right,' and turned to leave. As I reached the door the girl asked, 'Who should I say called when Jack comes back?'

I answered, 'Mrs Charlton, Jack Charlton's mother'. It was as if I had said a magic password. The receptionist's manner changed completely. She said, 'Oh, would you like a room with a bath?' I was infuriated to think that as an ordinary customer I couldn't have the room, yet as Cis Charlton I could.

I snapped, 'No, you can keep it,' and stormed out. Unfortunately I had just thrown away my only chance of a room and I had to travel down from the North East for the rest of the World Cup games until the final.

Just before England met Portugal in that crucial semi-final, Jack telephoned and asked me to have tea with him before the match. The team had been stuck in Hendon Hall Hotel since July 8 and he was aching to see a friendly face that didn't belong to the England party.

When I got there Alf Ramsey, England's manager, came over to me and announced that he had arranged transport to Wembley for me. He also added, 'You're not going home tonight either, I have booked a room for you here.'

I was really impressed to think that in spite of all the pressure he must have been under, Alf would take time out to think about me.

THE SEMI-FINAL in front of more than 90,000 at Wembley was indeed a classic. And England were too good. Nobby Stiles stifled Eusebio, handling the "Black Pearl" with his customary care; Jack matched Jose Torres' size and physicality, and Bobby Charlton ran the show, scoring two brilliant goals.

'At the end I was in tears as I hugged our kid. We were through to the final.'

Jack did give away a late penalty and England conceded their first goal of the finals. He handled a Torres header over Banks, denying a clear goal by palming the ball away on the line. Jack wasn't even booked, as yellow and red cards had not been introduced then. But in the modern game, he would have been sent off. And Jack Charlton would have missed the 1966 World Cup final. England met West Germany at Wembley on July 30, 1966.

The entire country was at fever pitch. Ramsey controversially selected Hurst ahead of a fit again Greaves. This time, Cissie insisted on Bob going to the game. She even bought him a new suit for the occasion, plus a trilby to replace his tatty flat cap. She was not impressed when her husband somehow misplaced his new headwear and he wore the flat cap to the final anyway.

This time *The People* newspaper picked up the bill and photographed her buying a new hat for the day. It was without question the greatest day of her life. And Cissie was devastated that Pat, her regular partner at grounds up and down the country, in all weathers, was not sat beside her, or got to meet Prime Minister Harold Wilson at the after-dinner party.

Pat was expecting Peter, nicknamed "World Cup Willie" because he was due on cup final day. She decided not to risk any unnecessary excitement away from their home in Leeds. It was probably a wise decision. Brother Gordon, who had once been on the Leeds playing staff but did not make it as a pro, also missed the final. He was working as a Navy engineer on board the Glengyle – 30 miles off Shanghai in the South China Sea. The match clashed with his shift so he missed the commentary of the game on the BBC, and had to rely on other crewmen to relay progress reports.

When Germany equalised in the dying minutes, one came down to yell at him, 'That bastard brother of yours has given a goal away!'

Jack was always confident of winning the biggest game of his life. 'So it was a terrible blow when we went a goal down. I remember it to this day. It was a fairly simple cross into the box, and instead of playing the ball on, the way he should have done, Ray Wilson headed it back up the middle, something you should never do.

'He mistimed it... it fell to Haller, who had plenty of time to shoot – though funnily enough, he didn't hit it that well. I remember standing there, and as the ball came past me I could have stuck a foot out and stopped it. But it looked as if it was going straight to Banksy. Now normally I had a very good understanding with Gordon, but as it happened, it sort of sneaked in between me and him. Maybe he thought I was going to stop it, I don't know.'

England equalised with a Hurst header from Bobby Moore's quickly taken free kick, then Jack nearly got in on the act.

'The second goal came after Geoff Hurst's shot ricocheted off somebody and came over the top of the centre back just as I was coming in behind. I was thinking to myself, this is coming to me – and then all of a sudden Martin Peters runs in front of me and knocks the ball into the net.'

With seconds of the game remaining, Jack gave away a free kick just outside the area and in the ensuing scramble Wolfgang Weber scored at the far post. Wembley fell silent. Extra-time beckoned.

Geoff Hurst's controversial second goal in the first half of extra-time put England ahead and he completed his hat trick in the second half, running on to Moore's long through ball before smashing the ball into the roof of the net past German keeper Hans Tilkowski. The stadium erupted.

'The final whistle went just after Geoff's goal, the game was over, and Geoff stood there with his hands in the air. I ran the whole length of the field just to get hold of him, but as I came near him he ran off and I was too knackered to follow.

'I flopped to my knees, totally exhausted, and my head fell forwards onto my hands. I don't remember saying a prayer – I probably just said something like, "Thank the Lord that's over".'

With Pat back home in Leeds, Jack was on his own after the official team reception. Rather than go with his teammates and their wives to a nightclub, he teamed up with Jim Mossop, an old journalist friend from the North East.

JIM MOSSOP

In the early hours in a Nottingham hotel, shortly after Leeds had defeated Manchester United in an FA Cup semi-final in 1965, Don Revie let slip a gem of information.

'Keep this to yourselves for now,' he told a couple of football writers he trusted, 'Alf Ramsey has been on the phone and he wants to call up Jack into his England squad.'

This was a stunner. Jack was just short of his 30th birthday and for a journalist to keep that under his hat was asking a lot. It was used as 'speculation' in print until confirmation came.

There was more than a hint of pride in Revie's voice. In his role as Leeds United manager he was often tested by Jack's stubborn contrariness. Jack knew it all, or he thought he did and there were times when Revie couldn't fathom him. Then it all clicked.

He played 35 times for England but the pinnacle of his international career was being part of England's 1966 World Cup win. When Ramsey picked him for his debut against Scotland at Wembley in 1965, it was with the following year's tournament in mind.

With Jack Charlton you got honesty, ambition and commitment. He was a winner with an immensely competitive streak. But he was also a man of intense loyalty. He knuckled down in Revie's early years, listened to his manager and buried his own profound opinions on how the game should be played.

After one match at Elland Road, Revie sent a message to the Pressroom via a steward who said to a journalist (me), 'Mr Revie wants to see you'. When the writer went to Revie's office, perhaps expecting a chastisement over something he had written, Revie handed him a beer and said, 'I hear you are a friend of Jack Charlton's. In that case you have a friend for life'.

That remains true to this day.

And there was a night out with Jack, in the hours after the World Cup win. Jack's wife Pat, was at home with the birth of their third child Peter imminent, when Jack emerged from the banquet and walked over to his friend and said they would have a night out.

'But I'm driving back to Manchester and I've only got a tenner on me,' I replied.

'Not to worry,' said Jack, who had £100 for wearing his boots during the finals. We would spend that, and the tenner as well. We struggled to spend anything other than a taxi fare to the Astor Club. We had jumped into an occupied cab but it was grid-locked outside the Royal Garden Hotel and we told the passenger already in the cab that we would drop him at his destination and pay his fare at the end of the journey.

The man said he was a classical organist on his way to play a recital. He said he thought there had been some 'footy occasion' and hadn't a clue of Jack's identity.

On entering the club, the band stopped playing and as we sat down the first of the bottles of champagne began arriving at the table from people who were celebrating England's win. A couple at the next table invited us back to their house in Leytonstone and we returned to the hotel the following morning.

A FRIEND drove Jack and his parents back north the next day, and on the way he insisted on stopping at a motorway services for egg and chips; not surprisingly he described it as the best meal he'd had in weeks. Less than a month later, on August 17, Jack and Bobby Charlton returned to Ashington.

It seems only fitting that Cissie should tell the rest of the story.

CISSIE CHARLTON

Civic leaders in Ashington decided that it was about time they paid their own tribute to two home grown sporting heroes by arranging a Town Hall reception and banquet in honour of Bobby and Jack. What a day that was!

The event was meant to 'kick off' with a procession starting from outside my home in Beatrice Street at six fifteen in the evening. But that official starting time was ignored by many people. They began to congregate in the back lane from first thing in the morning. Colourful bunting had been strung across the narrow street overnight. Posters, banners and flags were fastened to the high, yellow brick wall enclosing ours and neighbouring backyards.

By ten am children were beginning to gather outside my house and chatted excitedly. Youngsters who had climbed onto wall tops outside our house, as the day progressed, set up a cheer which was caught and echoed by several hundred people in the street below every time one of us came to the door. It was flattering – but also embarrassing. Our only toilet stood at the bottom of the yard and anyone using it had to do so with several well-wishers clumping around on the roof over their head.

At five pm the back lane was filled with a surging mass of people. Youngsters were standing on each other's shoulders to scramble on to the top of our yard wall in an effort to catch a glimpse of Bobby or Jack. By that time Jack and Pat had arrived with their children Deborah, John and little Peter in his carrycot.

Lancashire industrialist Donald Heyworth had read of the civic reception idea in a newspaper and offered to drive Bobby and Jack the half mile to Ashington's Town Hall in his 1926 open top yellow Rolls Royce. It was a terrific struggle, but first Bobby and Jack, then Bob and me along with their wives, heaved ourselves through the crowd of noisy well wishers to our waiting cars. Minutes earlier it had begun to rain, but no one seemed to notice or to care.

Jack made the most of that half-mile trip, perched there on the back of the rear seat. He waved and grinned all the way to the Town Hall, every inch of which was lined by cheering people.

Inside the Council Chamber, Council Chairman Tom Harkness formally welcomed us and presented Bobby and Jack with inscribed watches and silver tankards. Jack immediately slipped on his watch; then produced his World Cup winners medal. In the glare of the television lights it gleamed brilliantly.

After the official presentations we left for a banquet at Ashington's Hirst Welfare Miner's Hall. Somehow, instead of getting into the official car, Jack charged into one driven by a reporter Vince Gledhill. Rather than returning to the melee to await the official transport, they set off for Hirst Welfare in Vince's old Triumph Herald. Following close behind them was Roy Nuttall, Ashington's Town Clerk and the man whose carefully laid plans for this highly publicised event seemed to be going off course.

Halfway to the Welfare his worst fears seem to be taking shape before his eyes. Inside the Triumph Herald Jack was shouting, 'Stop! Stop the car!' The cavalcade behind them also slowed as the Herald braked. A mystified Roy Nuttall watched Jack climb out of the car and head for a workingmen's club a few yards away. Jack had taken it into his head to pop in for a pint and see some of his old mates, regardless of the fact that a banquet organised in his honour would have to be held up until he arrived. Red faced, Roy jumped from his car and ran to the club doorway barring Jack's path.

IT WAS not the first time Jack would veer off schedule to be with his friends and not just those with football connections. For as long as they have been together, Jack and Pat have welcomed people from all walks of life into their lives. And when they say come visit, or we'll visit you, they mean it. Jack's success with Ireland allowed him the opportunity to experience vast areas of the country at will. He wanted to visit these places, the people embraced him with open arms, and refused to let him pay a penny. Not surprisingly, he loved it and Ireland loved Jack. He was no different when he played and managed around Yorkshire, Teesside and Northumberland.

The list of friends Jack and Pat have made along the way is endless, almost as long as the players. And like the players, they are loyal and affectionate towards the couple and they are such an important part of the story. And so, in Dublin, Dallas or Dortmund, if someone he knew needed a lift to the game, or had popped down to watch training, they got on the team bus. And no one argued with the manager.

That can't be said of former Hunslet professional rugby league player Dave

Croft, who like Jack's other closest friends, had his humdinger rows with him...
and loved every minute of them. The secret is to remember Jack's always right.
And you can argue with him, because he likes a rant and he's never held a grudge.

The pair have remained close since their playing days when they would
regularly go shooting together around the Yorkshire Dales. Their families grew
up, went on holiday to the caravans in Filey, shared Christmases together. Uncle
Jack took Dave's daughter Jane on her first day at primary school, to the delight
of her Leeds United-supporting new classmates, and their parents, and had a
great relationship with her sister Ruth.

RAY BAILEY was former Shrewsbury Town chairman and a successful horse
owner. And he is a serious fisherman. They met at Oakwell one cold night. They
were the only three in the directors' box to make the unusual decision to turn
down the half-time Barnsley chops. It was Pat who initiated the conversation.

'"Are you not going in for the Barnsley chop, love?" Ray remembers being
asked. 'And I turned round and there was a well-wrapped up lady and Jack
Charlton. And I explained that I was settled and would have to give the meal a
miss. "We were just saying the same thing," she said. So we introduced ourselves,
and started chatting. And inevitably, with Jack, we moved on to the subject of
fishing. I asked if he had ever tried sea trout fishing. He hadn't. I said I had a
place on the west coast of Scotland and he should come over. He'd like that, he
said, and he got my phone number.

'The next morning, I was in the office and my secretary Lily Costello took
a call. "It's Jack Charlton," she said. "He wants to speak to you." She put him
through. "Hello Raymond," he said. "Were you serious about going to your
place for some sea trout fishing?" And so began a wonderful friendship, with
Jack and Pat, which has taken us to some beautiful places in the UK and Ireland.'

'And Pat is the most incredible woman. There is no way Jack could have
achieved all he has in football, if Pat had not been beside him with the check-list
in her head, whether he's going to watch a game, or meeting civic leaders. She
just wants to make sure everything is in place. Not that it mattered in Ireland that
much. People just accept Jack because he is the most wonderful, honest man you
could meet.'

Ray became more than a great friend, he became one of Jack's group of
'Fishermen Friends', a very important group that included Dave Hutton, Dave

Croft, Mac Murray, and Frank Gillespie. They are 'Fishermen Friends' with more than one tale to tell.

RAY BAILEY

We were on the River Eriff near Connemara, a good eight miles off the beaten track on a warm August day and not much was happening. Jack said, 'I tell you what Raymond, I'm parched'. I'm christened Ray, and I told him that but Jack still calls me Raymond. We'd spotted a halfway house about half an hour away, so I said I'd go get a couple of beers each. The house was a shop/pub/post office/house, and run by a lovely little old lady. I got half a dozen Smithwicks, paid her and headed back to Jack. I opened a bottle and handed him it. He took a swig, then turned to me and said, 'Have you seen the sell-by date on the bottles, pal?' They were four years out of date.

I think the Ireland 1990 squad troubled Jack the most.

Jack would often talk out loud about his team selections and before that tournament we went up to Galway for a few days. Willie Moran has the Oyster Cottage at Moran's Of The Weir there, serving 400,000 oysters a year at one point and he became a great friend. We liked to have a cigar – a King Edwards or a Villiger – and watch the world go by. Jack was anxious not to upset anyone, but deep down, he knew he would have to. 'I want to take them all,' he said.

We were never looking to stay in the best hotels or great luxury. Jack and Pat were happiest when they were in the little B&Bs where, as Jack said, 'You don't have to change for dinner'. We were out in the countryside near Connemara and passed a little sign for a bed-and-breakfast. Pat and I knocked on the door.

Jack stayed in the car and we checked if they had any vacancies. There were some; we looked at the rooms, spoke to the owner, who was a lady in her early 40s, with three kids. I said we'd go and get our luggage and additional guest from the car; she said she would make a pot of tea.

As she was bringing the tea in, Jack came to the front door. She didn't say a word, just stood there clasping her mouth and tears started rolling down her cheeks. Then she started running round and fussing over Jack and eventually we had to tell her to calm down.

We went fishing in some beautiful places, among the best in the world. We fished the famous falls at Aisley, and stayed at Aisley Lodge. Jack caught a lot of fish there over the years.

People always made a fuss of Jack, and he was always just the same. When we went to

Galway, we stayed with Ann and Martin Kerrins, they'd put us up in a dormer-bungalow. And every night, their children would come down, impeccably dressed, and perform the Irish dancing. It was so enchanting and lovely. Jack loved it.

It was just after Italia '90 and we were in Galway, staying with the Kerrins'. We were fishing the Golden Furlong. The man who ran it was a fella called Seamus Hartigan, with Jimmy Small. When you fish the Golden Furlong, you start up at the top and work your way down. It takes a while and it's quite perilous as the water comes through the gates.

Jack was 30 yards in front of me and 10 yards above the best bit; the water was boiling up. Jack said it was looking great for fish, and he got closer in. You could hardly hear yourself above the noise of the water. Just as he started, Seamus was shouting at me but I couldn't hear a word. He seemed to be indicating he wanted me to get Jack out of the water.

There was absolutely no chance. But Seamus was becoming very animated and very insistent. I decided I had no choice but to come out of the river and see what the fuss was all about. As I came up to the bridge, there were two Gardai and the bridge was nearly 20-people deep, and beyond that you could see the traffic was at a standstill. Jack was oblivious to it but the Garda and Seamus pleaded with me to get Jack out of the river.

I went back down and just about got him to hear me. I said, 'You've got to come out of the water, Jack'. His reply made it quite clear he was going nowhere. Then I told him to look up. There were people peering over the bridge trying to catch a glimpse. Well, that was it. Jack managed to catch a fish on the walkway as he headed out and Seamus netted it for him. It was the only way to do it in front of the whole town.

We were up at our lodge near Loch Striven and Cissie was with us, she was in her late 80s. She was such a lovely lady and you can understand why Jack is such a humble person and gets on with people from all walks of life so well. They were very similar. Jack and Pat had gone into the pub and I was walking in with Cissie. We walked up the steps and saw a swing with two rubber tyres on it.

Cissie wanted a go. So, I sat this 80 year-old woman in a rubber tyre and stood behind her giving her a good push, while she was whooping and laughing away. Eventually Jack came out looking for us and he was absolutely crackers.

'You daft old sod,' he shouted. 'Get off there.' Cissie just ignored him and told me to carry on pushing. Oh, never mind him,' she said. 'Bad-tempered old buggah.'

Jack loves shooting and one of his favourites is the Wenalt Drive near Llangedwyn, just over the Welsh border. It's a tough shoot because the birds go 50 to 60 yards in the air.

'I can't hit the f**king things,' Jack loved to moan, saying they were too high for him and he was never going to shoot anything. He persevered and brought this bird down and *the whole line stopped and applauded. He had a beautiful Purdey gun but the funny thing was that he would never shoot with it, preferring to use his Browning instead. He thought the world of the Purdey but didn't want to use his best one.*

DAVID HUTTON

We were in Ballina for the salmon festival and Jack had been asked to start a number of races for sheep, geese, pigs, chickens. There was one goose in its race and it had a sign round its neck... 'Dunphy'.

And the fella said, 'We thought you could give is a kick up the arse, Jack'. Lunch was a most incredible platter of seafood, a big loaf of soda bread and a pint of Guinness at Eddie Doherty's bar which was above The Ridge Pool. Eddie and his mother Ali became great friends over the years. We were ready to head off when Jack was asked to start one last race.

He headed back to the start line, and was handed a flag. It was the blind man's race, complete with guide dogs. 'What do I need the flag for?' Jack asked.

And the fella said, 'When you drop the flag... just shout go'.

FRANK GILLESPIE

We headed to Belfast from Limerick, via Ballina in Frank Smith's Jaguar, to watch Northern Ireland versus Latvia. As we came into Belfast, I said to Jack that we were running out of petrol. He looked across and the gauge was just below half. 'You'll be fine,' he said.

We went to the game and were an hour into the journey to Ballina afterwards when the gauge went from half to nearly empty in a short space of time. I knew we were in trouble and that I wouldn't hear the last of it. We started blaming each other when I spotted this closed petrol station, so I pulled in. Now when a stranger's car pulled into a petrol station in Northern Ireland back then, people notice. And I was travelling with Jack Charlton.

Suddenly these fellas came from nowhere, spotted Jack and started asking if they could help us out. Then the RUC arrived; they were all delighted to see Jack. They said they knew the lady who ran the petrol station, so jumped in the car to get her. When she came back she said she would only give us petrol on the condition that she could have an autograph. He posed for some photos and gave her the autograph, and got a packet of cigs.

As we left, he said, 'Don't you tell the players we ran out of petrol because they will love that and start giving me s***.' We had a night-cap and went to bed, and when I caught up with Jack late the next afternoon in Limerick, he was in a foul mood. He said to me, 'I thought I told you not to say anything about running out of petrol last night?' He showed me the newspaper.

There was an article saying the RUC had come to Jack's rescue. I said, 'I never said anything about it. It is nothing to do with me. It must've been them'. He was right. The players gave him some terrible stick.

He went to Mountjoy prison in Dublin to give a presentation to the prisoners. He asked me to go along, jokingly saying I could be his bodyguard. John Lonegan, Tipperary man, was the governor and he gave us the tour and introduced us to a convicted murderer. Jack wasn't happy.

He said, 'Take me to see the lads who are into football and want to do something with their lives.' John arranged for some pictures to be taken. They were lined up against the wall when suddenly Jack started shouting, and pointing at this lad.

'This guy has stolen my wallet'. I looked at Jack. 'Arrest him,' he shouted. When he said that, all we could do was buckle over and laugh our heads off.

'What's the point?' I asked him.

And Jack said, 'Fine bloody bodyguard you are'. He got the wallet back. There was no money in it. 'How much did you have in it?' I asked him.

And he said, 'I don't carry cash'.

He came to Boston for his 60th birthday and I arranged for Mick Byrne and Charlie O'Leary to come over for his party as a surprise.

So Mick and Charlie, dressed as two chefs, came up to Jack and Pat's hotel suite with a trolley and knocked on the door. I answered the door and backed them in, but Jack was stood in our way saying, 'No, no... sorry boys... not for this room... no, no'. So we were stood there for a few seconds jostling, the lads trying to get into the middle of the room when they finally managed to shout 'HAPPY BIRTHDAY!'

Jack fell back in the chair.

He actually cried.

DAVE CROFT

We were at the Inniscarra fishery after an invitation from John Banks. Jack took over, as he usually did, told me where to go and he went further down, which is the preferred spot. I caught a nine pound salmon, it was absolutely beautiful.

When I got back, Jack had taken my spot. You don't really do that, but Jack could get *away with doing what he liked. We were fishing for another hour, and I caught another nine pound salmon, in the exact spot where he'd been originally. You can imagine the shouting and swearing. The language was just choice.*

We posed for a couple of photos and Jack pretended to look glum while I held up the two salmon. The photo is on the wall of The Den in Jack's home.

Peter O'Reilly had arranged for Jack to have lunch at a garage/shop in the middle of nowhere. A couple ran the place and after sitting us down, we got talking and Jack asked if they had any kids. They had 12. They all lived at home and the eldest was 17. Jack asked if he could meet them? They came in, one-by-one, and the wife had scrubbed them all and they were in their Sunday best.

When they'd finished, Jack said, 'There's only 11. One's missing.' She said, 'He has the mumps.' And Jack said, 'Ah, go get him.'

He led the way for the good feeling there is between English and Irish people now.

He made people realise that we're not that different, and, without saying it, that we all wanted peace in Ireland.

There was a lot of trouble when we first started travelling over. We would drive from Larne to get to Ballina and we had to go through the barriers with the soldiers. They were poor times in the history of the relationship between the two countries.

I believe Jack laid the foundation for what was to come. We travelled all over Ireland and he was worshipped everywhere he went. And suddenly, a lot of Irish people started to realise that English people weren't so bad, and English people became more comfortable with travelling to Ireland and discovering its beauty.

MIDDLESBROUGH

JACK CHARLTON was still a Leeds United player when he was offered the Middlesbrough job. He knew his playing days were numbered after 23 years at Elland Road. Don Revie had even told him so.

'The problem with you,' said the Leeds boss, at the start of the 1972-73 season and a year before he left the club, 'is that you can now only motivate yourself for the big games.' It was one of the few conversations in which Jack didn't disagree with every word out of his manager's mouth.

Middlesbrough had not been in the top flight for 20 years. Stan Anderson had just quit as manager and club chairman Charlie Aymer rang Jack to see if he wanted the job. After taking in a game with Pat and being suitably impressed with the team, he agreed to meet the Board on his 38th birthday. The interview did not go according to their plans, or his. When he was called in, he sat before a dozen directors who started firing questions at him. Jack immediately halted proceedings.

'Wait a minute,' he said, 'I didn't come here to be interviewed for the job, I came here because I was told that you wanted me to manage the club, and that the job was mine if I wanted it.' He produced a piece of paper from his pocket.

It was in Don Revie's handwriting. His mentor had given him a list of manager's responsibilities, making it clear Jack would have a say in everything and the final say in all things relating to the team.

'I will just go and sit outside while you read it,' he said, 'so we won't need to have a discussion. If you decide that you want me to be the manager, okay, and if you don't, just let me know and I'll go.'

After waiting for 15 minutes, Jack became impatient. He knocked on the door, put his head round it and told them they had another 10 minutes, or he was off.

Five minutes later, he was summoned back in to the Board Room and told he had the job. But he had one final demand. He would not be signing a contract. He told his astonished new employers that he planned to stay for a maximum of four years and if either party wanted to terminate the agreement before then, it could be done with no hard feelings.

AS WELL as being able to turn to Revie at any time, Jack had the ear and wisdom of Jock Stein to rely on. The pair sat together at a Football Writers' Association banquet in London before the 1973 FA Cup final. Stein, who six years earlier had guided Celtic to victory in the European Cup, offered advice on the new job. Jack listened to every word.

He told him to take the team on tour as soon as possible, telling him he would learn more about his players in that time than during an entire season. Stein arranged pre-season friendlies for Boro in Scotland. When he returned back home, Jack made it his mission to get rid of 'two or three barrack-room lawyers'.

Stein also delivered one gem that was to serve Jack well throughout his managerial career. '"There will come a time", he told me, "when your players become complacent and start taking advantage. They might have done nothing wrong, just become a bit blasé about the results or their performances.

'"It is then that you have to crack the whip."

'It may seem a little hard at the time, but Jock was absolutely right – you've got to shout at your players now and again, just to stir them up a bit and make them take notice.'

His old pal and former England teammate Nobby Stiles left straight away. That was a blow. Jack tried to persuade him to stay, as he knew he would be a trusted ally and one who just happened to be more than capable of playing the vital holding and break-up role. But Stiles and his wife wanted to return to Manchester, so Jack arranged for him to join his brother Bobby at Preston North End.

'Our Bob had been at the same Football Writers' banquet when I sat next to Jock Stein. He'd already taken the Preston job, but he never mentioned it to me, which I found a little strange. The first I knew of it was when I read about it in the Sunday papers a few days later.'

STEIN ALSO bestowed one precious gift to Jack to fill the gap left by Stiles. Bobby Murdoch. However, despite the immediate friendship and bond with Stein, when the wily Scot offered his Celtic, European Cup winning, Scotland international midfield linchpin, who was still only 28, on a free transfer, with only a signing on fee to pay, Jack was still suspicious.

He asked Murdoch to meet him. What followed, Jack revealed, was 'one of the most honest and frank talks that I've ever had in my entire life'. Murdoch admitted he had a problem with his weight, which was Jack's main concern, but vowed to keep working to keep it down. Satisfied, Jack signed him.

'It was an investment which would be recouped over and over again in the years ahead.' After his influential role in Middlesbrough's record-breaking promotion from the Second Division, it was, however, Murdoch who was to cost Middlesbrough a place in Europe in Jack's penultimate season. Middlesbrough were leading 1-0 against Derby County in the last game of the season at Ayresome Park. A win was enough for a European place.

In the last minute, Middlesbrough had a corner.

Jack ran down the touchline, yelling at Murdoch to keep the ball there. He didn't listen; instead he knocked it across the face of the box where it went out for another corner. By now apoplectic, Jack watched Murdoch play a poor pass from the corner to the back four. Kevin Hector intercepted before it reached them on the halfway line. The Derby striker ran half the length of the pitch and slotted the ball past Jim Platt to equalise.

'I am afraid I didn't spare Bobby in the dressing room. It was the last game of the season, so there was no putting it off until Monday. Nobody had done more to put me right at the start of my managerial career, and now he was guilty of the schoolboy error which cost us Europe.'

JACK CHANGED the kit.

Believing in what had worked for Don Revie and Bill Shankly at Leeds United and Liverpool, where they introduced the distinctive all white and all red strips, Jack decided to make his mark too. Out went a red shirt with white trimmings. Middlesbrough now had their own brand. A bright red shirt with a distinctive white stripe across the chest. No other club had it. 'Old-timers thought I was crackers, but I knew my football and the value of being able to spot a teammate under pressure.'

Jack also gave Ayresome Park a makeover.

He moved the TV gantry to give more presentable views of action from the ground to the viewers, and spruced up the dressing rooms and the stands.

He went to the ICI plant in Billingham, who along with British Steel were the biggest employers on Teesside, and with a hardcore Boro following. They agreed to supply the paint. He wanted the seats in red and white. And Jack was more than a little peeved when his chairman interfered. He'd made the mistake, in a rare Board meeting appearance, of mentioning his little coup to the directors. Chairman Charlie Aymer said he'd give his friend at the plant a call. Jack pleaded with him to leave it. But Aymer insisted. And got a bill for the paint for his troubles.

It was the club's money, not Jack's. But he was displeased to say the least.

'I learned my first lesson in management. If you want things done, do them yourself and tell nobody.'

RAY ROBERTSON

Middlesbrough fans were delighted when the news was officially confirmed. They felt Jack could lift the team out of the doldrums and challenge Newcastle United and Sunderland for the back page headlines in the North East.

Jack laid it on the line when he met the players for the first time at Marton Hotel and Country Club.

'There are some good players, some poor players and some lazy players,' he said.

The players got the message and were determined not to finish in the latter category.

On a pre--season tour of Scotland, Jack asked me, 'Who is this kid Armstrong?'

David Armstrong was a local discovery on the fringe of the first team. 'He's a natural left footer who provides the perfect balance,' I said. Within six months he rated him good enough to play in the great Leeds United team of the day.

Meanwhile, Bobby Murdoch was one of the best passers of a ball I have ever seen. He was not the most agile of players but as one teammate remarked, 'He could win a game standing still'.

Middlesbrough swept everything before them and had promotion wrapped up with weeks to spare.

In recognition of Boro's success, Jack won a Manager of the Year award, though I think he was embarrassed by it. He thought it should have gone to Bill Shankly in the First Division.

To beat the offside trap, Jack devised a special plan so the midfielders would pull the ball back into midfield where Alan Foggon – the 'flying pig' to his teammates – would race through and score.

It proved very effective. Middlesbrough made their mark in the First Division, came within a whisker of qualifying for Europe, and could have won the title in Jack's final season. Skipper Stuart Boam publicly urged Jack to strengthen the attack but he had a tight-fisted approach to the transfer market. Jack later admitted he had been naïve.

Jack's reign at Ayresome Park was not all sweetness and light. He had frequent clashes with the Board.

When he was appointed, it was laid down that Jack would look after the football and the Board would handle all business matters.

The Board built up a "Charlton interfering file" and he told them he could no longer listen to their 'nonsensical views'. He did not attend Board meetings for another three years.

Everyone knows Jack loves fishing. He would regularly rush off from a morning training session to a river somewhere in the North East. But not many people are aware Jack also has a love of leeks. When Jack left Boro, I wanted to make a farewell gift in appreciation of his excellent cooperation over the years. A packet of cigarettes was out of the question and a bottle of wine or whiskey seemed inadequate.

In a moment of inspiration, I remembered his love of leeks. A friend of mine was the Durham County leek champion and I arranged to collect his prize examples at a hotel in Darlington.

When I took the leeks to Jack's house in Great Ayton, you would have thought I was handing over the crown jewels!

JACK CHARLTON built a good Middlesbrough side.

It was full of Boro heroes... Hickton, Armstrong, Boam, Maddren, Mills, Foggon... the list goes on. They still talk about that team today and with a fondness that even the cup winning side of the modern era couldn't match.

He built a generation of Middlesbrough supporters. Supporters like the present Middlesbrough chairman Steve Gibson and Gibson's best school pal Chris Kamara who played for Middlesbrough Boys, but neither of whom were signed as apprentices by the club. Gibson turned to business and became Middlesbrough's saviour, whose nouse took them into Europe after winning the League Cup in 2004, the North East's only trophy in 50 years.

Kamara left the town aged 16 to join the Navy before he was spotted and offered a contract by Portsmouth boss Ian St John. Now a popular *Sky Sports* pundit, Kamara played more than 600 games for nine clubs, including a brief spell on loan at Middlesbrough in 1993.

STEVE GIBSON

I was 16 when Jack joined the club and to have a World Cup legend at Middlesbrough was fantastic for us and I remember the excitement right across Teesside at the time. He was untried as a manager but the team had performed reasonably well under Stan Anderson. Jack took it to a different level. We won the old Second Division with months to spare and if only Jack had had the right backing then, who knows where the club could have gone.

It was great to see him at the Riverside on the day we went back up to the Premier League in May, 2015. He admitted he was slightly torn because his former player Chris Hughton was in charge of Brighton that day and could also have gone up, but they just missed out. It was Middlesbrough's day and it was wonderful that Jack could be a part of it.

You could see from the warm reception he received from Middlesbrough supporters at half time just how much he still means to the people of Teesside. Jack is still a colossus and it is always great to see him at the Riverside. He is still revered in Middlesbrough and around the town, as we saw that day and as are all the players from Jack's team. Unfortunately, some are not with us any longer, but they are all warmly remembered. Jack is fun to be with, and he is not just a good football manager, and a brilliant footballer, he is a great man.

CHRIS KAMARA

I used to train with Middlesbrough Boys on the pitches next to the first team on Hutton Road. In those days, the first team manager didn't concern himself with the youth team and there were no academies, or anything like that.

We'd be able to watch Souness, Hickton, Foggon… all that team training, with Big Jack shouting and bellowing at them, losing his rag.

He was great to watch in full flow. You could see even seasoned pros like Bobby Murdoch, who'd come down from Scotland, respected him and were scared stiff of him. Everyone was. Graeme Souness was one of the best players the UK has ever seen, and went on to do the business abroad, and Big Jack got the best out of him.

Jack's style of management was off-the-cuff and he was a one-off, but it worked.

Before that, Middlesbrough were in the Third Division, and you couldn't support Sunderland or Newcastle, so I used to go and watch Leeds United.

It was just packed with brilliant players, even the sub Paul Madeley.

If you studied Jack with Ireland and compared him to managers now, you would look at his style and think, 'how on earth did that work?' But it did.

And he had the charisma and that little extra something. Sometimes the players might be bewildered by it, or frustrated and even fall out with him, but he always did it his way. And it worked.

ANOTHER FUTURE *Sky Sports* pundit in the senior Middlesbrough ranks in 1974 was Graeme Souness. Jack liked him immediately. But why the teenager had been discarded by Tottenham boss Bill Nicholson and ended up on Teesside mystified him.

'Graeme Souness was a young Scots lad who had been tried and rejected by Tottenham. Harold Stephenson had signed him at the end of the previous season and it didn't need a genius to deduce that with proper handling, he could become a top-class midfielder.

'As a footballer Graeme had a mean streak – in the best sense. When he put his foot in for the ball he intended to win it. And he spared nothing or nobody in the process of doing so. Why Tottenham ever let him go is a mystery.

'Perhaps he didn't settle in London, or it may have been an attitude problem. But within days of meeting him, I had put my mind at rest on this second issue. I took him into my office and confronted him straight away.

'"You've a reputation as a bit of a wide-boy who likes the birds and the booze," I started. And before I said another word, he got in his spoke.

'"That's right," he said. "I am fond of the girls and a night out, but I will tell you this – I will not cause you any problems. I want to succeed in football, and neither women nor drink will get in the way. I will prepare for games as carefully as anybody. I am annoyed you felt you had to haul me in here in the first place."

'I liked that last bit.

'The lad had a bit of fire in him, and if his skill was as good as I'd been led to believe, I reckoned young Souness would make out pretty well. In that I was proved right – but only after a period of trial and error.

'Graeme, when he started with us, was a left sided midfield player. To my mind he didn't have the kind of pace needed to get up and down the flank. But I reckoned he could do the business in the centre and it was there in fact that he grew into one of the great talents in British football.

'As a distributor of the ball, he was already displaying some of the characteristics of Bobby Murdoch. But unlike Bob, he'd often play it backwards or sideways – and that needed urgent correction.

'Day after day, I preached the necessity of getting it to the front men, of looking up when he got past an opponent, of playing it into the spaces and then supporting. It was alien to his way of thinking, but he worked hard, and eventually he did precisely what I demanded of him.'

GRAEME SOUNESS

I remember that meeting well. My head was up my own backside. I thought the world revolved around me. When Jack came, I was in the reserves and I used to drive him mad, telling him I should be in the team from the age of 18 onwards.

And he said, 'Look, you've got the talent but I have seen hundreds of players like you in the history of football that have had talent and have not used it and wasted it. He said, 'There are two doors for you. There is one you can walk out of to use your talent, make something of yourself and perhaps be a player one day. The other one is to throw it all away.'

He was not an arm-round-the-shoulder manager; it was blunt, straight to the point. He said what he had to say in a very basic and straightforward manner. It was great for me at the time.

I see that as a real milestone in my career. If I had met a less demanding manager, who was not as confrontational and aggressive, I might have drifted even more. So I see it as a really important period in my life as a player.

I could play anywhere across the middle but I remember playing at Bournemouth in a pre-season friendly at left back because the regular left back was injured and there was no one else. I couldn't get in the team in midfield but Taylor, who was playing on the left, got injured. Willie Maddren moved over and Jack put me in the middle, and that was the start of it.

It was a good team. We had a nice mix. The two up front were very direct and honest, chased everything down. Hickton was very aggressive and had real pace. David Armstrong on the left was a very good football player. He could open a can of beans with his left foot, ended up playing for England.

And we were solid at the back.

Jack was pretty basic in his methods. It was about getting it forward as quickly as you could. He didn't want you to over-complicate it in the middle of midfield and the best ball for him was to get John Hickton in a race with their defenders, and he would use his strength when he got there.

He was fairly straightforward and easy to understand in telling you the way he wanted you to play. But there was no time for tippy-tappy football then, and you have to factor in that the pitches were s***. Teams didn't play with the ball across their own penalty box because you couldn't.

He definitely had an influence on me as a manager. I was lucky enough to work with some greats in the game and he is definitely up there. His style was, 'I'm the manager, I'll manage it'.

Would he survive today?

No. Because players do not like being told the truth. You have to pussyfoot around them today and that was not Jack's style. Jack believed that if there was something to be said… he said it, and he wasn't too bothered if you didn't like what he was saying. Deal with it. You're a man.

He liked aggressive players. And he liked everyone to have a right go. Aggression in football comes in many different guises. It can be the goalkeeper commanding his box or the centre forward running at full throttle in a race for a through ball and knocking people out of his way to get there. And he liked aggression in midfield and I enjoyed playing for him.

I needed strong management and he gave me that. He knew in those days we liked a night out. And sometimes we bumped into him in the same places. He enjoyed himself as well. There was a time for that, and a time to work hard. And we were all terrified of him, so we did as we were told. He was a big old boy and aggressive in what he said. He had a temper on him, which we saw a few times. But you knew where you stood with him. You just had to deal with it.

We really didn't have that many run-ins, one-to-one. I think he liked me. Once he laid down the rules early on, I knew where I stood.

I told him I would deliver when I played for him, and I did. He liked that. He didn't come after me much, because I did what he wanted on the pitch. And Pat liked me, so I think I got on his right side because of that. I don't know why she did? She just liked me. I think she saw the mischief in me.

He left too early because if you look at the age of the team, the majority of us still had some life in us. In many cases the best years were still ahead of us. You look at myself, David Armstrong, Willie Maddren, our best years were still to come. But I don't think he liked spending money.

We finished seventh in our first season and I just think if he had gone out and spent the dosh, and added a couple of players, things might have been different.

Our paths never crossed professionally after that, but of course they did socially. And every time you meet him, you still feel he is The Boss.

His time with Ireland was a success. It suited him. But international football is very different to club football. You are dealt a hand. You cannot buy players. You have to work with what you have been given. And his style did not suit certain players.

But it comes back to what Jack wants. There was only way… Jack's way.

He wanted to play a certain way. The players had to do it, or there's the door. And it is very difficult to look back and argue differently.

Ireland were successful.

MIDDLESBROUGH WON the inaugural Anglo-Scottish Cup in 1976 beating Fulham 1-0 over two legs to bring some rare silverware back to the North East, albeit in a competition no team wanted to play in, never mind win.

Jack bought Phil Boersma from Liverpool to replace Murdoch in the club's centenary season. But he was beset by injuries and failed to reach the standards Jack expected.

Middlesbrough reached the semi-final of the League Cup but after winning the first leg against Manchester City 1-0 at Ayresome Park, they blew their chances on a disastrous night at Maine Road.

The team coach got caught in traffic and was late arriving, and Jack felt the players never settled. 'We got well and truly stuffed, four-nowt. I remember thinking to myself, I can't handle too many more nights like this.' Jack also felt his team was being found out.

On a wet and windy night at Birmingham, the opposition centre backs barely moved from outside their own penalty area. That closed down the space for Alan Foggon to run into and Jack knew the game was up for his striker and that way of playing. His misery was compounded when Wrexham did exactly the same when they knocked Boro out of the FA Cup.

Jack's fourth season at Middlesbrough was another frustrating one. After finishing mid-table the previous year, he hoped to be back in the shake-up for the title. But after another good FA Cup run, which saw them knocked out in the sixth round by Liverpool, their challenge withered and Boro could only finish 12th. For once he had the money, but he refused to spend it.

'We needed to change the team pattern, which meant spending some money. That was something I never liked doing. I treated club funds like my own – how naïve can you get? I reckon that I was only two players short of a title winning team, and I could have got them by spending some of the money I amassed for the club in the previous four years. But for better or worse, I chose not to do so.' Middlesbrough remains the one big regret in Jack Charlton's managerial career. He knows he walked away a year too soon.

He knows he should have spent the money.

He did try, but when it came to spending £80,000 to sign David Cross from Coventry, Jack balked at the fee. Cross eventually went to West Ham for £120,000. Everyone, including Jack, including John Hickton, knew that the fans' favourite was waning. And Jack failed to replace him.

By February of 1977 he had had enough and told Charlie Aymer he would be quitting at the end of the season. 'Though I'd had a few rows with the chairman, none of them particularly serious, I reckon Charlie was the most surprised man at the club.'

DAVID ARMSTRONG

When Jack joined Middlesbrough I was in the team but I was still only 17 and weighed about three stone wet through. Jack told me I had to put weight on and he sent me to his mum and dad's farm at Leyburn with Bobby Hosker, another young lad.

He knew that to play at a consistent level in his team we needed building up so we went to the farm for a week-to-10 days and he told Cissie to feed us big breakfasts, lunches and evening meals. We just ate, went for walks in the beautiful North Yorkshire countryside and built our muscles up by working on the farm, doing odd jobs and then having a bit of craic with Cissie and Jack's dad Bob. We were well looked after. Cissie just loved her football.

Jack used to call me his 'little gem'. Mind you, he used to call me 'Neil' as well, which

I wasn't over the moon about.

Before Jack came we were quite happily going along. He had an aura about him. He was a World Cup winner and had won league titles at Leeds. He was a big lad as well, so not many people argued with him and because of the success that he brought to the club there was no questioning him; and everyone believed in the system and the way we played and, of course, you can't argue with his record at club and international level.

Jack saw that fortunately, because I was left footed, I made the balance of the team right. And it led to a very happy time, not only for myself but for the club.

I was a bit scared of Jack at times. We all were.

The principles of the game are simple. People in the game make it difficult. Jack was one of those people who made it very, very easy to utilise your strengths and cover your weaknesses by having a system of playing. For example, Alan Foggon was a fantastic runner, great going forward, a lot of strength and endurance, so he would run from deep and we knew exactly where to pass the ball to cause the most damage to the opposition.

Jack wanted us to play the ball up the field, win it in the opposition's half most of the time, and then we had explosive people in the team who could make things happen, by creating and scoring goals.

And home or away, it didn't matter to us. We approached the game in exactly the same way, knowing full well that we had quality players in the side who could win a game because we had a good work ethic, good formation and we could play. The London press didn't like us, but we were in our element and we were a good side, to such a degree that many players were recognised for the hard work and endeavours they put in for the club and got international honours, including myself.

Watching Leicester win the Premier League title in such a similar way last season (2015-16) reminded me of just how good we were 40 years ago. We did exactly what Leicester did. And in that regard, we were a year ahead of Nottingham Forest, who of course went on to win the league and European Cup twice.

Jack was renowned for giving us carrots. And you couldn't help but love the little incentives he had and some of the tricks he played on us.

At the start of the season he would set out five game blocks with rewards if we won a set number of points in that period. On one occasion we each got a suit, then shirts, club ties and shirts, all arranged through the tailor Jack knew in Leeds.

In five-a-sides he would have Scotland versus England games, or North versus South when you would play against your opposite number for a Mars bar. So whoever lost had to buy the other fella a Mars bar. So you would basically kick seven sorts of s**** out of each *other just for a Mars bar. But that was the professionalism he was bringing.*

And we wanted to win every game, including the five-a-sides.

The Manager of the Year award was sponsored by Bells and when he was in the running for the award, Stuart Boam jokingly said he should donate it to the players if he won it. When he did, he came into the club and presented the gallon of whisky to the lads, which we signed and auctioned for charity.

He took us on tour to Hong Kong, Bangkok, Tahiti, Australia and New Zealand after we won promotion, promising us we would have £6 a day spending money, and then, just as we were about to take off, he promptly announced it had been reduced to £2. It was still a fantastic, once in a lifetime trip. And he was in his element.

We moved into an era where we were rock solid in the First Division and it was a pity Jack left before that really. I know Jack always said he probably left a year too early. And I think he was right.

DAVID HODGSON

I had offers from other clubs to sign as an apprentice but I chose to join Middlesbrough, much to my father's surprise, because of Jack Charlton. He used to have a football coaching TV programme on a Saturday morning and he was brilliant.

I just loved the idea of this big, mad Geordie being my manager.

He was coaching lads of varying ability with George Wardle down at Framwellgate School in Durham. The cameras captured him in full flow and he was so good with the kids, even when they made a mistake. He was such a laugh and had such a lovely persona.

I wasn't to know he wouldn't really be involved with me because he was the first team manager, but we still had a couple of very funny dealings.

We were on the pitch next to the first team when Jack played in one of his last five-a-sides with the first team. John Craggs put him on his arse, right in front of the TV cameras. Almost as soon as he hit the ground, Jack got up and ran after Craggsy, who thought he was joking. But he wasn't.

Jack was going mental... shouting and screaming at him, and would not give up running. He must have chased him for 20 minutes, with the cameras still filming the whole thing.

Bobby Murdoch was our youth team coach and one morning Jack came over and asked which two players could afford to miss training, and Bobby said, 'Hodgy and Gary Briggs.'

So Jack called us over and stuck us in the back of his Landrover with two manky labradors and we headed off. We didn't have a clue where we were going but after an hour we were in the middle of the Cleveland Hills somewhere near Guisborough. We got out. Jack handed us two large sticks and got his gun out. Briggsy and I looked at each other.

What did he have planned?

Jack shut the boot and said, 'Right lairds… you're going pheasant beating'. And we whacked the bushes round the fields as Jack tried to shoot the birds. He wasn't even any good. We sent dozens up and he kept missing.

I'd been quite handy with an air rifle as a kid, so I said, 'Gaffer… give us a go, you're hopeless'. And he went absolutely berserk and told me I'd never play a game in professional football if I didn't 'shut the f**k up'.

In the end he got about half a dozen and gave them to us to give to our elderly landlady Mrs P. When we handed them over, she said, 'What the hell am I supposed to do with these?' and when we told her Big Jack had sent them, she was overjoyed.

He had an aura about him because he'd won the World Cup and we lived in fear of him collaring us. I'd been playing regularly for the reserves and scoring, so a week before the game, Jack asked me if I fancied playing in John Hickton's testimonial. Of course I did!

So he said, 'Here's the deal… you run me a bath and if it's the nicest bath I've ever had, I will play you in the testimonial'.

So of course, that was it. I made possibly the greatest bath I have ever made in my life – perfect temperature, suds up to the brim, nice and deep – and afterwards, sure enough, Jack said it was the best bath he'd ever had and I was in the team.

But when the team was named the following week, of course I wasn't even on the bench. Jack saw me the following day, and suddenly remembered our deal.

'Sorry son… I promised didn't I?' he said.

I nodded. 'It wasn't my fault,' he said. 'Hicky wouldn't let you play.' He was lying of course. He probably forgot, but you just forgave him because that was Jack. Just a great guy and a brilliant manager who lived up to my expectations, and more.

JACK DISCOURAGED his Middlesbrough players from calling him 'boss' or 'gaffer'. Jack was Jack, and 'Jack' would do. After the chase with Craggs Jack knew he was 'getting too old for this lark'.

'The lads were having a bit of fun at the expense of the new manager – but I drew the line when I got a bill for sixty-eight pounds for a broken skylight in a hotel we stayed in after playing a game at Grimsby. I confronted the players back at Ayresome Park, and after I had threatened to deduct the money from their wages unless the culprit came forward, a hand eventually went up at the back of the room.

'The player, who shall be nameless, said that he had succeeded in enticing a young lady back to his room, and once the word was out, his teammates, in the manner of these things, had climbed out on the roof to look through the skylight. Unfortunately, one of them got so excited that he fell through the bloody thing.

'I'm stood there in mock horror.

'I turned to the baby of the team Stan Cummins, a lad of seventeen, and said, "Hey, I hope you weren't up there on that roof?"

'"No, Boss," he says. "I were in the cupboard."'

CRAIG JOHNSTON

My parents sold the house to finance my trip (from Australia) and on the first day there was a trial game. We were losing 3-0 at half time and Jack Charlton walked into the dressing room and had a go at everybody.

'Where are you from?' he asked me.

And I said, 'Australia'.

And he said, 'You are the worst footballer I have ever seen in my life. Now hop it back to Australia'. But he didn't use the phrase 'hop it'. He said worse words. And that was the end of the dream. I went back to my digs and phoned my mum and she was so excited. She asked me how the trial had gone and if Jack Charlton liked me?

And I said, 'Mum, he thinks I am the best footballer he has ever seen and he wants me to stay', and I immediately hung up before I burst into tears.

I couldn't go home because of all the sacrifices that had been made for me. The fact was that Jack Charlton was not wrong. Compared to the sophisticated 15 year-old English, Scottish, Irish and Welsh kids, I was a laughing stock.

So then I had to basically put myself in jail and get up at seven o'clock every morning to clean the players' boots and cars. The only way I could hide from Charlton was helping them; the players would pay me money to clean their cars and they would shout, 'Charlton's coming' and I would hide in the car park among the cars until he had gone.

I did that for a year and a half, and spent six or seven hours a day practicing, shooting, heading, passing, all the things that it took to be a professional player.

So the dream was over after that first day but then came the hard work.

JACK WASN'T finished with Middlesbrough.

He was offered jobs after leaving Newcastle United many years later but turned them down. But in late March, 1984 he received a call from a desperate Middlesbrough chairman Mike McCullagh, an old friend.

The club was now skint, and heading towards receivership as well as relegation to the Third Division. His old TV pal Malcolm Allison had walked out with the club perilously close to the foot of the table.

They looked doomed and Jack did not need the hassle. But the loyalty to McCullagh was deep. When he discovered Jack and Pat had lost a substantial amount moving house between jobs a couple of years earlier, he had sent a cheque for £20,000 to cover the shortfall. Although Jack repaid his friend, he could not turn him down in his hour of need.

Middlesbrough won three and drew three of Jack's nine games in charge, and finished seven points clear of the drop. Job done. A grateful McCullagh started talking of plans and players after the final day goalless draw with Huddersfield Town at Ayresome Park.

But Jack apologised to his good friend and walked away.

SHEFFIELD
WEDNESDAY

JACK CHARLTON was recommended for the Sheffield Wednesday job in 1977 by his old North East mucker Len Ashurst. The only problem was that Ashurst was the Sheffield Wednesday manager. When director Ron Whitehead called Jack to offer him the job in October, he wasn't interested.

Only when Ashurst quit a few weeks later did Jack take a serious look.

The prospect of managing a club in the Third Division did not appeal initially. He had left Middlesbrough in the First Division, having struggled to get them there, and he knew the drop down the divisions would require patience with players of lesser ability. By his own admission he was not a patient football man. He bought a ticket for himself and Pat to watch Wednesday beat Brighton and Hove Albion 2-1 at Hillsborough. He was not overly impressed.

'Without putting too fine a point on it, they were bloody awful!'

But he met Wednesday chairman Bert McGee after the match and agreed to take the job that night. His first decision was to appoint Maurice Setters as his assistant. It was the start of a friendship and relationship that would last more than 20 years. The pair had met at Lilleshall on a coaching course and Setters had already worked in the Third Division as the manager of Doncaster Rovers. He liked Setters' blunt and abrasive style.

While Pat moved into a new house in Mexborough near Barnsley with the family, the two men trawled the country virtually every night looking for new recruits. They wanted a big goalkeeper, a big centre half, a big centre forward.

Jack also made sure the Wednesday directors knew who was boss.

He was friends with the former pit manager Jim Bullock who had chaired the first mine managers' union. He was the man who had advised Jack to quit Middlesbrough while the going was good. 'One of the gems of wisdom that Jim imparted was that you were never stronger in any managerial job than in the first few months of taking it. If you don't assert your authority in that period, you're living with a time bomb. I have never forgotten that.'

SO WHEN Jack heard that Bert McGee had been in the dressing room after a reserve team defeat to berate Setters and trainer Tony Toms in the early weeks of their reign, Jack acted immediately. He bolted from his office as Setters was still telling the story and stormed straight into a Board meeting, asking McGee to step outside. The astonished directors could hear Jack unleash a tirade at his chairman through the walls.

'You've been down to abuse my staff about results. Don't do it again,' Jack recalled in his autobiography. 'If you have any comments to make about the team, talk to me. And furthermore, it has come to my attention that certain directors are shooting their mouths off in pubs and golf clubs about players and the staff. That stops right now.'

'I could see he was shaken. He started to blurt out something but before he got going, I let him have some more stick. I know I can be a bit abrasive at times, and afterwards I felt sorry for upsetting him – but he had to be given the message there and then or not at all.'

Within a few weeks Wednesday suffered a humiliating FA Cup defeat to Wigan Athletic, then still in the Northern Premier League. Jack's mood was not helped when the team bus got stuck in the mud outside Priestfield.

He worked endlessly on set pieces on the training ground, devising and imparting the little tricks he'd invented, picked up or manipulated.

TERRY CURRAN

We played Newcastle at Newcastle and I was on free kicks. I scored nine goals from free kicks that season out of 23 goals but I couldn't score that day.

We battered Newcastle and lost 1-0. It was one of those games, when you come off the field and say, 'How the hell have we lost that game?' Jack was furious. He was a Geordie. He didn't want to lose at Newcastle. He came into the dressing room, there was cups flying about off the tray on the table in the middle of the room.

And he turned to me and he shouted, 'I'm telling you... you are not taking another f**king free kick as long as I live. And you're all in tomorrow.' And he storms out.

The next morning he walked on to the training ground in his tracksuit, which was quite unusual because he was usually suited and booted or in his waterproofs and wellies. The tracksuit bottoms came up to the top of his socks. He had one ordinary sock on his right foot, and a football sock on his left.

You could see he was still angry. 'Right,' he said, 'You remember what I said to you all last night? You're off free kicks'. And he points at me.

'Meggo (Gary Megson) is going to take them and you (meaning me) and Banno (Gary Bannister) are going to be in the wall.' He told us we were going to recreate a free kick at the edge of the box on the ref's whistle. He had a whistle in his pocket, ready to blow it.

He said, 'When the whistle goes, I want you two to come out of the wall, towards the ball, and I'm going to hit this ball at Banno; he turns round and it's going to come off his back, and go in the goal.'

This is the Gospel truth. He hits this ball perfectly, it skims off Banno's back and ends up in the back of the net. I just started laughing. And I could not stop. And it started to spread round the lads. Jack turned to me and said, 'You've caused all this... now, f**k off'. And he sent me off the training pitch.

GARY MEGSON

He was innovative and came up with ideas; some worked, some didn't, but he was never afraid to do something that was different to what everybody else was doing.

He had worked out one particular routine from a free kick at the edge of the box. He wanted me to hit the ball like a shot. It couldn't be one foot off the ground, or five foot, it had to be between two and four. McCulloch was then supposed to come in with a diving header as the goalkeeper is coming across, and put it to the other side of the goal.

It just wasn't working at all and I couldn't get this ball exactly at three foot. So he strode on to the pitch in his wellies, pushes me to one side and says, 'Here... this is what I want'.

And he plays this ball perfectly across for McCulloch to score.

JACK EVENTUALLY found his big target man in Andy McCulloch, signed from Brentford for £70,000, completing the deal while working for ITV during the FA Cup final between Bobby Robson's Ipswich Town and Arsenal. 'He proved to be one of my better investments.'

Another shrewd signing was Terry Curran from Southampton. Signed as a winger, Jack moved him to centre forward where he was a revelation. He encouraged Curran to play the same way he had as a winger, but rather than attack full backs he was told to go at central defenders. His goals were to prove vital, particularly in the famous Boxing Day Massacre. Sheffield Wednesday won the 1979 Steel City derby 4-1.

TERRY CURRAN

I met Jack and Maurice in a nightclub in Leeds Peter Stringfellow owned. We had played Leeds in the League Cup semi-final, a 2-2 draw. Maurice knew I was a Wednesday fan. We got talking, one thing led to another, and Jack said, 'Do you want to come and play for us and help us get Wednesday out of the Third Division?'

I would have signed there and then.

But Alan Ball, who was Southampton manager said, 'You are not going to Sheffield Wednesday'. Bally went absolutely ballistic with me when I said I wanted to go and play for them. He told me he felt it was a backward step for my career dropping down two leagues.

They were the team I supported as a kid and it was a big club, it still is, not with the things they have won but its tradition.

Jack used to say about me, 'You're not a centre forward'. But I had always been a striker, playing off the striker. Right until going into professional football I had been a centre forward and I'd scored 50-plus goals every season.

I didn't like playing on the wing. I preferred to play as a striker where I was allowed to do what I wanted to do. Someone got injured at Wednesday, so I ended up playing up front alongside Andy McCulloch and did well playing off him.

Then Jack signed Gary Bannister and told me I was going to be playing out wide again. I said, 'I'm not doing it'.

I look back now and think, 'What was I doing?' But I was 23, I didn't like it out wide and I wanted to play in the middle. We were playing Norwich City away the following day.

He said, 'You are playing out wide'.

'I'm not,' I told him. I remember he was wearing one of those sheepskin coats people

wore back then. He started to come towards me.

Jack is what… six foot three? I'm five foot ten… eleven. His face was getting redder and redder, steam coming out of his ears. He is still coming towards me and he said, 'You're going to f**king play on that wing tomorrow night and I don't give a f**k what you say'.

And, again, I said, 'I'm not. Play Muppet out there'.

All of a sudden he gets up to me and throws a punch and I ducked down, and as I did that I grabbed his coat and had him up in the air, with his arms flailing. Then before we know it there's 20-odd lads on top of us trying to pull us apart. I didn't play at Norwich; a kid called Gordon Owen, Muppet we called him, he came in, and we beat them 3-1. Jack was one of those who, when he was angry, he'd let fly, and then that was it.

He would always be friendly afterwards and come talk to you. He never sulked and let it fester like some managers. After the game we had a laugh about it and it was forgotten. He made decisions to win football matches and I like to think he knows I did my best for him. He's a lovely, fabulous, funny guy and I loved working with him. He's a proper football player, proper football manager, proper football fan. You could sit in a pub and have a pint with him, just talk football.

He'd cheat at cards. With his long bloody neck, he'd be looking over at your cards; he was the worst cheat in the world, but he would get away with it. If you pulled him up on it, he'd threaten to drop you and the way he said it, you just never knew if he was serious or not.

Jack will always be fondly remembered at Sheffield Wednesday and every time he goes down there he gets a standing ovation and applause that is second to none. They all think the world of him. They all admire him for what he did for Sheffield Wednesday, and no disrespect to Howard Wilkinson, but he took over the team that could play, added a couple of players, got promoted and the club enjoyed a golden period. Jack set all that up.

IN HIS first pre-season at Hillsborough, club trainer and ex-military man Tony Toms insisted on taking Jack's squad to Lympstone, the Royal Marines HQ on the south coast. The fortnight in barracks, with intense commando-style training, worked a treat. Wednesday were the fittest team in the Third Division by a mile. And they should have won promotion, but their league campaign was sidetracked by a good FA Cup run.

They reached the fifth round and met Arsenal and a certain Liam Brady. After a 1-1 draw at Hillsborough they drew by the same scoreline at Highbury. Two further games at Filbert Street failed to split the teams, before Brady inspired the Gunners to a 2-0 win in the fourth replay at Leicester.

'In the earlier games, Brady played from the back and we handled him without too many problems. Once he began taking the ball off the front two in the last game, instantly we were in trouble. I learned a lesson about how Liam could play most effectively which would stand me in good stead on other days.'

Jack, who added former Liverpool striker Ian St John to his coaching staff, finally got Wednesday out of the Third Division in his third season and the following year they finished mid-table in the Second Division.

He signed Ante Mirocevic, a maverick, socks-round-the-ankles playmaker whom Setters had seen in the Yugoslav Olympic squad, for a club record £250,000. The jury is still out on his impact at Wednesday. But Jack clearly loved him.

'I still reckon that Ante was a good signing, but there are those at Hillsborough who would dispute that to this day. In my book he was different to anything we ever had at Sheffield. For three seasons we'd huffed and puffed our way in the Third Division, matching the best in work rate but lacking real flair. Ante filled that void, and what's more, he gradually got those around him to play a bit more. The only problem was that he couldn't bear the cold weather.

'Tony Toms' commando courses were simply anathema to him. There was one day when Tony demanded that the players wade through a stream – but would Ante do it? Not on your life. He pretended he couldn't understand English when it suited him not to, but as I recall he never had many problems when the talk got round to money.

For the first couple of months of the season, while there was still a lot of grass on the pitches, he was brilliant. Then the winter came and Ante would turn up for training with gloves, a balaclava, two shirts, two sweaters and a tracksuit.

'I have never known a man who hated the cold more, but once spring rolled around, he was on his bike again.' Jack and Pat have always had an open house. Whether it's family, friends, players, colleagues, they invite them in, and life goes on around their guests. And if Jack meets someone he likes, and finds out they might need somewhere to stay, he invites them. As the future England manager Sven-Goran Eriksson discovered when he travelled from Sweden as a young coach to see the best up-and-coming Englishmen at work. After visiting Jack at Hillsborough, he also spent time with Bobby Robson. Jack insisted Eriksson abandon plans to stay in a hotel and he stayed for a week with the Charlton family.

ANTE MIROCEVIC

When I came to England Jack picked me up at the airport and he said, 'We don't want you to stay in a hotel on your own… you are staying in my house'.

So I lived with Jack and Pat and his children John, Peter and Debbie for three months, and then my family came over and we moved into a house on our own. My daughter Mia was only three, and Jack was very fond of her; he would play with her and do magic tricks. She is a cardiology doctor now and one of the top surgeons in Montenegro.

Jack's house was like a castle, with a snooker table and fishing rods everywhere. And they all made me so welcome. Pat would do all the cooking, so we would eat fish and chips every Friday. I still like fish and chips, although it is better in England.

He took me fishing to a lake near Barnsley a few times but I don't remember catching anything. And he would take me to the pub.

We would have a few pints; play darts and dominoes. Jack could have been world champion at dominoes. I liked lager and lime and Jack had his bitter, and before we went home we would have whiskey chasers. And then we would train the next morning.

Football in England was 4-4-2 and Jack wanted me in the team for something a bit different but every team played with a high line of defenders so it was difficult to get on the ball. But I loved my time in England. My son was born in Sheffield.

And I loved Jack. He was a very special man, and a great manager. I was so proud when he took Ireland to the World Cup in Italy and Ireland did so well. When he came on the TV, I said to my wife, 'Look… it's Big Jack!'

LOCAL YOUNGSTERS Peter Shirtliff, Mel Sterland, Mark Smith and Kevin Taylor were promoted to the first team to add to the experience of signings like Gary Megson. The following season they missed out on promotion to the top flight by a single point. What was particularly galling about that disappointment was that a Football League ruling was to deprive them of success.

Before the 1981-82 season the points system changed, from two to three for a win. Under the previous rules Wednesday would have been promoted. Jack was particularly unhappy that his side was denied what would have been a vital win against Luton in one of their last games, when the referee played seven minutes of injury time and their opponents equalised with virtually the last kick of the match.

GARY MEGSON

My dad Don knew him as a player. They were about the same age and my dad had played against him for Wednesday when Jack of course was at Leeds. He never interfered with myself or my career but he did come across to Sheffield when I was going to sign for Wednesday from Everton.

Jack was being his usual tight self and wouldn't give me what I wanted. It came down to a car. I told him that I got a car at Everton, and he said, 'Well... we don't do that here, so that's your problem'.

And I said, 'Right... I'm not coming then.' And I walked out. As I walked out with my dad we bumped into Maurice Setters and he said, 'All done?'

And I said, 'No!' And I told him why. So we walked back into the office with Maurice and he said, 'Jack, you've been chasing him for over a year and now you're going to fall out over a poxy bleeding car. Get it sorted among yourselves'. I signed on the same day he signed Gary Bannister. And two weeks later he signed Gary Shelton from Aston Villa.

We were altogether in the clubhouse before training one morning and the three of us went out, one after the other, and Jack said, 'Morning Gerry... morning Barry... morning Harry'. We were sure he did it on purpose.

He was a manager players wanted to play for. He used to connect with everybody, especially supporters, players and also his directors. Jack had this reputation of being really tight. Tight as a duck's arse. While I think he was pretty frugal with his club's money, my experience is that he was very different with his own. I know quite a few stories of him helping players out who were in financial trouble and he never asked for it back.

When he signed Gary Shelton, the club put him in a hotel, while Gary Bannister and myself were in a club house. After training Jack told us we had to take Gary Shelton out for a meal to make him feel welcome, so we arranged it and had dinner at the hotel with him. A week later Jack pulled out this piece of paper and said, 'What's this?'

It was a copy of the bill for the meal.

'I told you to take him out for a meal,' he said, 'not that we were bloody paying for it.' And he made us pay back the money to the club. And yet when he took us to Spain, and we were coming back, we were in Duty Free, and I really wanted to buy this Lladro figurine, but I didn't have the money. Jack insisted on buying it.

I was really disappointed with how things ended at Sheffield Wednesday for Jack, and the people at the club and the supporters. We did get promoted the year after Jack left but I was sad Jack didn't do it. To miss out by one point, when we'd have gone up under the two points for a win system was just one of those things.

As a player you are probably unaware of the things that he did and how they might influence you later, particularly going into management. But, for example, in pre-season when I first joined Wednesday, we were running up and down the pitch and it was boiling hot. Jack got the older players to do two thirds of what the younger players were doing.

One of the lads shouts over, 'How come they don't have to do everything we're doing?'

And Jack shouts back, 'Ey… when you know what you're doing you can join this lot.' We were staying away one Christmas Day night in a hotel and, of course, nobody wanted to be there. You're away from your families and the hotel is just about dead. He got us all together and we had a secret vote on worst trainer, ugliest player, worst dressed, manager's pet; about 15 categories, and it was just a brilliant laugh.

Then he gave the winner of each category a fiver, but you couldn't spend it because he'd written UGLIEST PLAYER etc across it.

The last time I saw him was at Carlisle. I was manager of Sheffield Wednesday. We were just about to kick off. I am stood there by the side of the pitch; everything is set up, the ref is about to blow his whistle, and I get this tap on the shoulder.

I turned around thinking, 'Who the f**king hell is this?'

And Jack is stood there, with that big Morecambe and Wise grin on his face. And I said, 'Gaffer! How are ya?'

And he wanted to stay and have a chat but I had to remind him there was a bloody game on and we'd kicked off! It was brief, but I was pleased to see him. And I think the crowd were pleased to see him. He got a lovely reception, not just from the Wednesdayites who hold him in great affection, but from everyone in the ground.

THE BLOW of missing out on a top flight return prompted Jack to consider leaving Hillsborough in the summer of 1982. He decided to give it one more season. It was to prove the most exciting season of his spell in Sheffield, but tinged with more disappointment.

He signed Mike Lyons from Everton and by Christmas Wednesday were top of the table and looking good for promotion to the top flight at last. But once again a decent cup run, or two, was to kill off their effectiveness in the league.

They reached the latter stages of the League Cup in January, which was when Jack suggested to his chairman that an early exit from the FA Cup might not do the club, and his threadbare squad, any harm. Bert McGee refused to sanction the idea. Although they reached the FA Cup semi finals, they lost Andy McCulloch and Brian Hornsby with long-term injuries and their threat in the league waned. Wednesday lost to Brighton in the semi-final. Ante Mirocevic scored to cancel out Jimmy Case's opener, before Irishman Michael Robinson scored the winner to set up that famous FA Cup final against Manchester United.

PETER FERGUSON

I was delegated to make the trip to Exeter for Jack's first game, and in those days the local reporters were welcome on most clubs' official coaches; Wednesday included. Not that it did any good in terms of an early steer from the boss on his choice of team. It wasn't that he didn't want to tell you, there was no great secrecy involved; more that he could never remember names too well.

On one occasion my paper, the Morning Telegraph, *needed a squad to go with the preview for the following evening's game, so I rang Jack at home (more of a small holding in reality. The coach would drop him off on the motorway near Barnsley and, on lighter nights, you'd see him clamber over the fence and start his yomp across the fields).*

Anyway, Jack rattled through the players' names, then added, 'Oh aye... and I'm calling up young Taylor from the reserves as well'.

'First name, Jack?'

'Ticker.'

'Sorry?'

'Ticker... Ticker Taylor.'

'I can't put that in the paper, Jack.'

'Why not? Everybody'll know who you mean!'

Kevin Taylor didn't play that time but went on to make 125 appearances and score 21 goals from midfield, and I suspect Jack never, ever called him anything but Ticker.

That first season at Hillsborough was memorable for two things. Jack quickly realised that the players at his disposal were an average Third Division bunch, and tactics and strategy would need to be tailored to their abilities, with a more direct approach the best option.

He has a capacity for taking the rough with the smooth, and was more concerned about getting Wednesday out of the Third Division doldrums, although not at the cost of his enjoyment of life. He loved a game of cards – if there was no deck to be found on the coach, somebody would be sent to the shop for a pack of Waddington's – and there were times when Jack's card school was slow to disembark because one last hand had to be played out.

But his great love was fishing. When there was no midweek game, Jack might prove an elusive quarry. He'd be off with his fishing tackle, leaving word for the chairman that he was 'looking at a player'.

Wednesday's Board, rightly, felt lucky to have a manager of Jack's calibre and, having been set straight early on in the forthright Charlton manner, he would do it his way, brooking no interference, and banned chairman Bert McGee from the dressing room.

And Jack's team were gradually improving as he shaped the squad to his liking, but Jack struck gold in his third season, the addition of winger-turned-striker Terry Curran from Southampton, and his 22 goals, clinching third place and promotion.

Now in the Second Division, Jack's progress continued, albeit slower than he would have wished. Tenth in their first season back, fourth the next – missing out by a point – and suddenly it was perceived to be crunch time. Jack had always said five years at a club was long enough, but he had overstayed in the hope of completing the job.

He steered Wednesday to an FA Cup semi-final at Highbury against Brighton, then of the top flight, but Mike Lyons, captain and centre half, needed a fitness test on a groin strain.

So Jack dispatched Maurice Setters with the skipper to Hampstead Heath for a quick once-over and, never the most delicate of players, Maurice proceeded to put in a few tasty tackles (in his street shoes) that had onlookers wincing. When they got back to the hotel, Jack looked up from his newspaper with a raised eyebrow. 'He's fine,' said Maurice.

The semi-final at Highbury was Wednesday's last hope of glory that season – their promotion challenge was to fizzle out to sixth place – but they lost 2-1. Nevertheless, on their way back to the Tube, Wednesday fans sang, Always Look on the Bright Side of Life, *the tongue-in-cheek tune Eric Idle croons from the cross in the film* Life of Brian.

Yes, they'd just lost the semi-final and they weren't going up, but it was still light years away from the gloom Charlton had inherited in 1977.

PAT CHARLTON

We helped out with the striking miners a little bit. We found out that a lad had broken his back in the pit, so we held a strawberry and cream wine day in the garden to raise money for him and his family. We didn't know who he was but knew we could help him.

During the strike, Jack lent one of the miners his car so he could still get about. We also gave a huge freezer to the food room in the village for miners and provided some food. We just felt it was the least we could do.

We became very good friends with Arthur Scargill, who lived nearby. He'd regularly call in for a cup of tea and a chat, and Jack really liked him. He was a lovely, quiet man away from the public spotlight. You'd not recognise him from the man who used to get up on the podium, shouting and trying to raise the miners.

BEFORE THE semi-final meeting with Brighton at Highbury, Jack informed his chairman that he would be leaving Hillsborough at the end of the season. Two days after the game Jack received a letter from the club offering him a new contract for the following season. But Jack refused to sign.

The death of his close friend Jock Stein during Scotland's international against Wales at Ninian Park had changed his perspective on football. He decided that night that he would never die in the dug out. He left Hillsborough and headed for the rivers of Northumberland. 'If I can choose the way I will leave this world, it will be clutching a rod, with a forty pound salmon on the other end of the line dragging me down the river!' he promised himself.

PAT CHARLTON

Jack has only ever taken me fishing twice.

The first time it was so cold that my line was freezing up. That was a lot of years ago. I remember Sean Connery fishing on the same river and he invited us for a drink. Another time on the Tweed in a boat we didn't catch a thing!

It's safe to say I don't like fishing.

NEWCASTLE UNITED

JACK CHARLTON was born to be manager of Newcastle United. It was his club, his ground, his city, and his people.

But he didn't want the job when it came and it turned out the fans didn't want him in the end.

He had enjoyed his first full year away from football for nearly 30 years. He indulged himself in fishing and shooting at every opportunity, rediscovering some of the haunts of his childhood and discovering new ones across Northumberland and near the family farmhouse in the Yorkshire Dales.

After-dinner speaking and TV work kept the money coming in and the rod was often packed in the boot of the car as his reputation as an entertainer grew in England and he travelled the country. One of the first ex-footballers to recognise the easy money to be earned from telling a few stories, particularly of '66, Jack never really honed his act. He just told it as it is. And people loved him for it, and loved the stories. He did not miss the daily toil of football management.

JOHN CHARLTON

He was one of the first footballers to do after-dinner speaking and for several years agents used to tell us that he was the most requested speaker on the circuit, and he even did a tour as a one-man stage show at one point.

I used to drive him up and down the country; so we might be away from home for three or four days on the trot, and in a week we'd go from the North East, to Barrow-in-Furness, to Blackpool, then down to Rhyl and end up in Cardiff before we'd head home.

If we were driving down, or before a gig, he would have a sheet of paper and he'd write down bullet points of notes to remind himself; there was never a script. It got to the point where he had done it that often, he could remember it off by heart and it was honed to such an extent during and after his Ireland years that he'd cover every part of his career… sometimes in the right order!

My favourite bit was probably his opening line. He would be introduced by the MC, or whoever, who'd pay tribute to my dad and say, 'Ladies and gentlemen, World Cup '66 hero, Jack Charlton'. And the audience would applaud. Then, my dad would get to his feet and say, 'Well that was better than some of the welcomes and introductions I've had. Like the time I went to West Brom. And this is a true story.

'I went to the Hawthorns and the place was in darkness, not a soul there. And I saw the groundsman and he said, "Hello, Jack… what are you doing here?" And I said, "I'm supposed to be doing a dinner here, at the Hawthorns."

'So the groundsman said, "Well, there's nothing on here for definite. Why don't you try the pub on the corner, they sometimes do them."

'So I went to the pub, and sure enough the event's in there. And the guy gets up to announce me to the pub and he says, "Ladies and gentlemen. I'd like to introduce you to Jack Charlton. He played 700-odd games for Leeds United, he won the league twice, the FA Cup, the World Cup in '66 and 35 England caps, he was booked over 40 times, sent off six times. People up and down the country thought he was a credit to his working-class background and an honour to the game. But here at West Brom, we always thought he was a c***. Ladies and gentlemen, Jack Charlton."'

I always knew what was coming, and the audience would have no idea it was going to end that way, but the way he delivered it, he got a laugh every time.

JACK MILBURN made the first call on behalf of Newcastle United.

Jack turned him down initially. But his uncle was persistent. He played on the family ties to the club and repeatedly asked how a Milburn, a Geordie, could turn down the opportunity to manage Newcastle United?

JOHN CHARLTON

My uncle Jackie had been pestering him to take the Newcastle job, but my dad said he wasn't interested. He refused to go to St James' Park to meet the Board and once told him he was opening a double-glazing company in Consett and said, 'If you want to talk to me, meet me there', but of course nobody showed. Jackie Milburn and my father used to meet every few weeks for a bit of lunch, and they arranged to meet at the Ramside Hall Hotel, near Durham. They were sat having a bite to eat in one room, talking about the job.

He still didn't want it. Then, about halfway through the meal, Jackie says, 'Well… look, the Board are here. Will you go and speak to them at least?'

And he pointed to this door, stood up, opened it and the Newcastle directors were all there. He was set up. He went into another room, and the chairman Stan Seymour said, 'Jack… we have nowhere else to turn. We need you to take the job'. They told him they just needed him to make sure they didn't get relegated. After Kevin Keegan had left at the end of the previous season, having won promotion, Arthur Cox had gone and they were in a mess. But they just needed to stay up. In the end, Jackie and the Board wore him down.

He agreed to take the job eventually, and he was going to be paid more than he'd been paid at Wednesday. But he wouldn't sign a contract. He never did. He said, 'Here's what I'll do. I will keep you in the First Division, but then that'll be me gone at the end of next year. You sort it out and get a new manager'.

He signed a few players early in that season, took lads like Pat Heard and Gary Megson who had been with him at Wednesday, and strikers George Reilly and Tony Cunningham. But there was not a lot of money to spend. They were comfortable and safe at the end of the season, and they had some good young players like Gazza, Beardsley and Waddle.

But he could see the danger signs, especially when Waddle left. When it got towards the end of the season, it was obvious there was nothing in place to replace him and that they had no intention of getting anybody else. He agreed to stay on but it all changed in a meaningless, pre-season friendly against Sheffield United.

Funnily enough I was over from Australia, and I was at the game. There was a small section at the far corner of the Gallowgate, not a massive amount, maybe 500 to a thousand people, and they were booing and calling for his head. He listened to that and thought, 'F**k this'. I was sat next to my mother at the game and she was almost in tears. He went straight in after the game, said, 'That's it… I'm off'.

I don't think my uncle Jackie was best pleased, and they didn't speak for a while and had a falling out over it, by all accounts. But I'm not sure he was bothered.

THE APPOINTMENT did make absolute sense initially. Newcastle was Jack's club after all, and they desperately needed a manager.

Arthur Cox had left having just secured promotion to the First Division. Cox was the man who had delivered Kevin Keegan to the Newcastle public the previous year, and told him to go out and play. He helped create the Geordie legend, but Keegan had just left. Although he was to return as a manager, with Cox as his assistant, to take the club to unimaginable heights, at that time Kevin Keegan left a club and city in turmoil.

Newcastle were £700,000 in debt and only £200,000 was available to find Keegan's replacement. Jack knew immediately he had no Kevin Keegan in his midst. Keegan's pal Terry McDermott had been in a contract dispute with Cox. When Jack simply refused to improve the club's offer at their first meeting, within days of his appointment, McDermott left.

But he did inherit the emerging, and local, talents of Chris Waddle and Peter Beardsley, who were to play significant roles in Jack's brief tenure. Though when he took one look at the rest of his squad he decided First Division survival had to be the priority. And with little money to spend, he had to work with what he'd got. The team would have to play accordingly. The Board agreed.

'The England World Cup winner filled the breach and knuckled down to make sure United stayed in the First Division,' wrote Paul Joannou in *Newcastle United the Ultimate Record 1881-2011*. 'Without the flair and razzamatazz of Keegan, Charlton relied on the further development of Beardsley and especially of Waddle, who rapidly rose to England recognition.

'United's boss also brought in lanky strikers in George Reilly and Tony Cunningham and this made sure the ball was more often in the air, tactics which did not go down too well. Yet Charlton achieved his objective with comfort, United finishing 14th in the table.

'In the process he also guided United to a rip-roaring New Year's Day derby success over Sunderland at Gallowgate. Peter Beardsley – not far behind Waddle in international recognition – grabbed a hat trick in a match which saw six booked and two Wearsiders sent off. There was also the assurance of more talent being developed as United's kids lifted the FA Youth Cup – with a very special teenager making the headlines, Paul Gascoigne.'

PETER BEARDSLEY

When he first came, he had such a positive attitude, nothing was a problem.

We were not a great team, and I don't mean that in a horrible way, but he had a way about him and he just found a way to win games. We were top after three games. And it was all down hill from there really. He never, ever put his kit on. I never saw him in his training kit. He wore a suit, shoes and flat cap.

Before pre-season in the promotion season, Malcolm Brown snapped his Achilles so he was out for the season before we'd even kicked a ball.

So Malcolm returned for the start of the following season when Jack came in and we were training one day; 11 v 11 in a session with Willie McFaul, who did most of the training. Jack was standing at the side in his suit and shoes and suddenly he steps on to the pitch, stops the game and shouts… 'Hang on'.

He walks over to Malcolm and he takes him by the hand, takes him into the right back position and he says… 'What I want you to do young 'un… is to boot that ball as high as you can into that corner.

'Because what's up?' and he points up to the sky.

And Malcolm went… 'Clouds?'

And Jack said… 'No son… God's up there.

'We play one-two with God.'

And with that, he flicked his shoe off, grabbed the ball and, standing there in just his sock, he booted this ball high into the sky. It was unbelievable. He could not have picked the ball up and walked over there and placed it any better in the corner of the pitch. It dropped and died in the corner. 'That's what I want,' he said. And then he picked his shoe up, slipped it back on and walked off.

We played Arsenal away midweek in his fourth game, when we were top, and we got absolutely battered. And we were going to Old Trafford on the Saturday.

As we were leaving Highbury, he said, 'I'll see you at Old Trafford on Saturday lads'.

And we were all looking at each other thinking, 'He's taking the piss… isn't he?'

But he says, 'I'm off grouse shooting'.

We really thought we'll see him tomorrow, or we're bound to see him at training on Friday. But no, sure enough, we didn't see him until the Saturday when he came into the dressing room at quarter-to two. He didn't even come to the pre-match meal at the hotel.

People think I had a problem with him, but I really didn't.

He's a smashing fella. I didn't agree with his philosophy in terms of what he wanted and how he wanted to play the game, but I never had a problem with him. I loved him to bits.

He told me and Waddler early on that he wanted a big lad up front. He didn't tell us who and he certainly didn't ask for our opinion, not that we expected him to, he just said, 'I've got you two wide, and I'm getting a big laird in'. And it was a doddle for Waddler. He was a brilliant winger who could go either side and cross with either foot and it was natural for him, but it was not easy for me and I found it difficult playing in that role. So he told Maurice Setters to go out and get him a big striker, so he signed Tony Cunningham. And then he signed George Reilly and went 4-2-4.

He came on to the pitch to remonstrate with me against Luton. In front of the fans, in front of the press. We were 1-0 up with a minute to go at St James' Park and there were no boards or fourth officials in those days to tell you how much injury time was going to be played, you just got on with it.

I got the ball in injury time and I tried to go past the Luton left back Mal Donaghy and he tackled me right in front of the dug out. I did the right thing, I think, because Luton were pressing at the time and I was clear and I should have got past him, but he won the ball and launched it down the Luton left wing just as the final whistle went. I was stood about 15 yards from the halfway line and Jack stormed on to the pitch towards me. And I remember looking at him coming on, thinking, 'Where the hell is he going?'

He came right up to me, he grabbed my arm and he said, 'Just while it's fresh in your mind... don't ever do that again. He got the ball off you there, he could have got that into the area and they might have scored and made it 1-1'.

And I said, 'Yeah... but they didn't'.

And he said, 'Well, I'm just telling you, for next time'.

And of course because he'd come on to the pitch, everyone saw it and afterwards the press were all asking me, 'What's all that about?' as if there had been a bust-up? But that was just his way of making sure it didn't go out of his mind, and he'd got his message across to me.

The following week we were playing Watford at home, which was quite unusual in those days to have consecutive home games. We were 2-1 up with about a minute to go again. We got a free kick on the edge of the 18-yard box on the right hand corner. I swung the ball into the area and George Reilly scored to make it 3-1. Everyone is absolutely delighted.

When I go into the dressing room, Jack pulled me again and he said, 'What did I f**king tell you last week?' And I said, 'What are you on about? We've just scored. Everyone has gone home really happy'. And he just said, 'Aye... but what did I f**king tell you last week? You should have put it in the corner and killed the game'.

He once took us on a trip to Benidorm where we actually went to see Valencia play. Before we left Newcastle airport, he told everyone to make sure they had a partner. When we got to the airport, he said, 'Does everyone know who their partner is?'

Everyone says, 'Yes, no problem Jack… we all know'.

And then he says, 'Good, right now number yourselves… one and two'.

At this stage we have no idea why we have to have partners, one and two, until we have landed, got on the bus and are heading to the hotel. It turns out that we had booked two hotels. But we had no idea until we got to the first hotel, when the bus pulls up and Jack goes, 'Right Number Ones get off… Number Twos stay on the bus'.

Steve Carney and Waddler roomed together all their Newcastle lives and did everything together. And they both started to get off the bus together. Jack was sat at the front next to Pat and his mam Cissie, all three of them were there, and he says, 'Where are you two daft buggahs going?'

And Steve said, 'We are not splitting up, we're going together' and continues to get off the bus. So Jack gets out of his seat and follows the pair of them off the bus and he is full of hell now. He said, 'I don't care which one of you it is, but one of you is getting back on that bus'. And Steve said, 'No chance, you can f**k off. I'm not going anywhere without him,' pointing at Waddler.

And before you know it, Steve and Jack are standing by the side of the bus arguing with each other, ready to come to blows, ready to kill each other.

It was like the Only Fools and Horses *episode on the jolly boys' outing, everyone peering out the window to see what's happening. It was right next to the door of the bus, with Pat and Cissie in the front seats overlooking the whole thing, laughing and going… 'Look at that daft bugger'.*

Eventually Steve got back on the bus and came to the second hotel where I stayed. The first hotel was lovely; the second one was an absolute s***-hole. They had boiled egg soup, horrific. And Jack took us to a lovely restaurant for some 'chicken' that turned out to be 'rabbit'.

JACK WANTED to build his team round Waddle and Beardsley.

Both had their differences with their manager about the style of play, and just how effective they could be within it. The whole club and its supporters had been spoiled by the presence of Kevin Keegan, and those two in particular had blossomed by providing him with the ball.

But they had to learn to play Jack's way now. Jack was often infuriated with Beardsley, sensing he would never 'get' his policies, as other talented players had, and others would later for Ireland. That exasperation had blown over when he had grabbed Beardsley on the pitch in front of the entire ground after the Luton game.

Cissie certainly wasn't impressed. She was at every Newcastle home match, having moved back to Ashington, and she was watching her son's every move.

'I have to confess that of my four sons, Jack's nature is the closest to my own,' she observed. 'He is very straight-talking and doesn't soft-pedal if he thinks I am wrong; while the others would perhaps try to spare my feelings.

'By the same token I like to have my say too, especially when it involves football. I told Jack he was wrong to give Peter Beardsley a public dressing down on the pitch at the end of the match late in the season. Jack was angry with what he said was Peter's lack of commitment during the match.

'The fans didn't like it, neither did I and I told him so. "You should have waited until you were back in the dressing room," I said.

'He explained, "I just had to get it off my chest" and I knew what he meant.'

Waddle, on the other hand, did listen, and as a natural wide man, was probably better suited to Jack's tactics and instructions, whether he liked them or not. But when Waddle sought an escape route and started to head for an exit door to Spurs, Jack did his best to shut it, despite knowing it was futile. Fuelled by bloody-mindedness as much as realism, Jack made the move to White Hart Lane as difficult as possible.

'At the start of the season, I had two exceptional players, Waddle and Beardsley, players around whom I hoped to construct my team. One of them was off to Spurs and the other, I suspected, was merely biding his time at the club.'

WADDLE WAS a sausage factory worker playing amateur football for Tow Law Town in the Northern League when he was spotted by Newcastle. He was signed for 500 quid and a set of tracksuits in 1982. His brilliance in his first season in the top flight did not go unnoticed. England manager Bobby Robson saw Waddle's hat trick at Loftus Road with his own eyes.

He eventually made his England debut on March 26, 1985, ironically against the Republic of Ireland, then managed by Eoin Hand.

His potential was noted by other suitors. Waddle was also one of the first English footballers to sign an agent. Jack's reaction to the news was to tell the Board that he would negotiate the new contract for Waddle. Predictably, the talks were not productive for either side. Agent Mel Stein wrote Waddle's memoirs and the frustration with Jack's negotiation tactics poured out.

'The more he (Waddle) was exposed to the world outside the North East, the more certain he was that he had to get away. He was no longer the dorky, naive kid who had been prepared to do exactly what he was told by who ever happened to be in charge at the time.

'Whether or not (the negotiations) would have been better handled by the likes of (chairman) Stanley Seymour, who can say, but the fact of the matter was that his first offer to Chris was nothing short of insulting. The interests of other clubs were now public knowledge, with Chelsea leading the way and Spurs not far behind. They were soon to take the lead.'

Seymour tried to intervene but he knew Newcastle couldn't and wouldn't match Spurs' offer. And he knew Jack knew it.

They were all new to the idea of a third party representing their player in negotiations. It was not a situation Jack was happy with and he knew Waddle was leaving. It upset him that Waddle was booed by Newcastle fans. Jack knew Waddle wanted away because he felt he was better than Newcastle. And Waddle was right. Jack may have gone into those talks holding no grudge with his gifted young player, but with the idea of being as difficult and obstinate as possible with Waddle's London advisers, and loving every minute of that.

It was no surprise when the North London club came in with an offer for Waddle and his high-powered team quickly met then Spurs chairman Irving Scholar. Once he was shown around White Hart Lane, 'a far cry from the dilapidated St James' Park' as Stein put it, Waddle's mind was made up.

The divorce was acrimonious and went to a transfer tribunal meeting at the Football League. Jack stormed out. But the warring couple at the centre of the split were on friendly speaking terms the next time they met, at the European Championships finals in Germany.

CHRIS WADDLE

Jack as a bloke was great company; you could sit and have a beer with him and talk football. He was like a player and he had that respect because he was a World Cup winner, and although you knew he was the manager, you could have a laugh and a joke with him, and he was like one of the lads; but if you stepped out of line, he would be on you like a tonne of bricks. He didn't suffer fools and you knew when he wasn't happy.

Peter and I told him that we needed a big number nine and he really wanted to sign George Reilly, but he wasn't available. So he signed Tony Cunningham. And then when George became available, he bought him too. So we basically played with two big centre forwards, with Peter and I on the flanks.

He was brilliant with names.

He was going through the Ipswich team and he said, 'Ruurmeoo Zinderden' and someone said… 'No gaffer… it's Romeo Zondervan'.

And he said, 'Ruurmeoo Zondervan? That's not a footballer's name… you shouldn't be on the pitch with a name like that'. And then there was George Reilly's first game. Jack came into the dressing room on the Friday as he usually did to name the team.

We were all sat round waiting.

And he goes… 'Right… ghoulkeeper is the ghoulkeeper. Right back is the big laird, two centre-backs… the big laird and the big laird, left back, (which was Kenny Wharton) the little laird. Right wing (me)… the big laird, centre mids… the two big lairds, left wide (Peter Beardsley)… the little laird, up front… the big laird and…'

And he started to click his fingers as he looked at George Reilly.

And he said, '…and up front… erm… erm…erm…

'… what's your name son?'

Still clicking his fingers. George Reilly looked at the rest of us as if to say, 'Is he serious?' And then he said, 'You signed me yesterday from Watford for £200,000… I'm George Reilly'.

And Jack said, 'Aaah… is that your name? I always knew George Reilly as the big laird'. He took us to Benidorm after we had been knocked out of the cup. We were away for five days and after three days everyone was skint. Jack was sat in the bar and the lads told me to go to him and ask for a sub to see us through the last few days.

They said, 'He likes you… you go'. So I went over, he saw me and said, 'Hello Chris lad, how are you? Do you want a coffee?'

So we had a coffee and sat chatting for 10 minutes, and eventually I got round to the subject of him lending me some money. But when I asked him for a couple of hundred pesetas – about 50 quid – he spluttered… 'You are f**king joking?'

Then sat patting his pockets and said, 'Anyway… I'm f**king skint'. So I pleaded with him, and promised to pay him back. And he took off his flat cap and bundles of notes fell to the floor. He picked up about 100 pesetas, handed it to me and said… 'Now, p*** off''.

The rest of the lads were round the corner watching us, p***ing themselves, and when I showed them my 100 pesetas, the others decided to have a go. So over the course of the next *day, one by one, they went through the same routine before he took the money from under his flat cap and told them to scatter. In the end, eight of us borrowed some cash.*

When we returned to training the following week, he pulled me to one side and said, 'Hey Chris, did I lend you some money in Spain?'

And I said, 'Who… me gaffer? No gaffer. It wasn't me'.

And he said, 'Well I lent somebody some bloody money but I can't remember who it was. And I'm down 600 quid'. And then he pulled in every one of the lads asking the same question, and everyone denied it.

We were 4-1 up at QPR and we went in at half time celebrating and shaking hands. Everyone was smiling when Jack walked in. He said, 'I don't like it… I do not like it one bit'.

And we were like, 'Hold on… we're winning four-one here'.

But he knew what teams are like when there were 4-1 up. You get complacent and start thinking the game is won. So he said we had to go out and treat it like it was 0-0 and do the same again. We drew 5-5. He kicked the living daylights out of the advertising hoardings when the fifth one went in. He tried to kill the goalkeeper Kevin Carr in the dressing room. He went mad. I mean absolutely unbelievably off the scale… mad.

He laid into every player in the dressing room, in the showers, on the journey home, individually and as a group. Eventually he got up and went down the carriage; then five minutes later came back with a crate of beer. He dropped it on one of the tables and said, 'Here. Not that you bloody deserve it'. And as he turned and walked away, someone shouted, 'Well, you did say before the game that a draw at QPR was a good result'.

And he turned immediately to try and work out who had said it, and we all sat there silent and still. And he just looked at us, then turned and walked away.

I was a young lad; I had just become an England International and I couldn't see the club changing. The club let Jack deal with all the contract negotiations and when he made his offer, I just thought, 'Do you really want me to stay?'

Players talk about what money they're on, and there were a lot of players on more money than he was offering me. And he knew clubs were after me.

We didn't fall out but Jack wasn't happy at the tribunal (that settled the transfer fee) and stormed out. The club paid about £20,000 for me and sold me for £590,000. I don't know how he'd deal with agents now. He'd probably end up chinning one or two.

THE TRIP to Spain was intended as a mid-season lift for Newcastle's players after their predictable fall from top spot after three games to mid-table after a dozen. They briefly fell as low as 17th, causing a little concern, but they were to return to a finish 14th.

If Jack was to succeed at his club, he knew he needed to build his team round Waddle and Beardsley. He also knew he had a player to nurture in Gascoigne. He took the 16 year-old under his wing, as did many people at the club. But Jack's guiding hand was particularly influential. He gave the chubby mischief-maker his first professional contract of £200 a week, which was a decent wage. He gave him his debut against QPR on April 13, 1985 sending him on as a substitute for the last 10 minutes of a 1-0 home win.

He turned to the teenager on the bench.

'Gaz, get stripped… you're going on,' Jack said. 'Enjoy.'

Concerned at the youngster's already notorious Mars bars consumption and addiction, as he struggled to keep his weight down, Jack tried to improve Gascoigne's diet. When he discovered Gascoigne calling in at the Oven Door in Fenham for hamburgers and chips, followed by cakes, Jack went to the café and banned the fancies. He gave the owner a list of foods for a healthier nosebag when Gascoine called in and the club picked up the tab.

Despite his age, Gascoigne was a nuisance to the senior players even before he had made the break from the youth team to the firsts. Let loose on the first team dressing room with his scissors and anything else he could get his hands on, Gascoigne was a nightmare. Glenn Roeder was forever in Jack's office complaining about his pranks, threatening to 'chin him'. Fed up with acting as peacemaker, Jack eventually took Gascoigne behind the training ground changing rooms and stood him against a wall.

'I told him with as much sincerity as I could muster, "If you don't start treating the senior pros around here with a little respect, you're out the frigging door and I'll see that you never get another club".'

Jack knew that Gascoigne failed to curb his behaviour.

He just got cuter at hiding it, and as he got even dafter his behaviour was just about tolerated. But Jack knew Newcastle had a real player. They all did. He even asked Jackie Milburn, then a journalist with the *News of the World*, to have a look at him. His uncle was so impressed, he recommended him to Bobby Robson as one to keep an eye on.

A goal in the Youth Cup final win over Watford proved the point.

'Paul got the second of the goals with an orthodox header and then, late in the game, produced a stroke of genius. He went for a throw-in on the right, and as he ran for the ball, checked and ducked and the ball went over the player who was marking him. Then he started running diagonally towards the corner flag on the other side of the pitch, before suddenly stopping at the angle of the penalty area.

'His chaser slid past him, and now the ball was between his feet. Your ordinary player would at that point have shifted it to one or other foot and tried the shot. But Paul looked up, saw the keeper off his line, and with the ball still lodged between his feet, swung his leg and with just the outside of his right boot, got it up, over the keeper and down just beneath the crossbar.

'The ball was struck while he was totally off balance.

'To do it, he had to produce the kind of intuitive skill that you perhaps see once in a lifetime. I remember turning to Maurice Setters who was stood beside me and saying, "If you live to be 100, Maurice… you'll never see a better goal than that".'

THERE IS a signed picture of Paul Gascoigne in John Charlton's Bar, in all his fist-raising, beaming, sweaty Italia 90 glory.

"To Jack, My 2nd Dad, Love Gazza"

PAUL GASCOIGNE

I liked the idea of having a Geordie in charge of the Toon. But he obviously didn't like the idea of me, from what I had been told or from what he'd seen of me. He hadn't been there long when he called me into his office. He didn't ask me to sit down, so I just stood there, waiting to find out what he had to say. He reached out and patted my stomach, as if I were a woman expecting a bairn.

'I hear you're a cheeky chappie,' he said.

I just mumbled.

'And I also hear there's a bit of skill underneath all that fat. Well, you've got two weeks to get it all off. If you don't, you're out of the youth team and out of the club.' I left the room in tears and run home, feeling really scared. The next season, Jack made me captain of the youth team.

We set off on a really good run in the Youth Cup. We thumped Everton 6-0 and beat Leeds United and Manchester City. What was especially great was that we were getting big crowds at home for all our matches. We hammered Coventry 3-0 in the fifth round and in the semi-final we trounced Birmingham City 7-2 on aggregate, earning a place in the final, where we were due to meet Watford, then managed by Graham Taylor.

We were expected to hammer Watford but they held us to a goalless draw at St James' Park. However, in the replay at Vicarage Road, we beat them 4-1 in front of a crowd of 8,500, many of whom had come down from Newcastle. I scored twice. As captain, I received the trophy, holding it high in the air, imagining I was at Wembley, winning the World Cup.

On the coach back to Newcastle we were allowed fish and chips, still wrapped in the newspaper, as a special treat. And before we got off the bus, Jack told me he was going to offer me a two-year contract as a full professional. I was going to be 18 in just a week or so, so I'd been on tenterhooks about whether or not I'd be signed. I never asked him about the details. I had no agent or adviser to discuss it with or negotiate the best terms.

I just said yes. At once.

My wages went up from £25 as an apprentice to £120 a week as a pro. I was thrilled. I would also earn another £120 a game in appearance money, which seemed even better. In my contract, Newcastle insisted on a further two-year option on me. I should never have signed the contract with that clause in it. Needless to say, I didn't fully understand it. But having said that, if I were 18 again now and being offered that contract, I would probably do exactly the same. I'd have signed anything they stuck in front of me.

Big Jack was brilliant to me. He took me fishing with him one day. I'd just bought some new gear which had cost me £120. I had to take out a loan to get it. But he took one look at it and threw it in the river, saying it was rubbish. He then told me what sort of gear I really should have for proper fishing.

Then Big Jack resigned.

I'd been sitting beside him on the bench for the game, for which I was sub, and had to listen to the crowd starting to chant… "CHARLTON OUT". I could hear him saying, 'I don't need all this'. Not long afterwards, he jacked it in. He wished me all the best when he left. I was sorry he never managed England rather than Ireland. I feel he would have done a good job, but I could see that the establishment would never take to him.

After taking the Ireland job he'd asked me if I had an Irish wolfhound?

I said no, I hadn't – but why was he interested?

'If you had an Irish wolfhound, you could qualify to play for Ireland.'

THAT WAS the claim Gascoigne made in his autobiography. He would later admit that Jack looked into his ancestry within days of taking the job, and discovered he qualified for Ireland through his grandmother. By the time he had unearthed this gem, however, and confirmed it to Gascoigne, who was keen to play for Jack, the youngster had played for England Under-21s. Jack and Ireland missed out by a week. Gascoigne was eventually to become the third local lad to leave St James' Park in quick succession, and not long after Jack's own departure. Before them, Waddle and Beardsley left Tyneside. And there was nothing Jack could do about it.

He had achieved his target in his first season. Newcastle finished 14th, scoring 63 goals, so another season of the First Division football beckoned.

But the 78 goals conceded horrified him. 'Towards the end of the season, I was beginning to sense the futility of it all,' he confessed.

JOHN ANDERSON

I played 41 of 42 league games in the promotion season but when he came in, I was out of the side. The club had signed Malcolm Brown for £150,000 and he missed most of the season with an Achilles injury but he was fit again for the new season, and he was picked by Jack on the Friday before the first game against Leicester.

So I knocked on his door, sat down and said, 'What the f**k's going on? I've played the majority of pre-season… 41 games last year, why am I not in the team?'

And his words to me were, 'This club can't afford not to play Malcolm Brown. But I'll tell you what, you can be sub'.

So I said, 'F**king sub… I don't want to be sub. I want to f**king play'.

And he said, 'If you want to be on the bench, you're on the bench. If you don't, you don't have to be. Up to you?' I was sub the next day.

He knew how to look after players. He looked after Gazza, but then we all did. Jack decided he couldn't really be trusted with his wages, which weren't bad I don't think for a young lad, so he set up a trust fund for him, and used to give him a little bit every week to see him through.

Gazza was a nervous boy and always a bit daft and unpredictable, but he came alive when he had a ball at his feet. He was a bit chubby, he had a few run-ins with the older pros, but you could see from the first time he stepped on the training ground that he was going to be an exceptional player. And Jack had been round the block a bit, and he knew a player when he saw one.

I am sure he knew he was going to be one of the best players in the world. We all knew he was going to be great. He could do unbelievable things with a football and it was totally natural. He had a great attitude to training, he worked hard and he loved Jack.

The club should have built round him, Waddle and Beardsley. But there was no money and no ambition. I think Jack realised that pretty early on and there were times when you could tell his heart wasn't really in it.

There was a warm day at Filbert Street, when we'd lost.

Before the game, Jack came into the dug out last, wearing his tweed jacket and his cap. He let out a big sigh, turned to Willie and said, 'Do you know what… I could be out shooting today. In fact I'd rather be out shooting today.'

GLENN MCCRORY

Jack has always been a big boxing fan and first I got to know him and the whole family was when I was a young fighter. You can imagine what that was like as a 16,17 year-old kid. We come from very similar working-class, coal-mining upbringings and of course football and boxing are our link. We went to a dinner and I was sat there with Jack, Jackie Milburn, Colin Milburn and Cissie. It was just magical. Cissie was a very matriarchal character, a very strong but very nice woman who loved being round football people.

When we were at the dinner, Jack, Colin and Jackie were all trying to persuade me to have a pint. Cissie was having none of it.

'You leave that lad alone,' she said. We're great friends now and just a few weeks ago we were having Sunday dinner, and Jack was outside playing football with Aidan, who is one-and-a-half, running round in his Ireland kit. Then they just sat there in the garden… Aidan in his kit on Jack's knee. Of course Jack was just being Jack, like the grandad he is, but, especially for someone with a big Irish family like mine, it was just lovely.

Jack loves telling the story about the first time he took me fishing when I went with my brother Shaun. We went out on the River Tweed at six in the morning. Jack drove us there, parked up and started walking down towards the river; me and our kid behind him. For some reason, Jack stopped on a ledge. I thought he stopped to let me past, so I edged past him… and fell straight into the river Tweed. I fell in over my head and came up under my hat. As I stood there in the river, Jack just looked at me in absolute disbelief and shook his head. My brother was absolutely mortified that I'd shown him up.

Jack got us down to the river and started fishing but, of course, I was soaked to the skin, my waders full of water, and I was absolutely freezing. But I thought, 'I can't not go fishing with Jack Charlton… so I carried on'.

But I was convinced I was five minutes from death. Eventually, after a couple of hours of standing there, no sign of catching anything, I turned to Jack and said, 'Sorry Jack... can I have the car keys, I'm going to have to go'.

And he just said, 'What took you so bloody long?'

Jack is the Deputy Lord Lieutenant of Northumberland, which is a role to assist the Duchess of Northumberland in public duties around the region.

Unfortunately, you have to retire from the position at the age of 75, so Jack had to step down for a younger model. Out of the blue I got an official letter from the Duchess inviting me to be her new deputy at Jack's behest. I don't know what was the greater honour; getting the title of Deputy Lord Lieutenant of Northumberland, or being nominated by Jack in the first place.

JACK RESENTED the continued speculation that he spent more time on the river than on the training ground. He fell out with everyone about it, particularly the local press. His version is that it never interfered with his ability to do his job, and he and Maurice Setters spent more than enough time scouring the country for new players to justify time dipping his toes in field sports.

'I was coming back from some bloody match in Manchester. I'd been driving along the motorway for six hours and was knackered. Suddenly I realised I was falling asleep at the wheel and I thought, "What am I doing this for?"

'Over the years I had to put up with quite a bit of flak about my love of fishing; I can't really understand why. If I played golf, like so many sporting so-called celebrities, no one would even mention it. There was this endless rubbish talked about my hunting, shooting and fishing image. Football's my first love – the one thing I've always done is to work at this game.

'And when I'm not working and coaching I'll take a day off and go fishing or shooting. Some folk play golf; I fish and shoot. That's it.'

What didn't help was the animal rights' protests which dogged Newcastle that year, particularly in London, and which led to glass being thrown on to the Highfield Road pitch the night before a game at Coventry. It is no surprise that Jack stood up to the protestors, defending his right to shoot, and his love of the countryside and its protection, as he has throughout his life.

The end, when it came, was before the second season, 1985-86 started. He had just missed out on signing Eric Gates from Ipswich Town, having met the player and refused to meet his wage demands. Sunderland may have finished eight points behind Newcastle the previous season, and been relegated as a consequence, but they had the cash.

Gates signed for them instead. It was against that background that Newcastle faced Sheffield United in a pre-season friendly at St James' Park. The visitors won as home fans sang... "SACK JACK" and... "CHARLTON OUT".

Angry, disappointed and hurt, Jack turned on the supporters at the final whistle, leaping over the fence to remonstrate with one group, and almost coming to blows. He didn't even bother going to the dressing room after the game. He went to the Boardroom, told Stan Seymour he'd had enough and walked out, never to return as manager. The Newcastle directors did try to dissuade Jack from walking out but he was too raw and too angry to change his mind. He spent the following day with Pat in the Dales, and returned to St James' Park on Monday morning to collect his belongings. When he pulled into the stadium car park, he was stunned to see around 400 people outside.

They had turned out to persuade him to stay.

But if he was wavering, his mind was made up once he met Joe Harvey, still the club's chief scout and a former player who had also managed the club to the 1969 Fairs' Cup final success – still Newcastle's only major silverware in nearly half a century. He asked Harvey if he had done the right thing, or acted too impulsively?

'Once that crowd get after you,' Harvey said, 'they're never going to stop.'

'If I had any doubts about my decision, that settled them,' Jack insisted.

Word spread quickly among the throng outside that Jack was still quitting. He was booed at he made his way back to his car, and to freedom.

'I didn't make many friends in Newcastle by doing what I did.' And the people he arguably most upset were closest to home. It would be some time before Jackie Milburn took a call from him and they returned to having their regular lunches.

While Cissie was sympathetic, she was also distinctly unimpressed.

CISSIE CHARLTON

Jack had always said that he would only stay with United as long as the fans wanted him there. So, when they called for his resignation, he gave it, typically for him, on the spot.

Although Jack left under a cloud and not the way I had hoped for, I can't say that it took me completely by surprise. From the day he joined Newcastle, I had been uneasy about how things would work out. I was delighted, of course, that he had come back to the North East, but I felt that somehow the job was just not right for him.

For one thing, I knew that he hadn't wanted to go into football management again. But when the offer of the Newcastle job came up he decided to give it a go. Even so, he was never comfortable with the job. He had been much happier at Sheffield and Middlesbrough.

When Jack took over at Newcastle, Kevin Keegan had just left. Kevin had spent two seasons with Newcastle and had been the darling of the fans who looked to Jack to find an instant replacement for him.

The fans wanted Jack to go out straight away and buy another big name, even if it got them into debt. But Jack did the exact opposite instead – he put the club onto a better financial footing than it had been for years by not spending. Unfortunately when he did have the money to spend, the right players either weren't on the market, or didn't want to come to Newcastle.

I had been on holiday in Wales with my son Gordon when I heard on the radio that Jack had resigned. I was pleased that his decision had been quick and clean. Many years earlier I had told both Bobby and Jack that when they felt they were coming towards the end of their playing careers, to get out straight away while they were at the top.

'Don't stay until the crowds begin to barrack you,' I told them. 'There is nothing worse than hearing fans barracking someone who has been the best in his day.'

I had my cousin, Jackie Milburn in mind when I said those words.

I didn't want to see what happened to him, happen to my sons. I have always been a Newcastle United supporter and watched many a Magpie match in the 1950s when Jackie was playing at his best. In those days he was nothing short of a God to United's fans. Then, when he passed his peak, the fans turned on him.

What short memories they have!

I listened to what they were saying about Jackie Milburn and it hurt me to hear it. It is sad how soon supporters forget the good things players have achieved and want them kicked out. They did it with wor Jackie and they were trying to do it with my Jack.

JACK WASN'T bothered.

He knew he'd made the right decision.

The bigger hurdle was convincing Pat it was the right decision. They had after all just bought a property in Northumberland, after months of searching, and she was not about to start all over again, or return, as Jack suggested, to Yorkshire.

'I told her not to worry,' he said. 'I may have left Newcastle United, but we are not leaving this house.' Jack and Pat Charlton still live in that house today.

PAT CHARLTON

Jack has never really asked for my opinion over the years, as he knows what is best for the football decisions. The only time I said anything and got annoyed with him was when he walked out of Newcastle United.

We had come up from Sheffield and it took us a year to find a house. We hadn't been in the new house more than a month when he came home and told me that he had quit. He could see I was annoyed. So he suggested we could move back to Yorkshire. I put my foot down then. I said, 'We are not moving again!'

We are still in the same house now. The great thing was it was so convenient when Jack took the Ireland job because it's not far from Newcastle airport.

LADY ELSIE ROBSON

When Jack told us he wanted to get involved with the Sir Bobby Foundation, of course we were delighted. Jack has a lot of gravitas in the North East and the people just love him. You can't help but love him. He will always say that he is happy to do his bit for his old friend Bob because, 'he was a good lad'.

Jack has certainly done his bit for the Sir Bobby Foundation. And we have a large photo of him, fair-haired, young and smiling, in all his glory in his Leeds United days in the Football Corridor leading to the Sir Bobby Robson Cancer Trials Research Centre. It's right in the heart of the Northern Centre for Cancer Care in Newcastle's Freeman Hospital.

He was delighted to be the face of Northumberland Tea, a company set up by his friends Bill and Helen to raise funds for the foundation. And I know he pesters Bill to take him out on the delivery trips to the tea shops around Northumberland.

It's no surprise that he always makes an impression on his visits.

When Jack walks into a room, you know about it. But he doesn't mean to attract attention to himself; he just does.

He's so tall of course for a start, so he stands out. But then you hear that lovely, friendly voice, and you just feel in the company of an old friend. I have been in his company many times with the foundation and everybody makes a bee-line for Jack and has a little chat with him. His lovely wife, Pat is always there of course, as she always has been.

And he's always just Jack. He just loves meeting and talking to people, and hearing about their lives and their stories. You can tell people of all ages are delighted to meet him, particularly the younger ones,

He knew my Bob for years. And when they came to play each other, they just got on with it. I know Bob had a lot of respect for the teams that Jack built with Ireland. They were always hard to play against. And I think they enjoyed those battles. They would talk about it when they met up and they would often meet for a chat when Bob was Newcastle manager and also when Jack was involved with Ireland.

Throughout all of Jack's career, Pat has been there and she has been so, so good for him. I'm sure she has played her role in keeping him grounded. That's Pat and Jack. Nothing has phased or changed them. It's only really through our work for Bob's Foundation that Pat and I have got to know each other, which seems strange when you consider we were in the same stadiums, perhaps just feet away, in Germany and Italy.

A football manager's life really is 24/7, 365 days a year. It is a fact of life for his family, so you just live that life. That's the way it was with Bob and I am sure it was very much the same for Jack, Pat and their children.

As two proud North East men, from hard-working families, they expected to go out and work hard and prove they were the best in their profession, which just happened to be football. It helped, of course, that they loved it.

And it helps that they were both very good at it.

BOB CASS

There is more than a touch of irony in the fact that, having been accorded almost legendary status with followers of the Republic of Ireland, Jack Charlton was hardly regarded in the same light by those who lived in the area where he was born and bred and where he has made his home.

Newcastle United supporters had long memories and as far as they were concerned he was just another manager who failed. The contrast was vivid but clearly evident to people like myself who were able to witness Jack as a football prince at the same time he was a pauper.

Travelling with his team provided an opportunity to observe the contrast from close range and never was it made plainer than on the evening of November 17, 1993 and that never to be forgotten climatic football showdown when there were enough mathematical qualifying permutations to baffle Euclid.

Jack Charlton with his teammate, foe and future inspirational team manager Don Revie in the early days before Leeds United changed to all white.

A young Jack looking dapper in his early Leeds days (above); Holding his young son John high (top); and Pat with John and Debbie.

Jack heads it to the back of the Manchester City net (top) and rises highest in the Manchester United box for another trademark goal.

Jack and his longtime partner in the Leeds defence, Norman Hunter take the train down south (top) and despite the best efforts of Leeds midfield maestro and friend Billy Bremner, Jack goes into the referee's book.

Jack and goalkeeper Gary Sprake hold Billy Bremner aloft as Leeds celebrate their victory in the League Cup final, while John Giles is ready to start the team celebrations.

Bobby and Jack make their first appearance together in an English shirt (top) and Jack sees the funny side of life as he and his English teammates find themselves in the company of actress Britt Ekland before the 1966 World Cup finals.

Jack and Pat Charlton at play with their children, John, Peter and Debbie in the mid-70s (top); John hard at work polishing his dad's replica World Cup trophy (left) and (below) Jack and Pat celebrate a big day with another generation of the Charlton family at their granddaughter Emma's wedding in 2015.

Jack and Pat on their wedding day.

Jack's first foray into management brought him to Middlesbrough where he got to work with Graeme Souness (third from left, front row) and David Armstrong (third from right, front row) amongst others in a team that quickly became noticed.

Jack celebrates with his assistant Maurice Setters after Ireland had beaten England in Euro 88 in Stuttgart (top) and the Irish team that took on the Russians in the same tournament, earning a draw and bringing so much honour home.

Jack walks with his old friend Bobby Robson after Ireland drew with England in the 1990 World Cup finals in Italy (top); Mick McCarthy and Kevin Moran celebrate after defeating Romania to reach the quarter-finals (middle); and Packie Bonner pumps the air after the sensational penalty shoot out that sent Ireland into the quarter-finals against Italy.

Alan McLoughlin (top)celebrates with John Aldridge and Denis Irwin in Windsor Park after the former had scored the goal that secured Ireland a place in the 1994 World Cup finals in the USA, and (bottom) Ray Houghton scores his memorable goal in the Giants Stadium that gave Ireland an historic opening victory in the tournament.

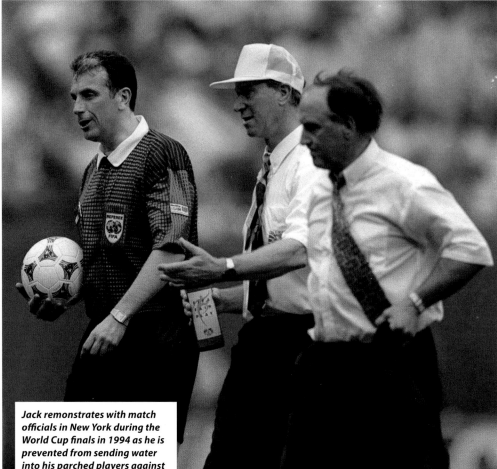

Jack remonstrates with match officials in New York during the World Cup finals in 1994 as he is prevented from sending water into his parched players against Mexico (top) and he sits it out in the game against Norway as a disciplinary measure.

Jack in his latter days as Ireland boss in 1995 with a young Roy Keane.

After losing to Holland and failing to secure a place in Euro 96, Jack waves to the Irish supporters in Anfield (top), and with Ronnie Whelan and John Aldridge at a team reunion in 2008.

A long day on the North Sea is too much for Jack who takes a nap while the fish are not biting (top) and looking over waters closer to his home in Northumberland with one of his best friends and fisherman buddies Bill Logan.

On an emotional day in the Aviva Stadium in 2015 when Ireland played England, Jack looks on with his wife Pat and the great Paul McGrath (top), and waves to the Irish supporters before being overcome by emotion.

England were in Bologna, Italy, where their only worries were whether, (a) they could score the seven goals they needed against San Marino; and (b) if they did, hope Poland would win their home match against Holland.

I was in Belfast for the infamous North-South match where my only worry was whether I would get out of the city in one piece!

In all my time reporting football, I have never known a more terrifying build-up to a game or a more intimidating atmosphere than there was in Windsor Park that night. Jack described it as the 'most hostile' he had ever known in any country he had played in. The match took place at the height of The Troubles; a month earlier 23 people had been killed in a series of shootings and bombings.

In order to safeguard to security of the players, staff, officials and media representatives such as myself (no Republic supporters were allowed to travel), the Irish FA had chartered a plane from Dublin to Belfast Airport from where we were whisked to the ground in a convoy of coaches and jeeps, manned by machine-gun toting military.

Vitally important it might have been, but the game was still almost incidental as far as large sections of the crowd were concerned. Without any opposition supporters to bawl at, all thousands of home fans were interested in was venting their spleen in the direction of the areas in which was seated anybody who appeared to have any connection with the visitors.

The astonishing news that San Marino had taken an eight-second lead against England provided a mild and, in Republican eyes, highly amusing diversion from the serious stuff going on in front of us. Subsequent euphoria at their qualification, coupled with Taylor's team's exit, quickly evaporated in the face of the more urgent priority of returning to the airport unscathed.

The celebrations back in Dublin involving players, management, back-room staff, officials, supporters and media alike were due to relief as much as triumph.

Covering an Ireland side which took its cue from their laid-back boss, I applauded that musketeerial sense of being all in it together which I rarely, if ever, came across with England – not that there was ever much to celebrate. The FA's policy of almost total isolation eschews social contact with the media. It would be really something if such demarcation could be justified by England's results.

The contrast in hospitality and co-operation offered covering Ireland or Wales could not have been more marked. Unburdened by delusions of international grandeur, players, many rated as high if not higher at club level as those who wore the three lions badge, were sociable, easily approached and not averse to enjoying a glass or two after a match. For instance, it was the regular routine for myself and a couple of other journos to join the Irish players as they wound down, particularly after a match in Dublin when we all repaired to a favoured venue in Leeson Street.

Either that or prop up a bar with the boss and his assistant Maurice Setters in the team hotel at Dublin airport. That usually happened when there was an early flight to Newcastle the next morning.

Often, when big Jack and I were on the same plane, he would depart the Emerald Isle a feted celebrity and return almost anonymously to his native Tyneside. A local World Cup hero he might have been but Magpie followers never forgot he walked out as manager after only one season in charge.

PART
2

IRELAND 88

JACK CHARLTON was reading in the den at home, four months after leaving Newcastle in August, 1985. The phone rang; he put down his book, and picked up the receiver.

'El-low?' grumped one of the most recognisable North East voices in football.

'Is that Jack Charlton?' said an unrecognisable Irish voice.

'It is,' was Jack's reply.

'This is Des Casey, president of the Football Association of Ireland. Would you be interested in doing the job?'

Jack's brow furrowed, he took off his glasses. 'What job?'

'Managing the Ireland team.'

'Yes,' said Jack, unaware that he was about to start the most incredible and unexpected journey of his life. And then the line went dead.

Casey called again a few weeks later.

'Are you still interested in the job?'

'Yes.'

Line dead. He was so amused and bemused at the same time that he told Pat straight away. They both laughed, shook their heads. He was still interested enough to agree to meet a party from the FAI after Casey made his third and final call before Christmas, this time with more clarity and details. A date was set for a Manchester hotel meeting.

The idea of international management appealed to Jack after walking out on Newcastle, and spending a few months back in the rivers and fields of

Northumberland and Yorkshire.

The only job application he ever wrote was for the England job when Don Revie quit in 1974. And the FA didn't even bother to respond or interview him.

That snub angered Jack. He never understood why the FA hadn't appreciated his credentials – World Cup winner, former England international with 35 caps, League title winner, experienced European football campaigner, respected and successful club manager, 20 years as one of the FA's first and now most decorated coaches. Instead, they appointed Ron Greenwood, overlooking Brian Clough in the process, as well as Jack.

While he had never been given the opportunity to put his theories to the test as an international manager with England, he was convinced they would work somewhere close to home.

When Des Casey made that first phone call to Northumberland, Jack was very much the outsider among the nine candidates identified by the FAI management committee.

Casey had decided Irish soccer needed a shake up and convinced his management committee that the manager should live in England. While Northern Ireland, under Stockport-based Billy Bingham, had enjoyed their first World Cup finals in Spain in 1982 and followed that with qualification for Mexico four years later, the Republic of Ireland, for all its talent, had once again just failed to qualify for those 1986 finals.

A shocking 4-1 defeat to Denmark in Eoin Hand's final competitive match had followed a dreary goalless draw with Mexico at a soul-less Dalymount Park; the lowest attendance for an Ireland home game. The seeds of failure had been planted long before Hand handed in his resignation. Ireland missed Jack's finest hour in 1966. They failed to qualify for the World Cup finals, losing a play-off after the FAI rejected taking a UK venue for the clash with Spain. The Spanish FA offered all the gate receipts if the game was played in Paris. They lost 1-0 in front of a predominantly Spanish crowd but pocketed £25,000.

Prior to Jack's arrival they were skint. The £20,000 a year salary they eventually compromised on, after he had been appointed and anointed, was as much as they could afford.

In his seven years in charge of the Irish team, Johnny Giles from 1973 had tried to instil some professionalism and a style of football he felt reflected the talent available, including his own. But Giles wasn't able to work any magical change. The FAI's lazy attitude didn't help. Eoin Hand had the same difficulties. And there was a perception that a hierarchy had developed within the squad, leading to players among the bigger English clubs calling the shots.

When he quit after the Denmark debacle, Hand was a shadow of the young, ambitious coach who had enjoyed rubbing shoulders with Europe's elite. Sadly, he knew he was close to getting it right with a good group of players.

With no money and no manager, Casey faced a tough task sweeping a new broom through the FAI corridors. He did at least have an executive who were equally sick of Ireland being the poor relations among the British and Irish football associations.

To maintain a new level of professionalism, and to feed the media, the FAI drew up a list of candidates for the team manager position to at least give the impression they were going through the process properly. As outlined, there were nine names on the list and Jack was among them, somewhere below six or seven.

Intrigued and amused by Casey's calls, Jack agreed to meet a trio of officials led by FAI president Joe Delaney in the Excelsior Hotel in Manchester in early December, 1986.

Jack was the first to be interviewed on the group's English tour after he returned from a family holiday in Spain. They had already spoken to three respected League of Ireland managers; Liam Tuohy, who had held the post for two years until 1973, Paddy Mulligan, and Jim McLaughlin. After Jack, they spoke to Paddy Crerand, Gordon Lee, Terry Neil, Theo Foley, Billy McNeill, and Johnny Giles.

A shortlist of three was drawn up for the FAI council's meeting of the 19 executives, including Casey, on Friday February 7, 1986, at their headquarters in Merrion Square. And then it gets complicated.

And the meeting got very heated.

Jack was on the list with Tuohy and Giles. There was some concern in the room about the circumstances of Jack's sudden exit from Newcastle just five months earlier, but he had explained those to Casey in their meeting, satisfying those who wanted a non-Irish manager. There was an acrimonious split between the two camps supporting the two Irish candidates that could not be resolved. And then, just as it went to the first vote, Bob Paisley's name was thrown into the equation and the voting process. His introduction at the 11th hour caused uproar.

Although the meeting was held in camera, and the source or sources of that discontent and the exact votes have never been fully revealed, what is known are the numbers. On the first vote, Paisley received nine and the other three got three each. Casey could not use his casting vote yet, however.

A second ballot was held to eliminate one man and Liam Tuohy was the first to go. In the third ballot, the votes were Paisley (9), Jack (5), and Giles (4). Giles was out. For the first time, a non-Irishman would be manager of the Republic of Ireland. It was down to a straight fight between the two North East ex-miners. And Casey now had his casting vote at the ready.

DES CASEY

The first man we interviewed was Jack Charlton. When he talked about the job he was able to rattle things off and he said he couldn't understand how we hadn't qualified for the World Cup with players like Dave O'Leary, Liam Brady, Frank Stapleton,Kevin Moran and Paul McGrath. He mentioned them all ... he said, 'if I had those players, I would certainly do something with them'.
He was number one on our list.

WHEN CASEY arrived for the executive meeting he was told by other officials that Bob Paisley had thrown his hat into the ring. Casey, who had established strong connections at Liverpool over the years, dismissed the idea, saying that he contacted the club's chairman Peter Robinson at the outset of the selection process and had been told that Paisley, who would later be diagnosed with Alzheimer's, was already believed to be unwell. Casey elaborated further in an interview with The Irish Times.

DES CASEY

I was told from inside the club, from the top of Liverpool that Bob had health problems and that he wouldn't be coming back into football management. So I said, 'right, get Bob on the phone'. I knew him personally and asked had he applied for the job. He said, 'I've been asked and if I was offered it I'd have to consider it'.
So I left it at that but I had a set to with the others. I told them that he wasn't on the shortlist because I had excluded him but they more or less said that now that he was interested, we couldn't ignore it. I said that was fair enough but I was going to put it to the executive.

So, it was put to the vote. Liam was eliminated, then John Giles. Paisley was stuck on nine votes and I was asked from the floor by somebody, maybe it was Milo Corcoran, if I was recommending Bob Paisley and I said, 'most certainly not'. I said that as far as I was concerned he wasn't interviewed by Tony and myself because I had been given a clear indication by Liverpool that he would not be coming back into management. So another vote was taken and Jack Charlton, who had remained static, got the vote by 10 votes to eight. He was getting the job.

AND SO the FAI was left to appoint a manager they didn't really want. Jack polled just three votes from 18 in the first round and got the job thanks to a power vacuum in a tiny room that had split and nearly destroyed Irish soccer.

Casey spoke to the press. 'He (Jack Charlton) indicated to me that he would be available to accept the position immediately and I anticipate that he will travel to Dublin in the coming week to outline his plans for the team.

'The terms of his contract have not yet been finalised and this is one of the items we will obviously discuss during his Irish visit. Jack Charlton is a man who operates on trust – many of his appointments in football have been uncontracted.'

Not only was Jack unaware of any pending furore over his appointment; he was unaware he had the job at all. The FAI only had his home number but Jack, oblivious to the drama in Merrion Square, was away at the house in Yorkshire. They didn't confirm with Jack that he had the job prior to their announcement.

When the home phone went unanswered, Casey trusted his new friend. He clearly took the view, early on from his dealings with Jack, that he would not go back on his word.

Thankfully Jack's old friend and England '66 teammate Jimmy Armfield had his number. He was working for the *Daily Express* and got the scoop of his life.

JIMMY ARMFIELD

A guy from the Irish FA rang me and he asked me if I knew how to get hold of Jack Charlton and I said, 'Probably'. He told me he didn't want the news broadcasted, but that Jack had got the job. I said, 'Oh no, I won't broadcast it'.

I knew he was down in Yorkshire, so I rang him there and I said, 'Congratulations, you're the manager of Ireland... if you want it?' So I asked if I should write the story. He didn't tell me what he was thinking, he just said, 'Get on with it'.

I was his ghost writer for two or three years for the Daily Express. *We were a good partnership; in fact a lot of the time I had to drag things out of him but when it came it was invariably quite good. We have always got on very well, never once falling out.*

Jack was a good manager. His was a very simple style. He was very good for Middlesbrough. He was forthright, strong; he said his piece and he liked everything straightforward and simple, and players who did that got to play for him.

He was suited to international management, because he'd worked out a system and a style of football that worked, and that had never been seen before.

He could also have time off to fish, and where better than Ireland?

Once he had made his mind up about how that unit was going to play, that was it. If two players pulled out in the run up to a game, he would bring in a couple who could play equally well in the system; his attitude was that they'd patch up and get on with it.

JACK TRAVELLED to Dublin for the first time as Ireland manager five days later. He didn't want a contract and he didn't even discuss it, never mind sign one.

He was introduced to the uninspired and largely cynical Irish media at the Westbury Hotel in the city centre. Dressed smartly, in blue blazer and red and blue tie, he was in good fettle in the build up, handing out his home number to anyone who wanted it.

He was delighted to be there, to have the job, and he spelt out his plans for success. From day one, Jack Charlton told the Irish people how it was.

'I am what I am and I can only promise to use the knowledge I have picked up in the game to achieve the right results for the Republic of Ireland team. My pedigree shows that I know the business and I'll be perfectly happy to be judged on what I do in the job.'

To his right was Casey, beaming and laughing when Jack got his title wrong and apologised. But this was the president's first meeting with the media since the previous Friday's announcement. There were many unanswered questions surrounding Jack's appointment and that explosive meeting preceding it.

Peter Byrne would become a close friend of the Charltons and the author of his autobiography and his World Cup diaries. But their relationship hardly got off on the right footing. The esteemed football correspondent of The Irish Times wanted to know more about the circumstances surrounding Bob Paisley's late, and failed, introduction to Friday night's proceedings. He was not alone in believing Jack's appointment was the outcome of a typical FAI debacle.

Casey may have been about to mount a defence, and suggest there was a time and a place for such a query, but he was not given the chance. His new manager took control, telling him… 'he didn't have to answer that question'.

But one man in the room disagreed.

And in that moment a stand-off with Eamon Dunphy began. After dispensing with the formalities, Jack offered to resolve their differences away from the cameras.

Jack immediately brought the press conference to a close.

Day One.

Jack's Way. And it would never change.

JACK CHARLTON took charge of the Republic of Ireland for the first time on Wednesday, March 26, 1986. It was a friendly against Wales, the venue was Lansdowne Road and the attendance was 16,500.

The fans were curious rather than convinced by his appointment; the majority of the media still miffed that Ireland had missed out on Bob Paisley. The game was only notable for an injury to Welsh goalkeeper Neville Southall and a typical Ian Rush finish for the Welsh winner.

Jack had a turbulent introduction to the business of running the Ireland team. Liam Tuohy was so peeved at Jack's honest intervention during half time in his Under-21 side's defeat to England in late February that he quit as his No.2 the following day. Jack insisted he had been invited to say his piece; Tuohy disagreed.

Jack did not see any issue, as he was the manager of the senior team and, therefore, technically manager of every Irish team. But he still described it as a serious setback. He was relying on Tuohy's infinite knowledge of the Irish game and its players, and had always been open to retaining the coaching staff he inherited in a new job. When the appointment of a new assistant came, it was swift and it was Maurice Setters. The FAI had tried to encourage Jack to appoint an Irishman after Tuohy's exit, but he declined.

Jack had known Setters since the 60s when the pair had played against each other, and of course they had worked together at Sheffield Wednesday and then briefly at Newcastle. Setters had the knowledge and the location, near his Leeds home, to see plenty of games and players; and he was handed responsibility for the Youth and Under-21 teams after Jack had handled matters for one underage game against Scotland.

Jack's first squad for the Wales game raised some eyebrows. He recalled John Anderson, whom he knew from Newcastle, and left out Gary Waddock. But it was the inclusion of uncapped Oxford United pair Ray Houghton and John Aldridge, and the omission of one Mick McCarthy that stood out in that first list.

Jack gambled on Houghton and Aldridge, naming the pair in his original 26-man squad, even though their Irish qualification had not being fully authenticated. The pair still didn't have an Irish passport by the time of the Wales game. But with the Ireland squad down to 19 due to injuries, Jack had to rely on the reluctant goodwill of Wales' manager Mike England, who allowed them to play.

Jack had gone to the Manor Ground to watch Aldridge within days of accepting the job. The Liverpool born striker, who scored twice that night from two Houghton assists, actually tipped Jack off about the Glaswegian midfielder's Irish ancestry. Jack got a lot of stick, particularly from the British media, over the number of non Irish-born players in his teams.

But it was not a Charlton phenomenon. When Ireland played Wales in 1981, five years before his appointment, there were six English-born players in the side; McDonagh, O'Callaghan, Hughton, Grealish, Waddock and O'Keefe. Michael Robinson became the seventh shortly afterwards.

The decision to leave out McCarthy caused some consternation in the Irish media, which the future Ireland captain and manager now finds very ironic. After missing just one World Cup qualifier under Hand, and performing well for Manchester City, many perceived his absence as harsh and perhaps the end of his Ireland career. In fact, Jack had deliberately left McCarthy out, on the basis that he was one of the few he really knew in the squad. When the injuries kicked in, McCarthy was asked to join up for the opening night.

MICK MCCARTHY

I had been to the PFA dinner on the Sunday and as tradition would have it, had a few scoops with my mates and some of the lads, and I came back home to Wilmslow on Monday night… got in, and Jack was on the phone.

I used to go have a pint and play pool with him in The Red Lion, *long before he got the Ireland job, so his thinking was, why should I call him up? He'd seen me play dozens of games for Barnsley when he was Sheffield Wednesday manager, so he knew me.*

But he was on the blower, asking if I would come in, so I jumped on a flight on Tuesday morning and went on as a sub for John Anderson. And I played just about every game after that. We never even discussed the Ireland job. It was a total surprise to everyone, including him. As far as I was concerned, he was the manager, I absolutely loved him as a player in that Leeds team and I thought it was a great appointment.

Eoin Hand did his best. He was great with me. We were probably two birds of a feather; two centre halves who were not the most graceful footballers in the world, but did what it said on the tin. I know that he appreciated me for how I played but it was a tough time for him.

We used to come into the team hotel on the Sunday, and there would be me, Chris Hughton, Tony Galvin, Gerry Peyton, Seamus McDonagh and Eamonn O'Keefe sitting around having a beer and the others would all go home to their families.

As soon as they got in, a fleet of hire cars would arrive, and they would disappear. And we wouldn't see them again until we trained on Monday morning, and then as soon as training finished, they would all go off again and have meals at home with their families. It was the norm when I joined, but when I look back now, it was carnage.

As soon as Jack came in, it all changed.

Everyone came in and you stayed with the team for the entire trip. We ate together, we went to the pictures together and it was just a lot more disciplined.

It needed it. There were too many people who liked to have an opinion and an influence, and he took all that away. He was the star of the show. He wasn't bothered about what anybody thought. Fans, media, players, he did it his way. Reputations meant nothing.

From day one there was a structure to everything. And it was clear what you did and what you didn't do. Well, it wasn't what you didn't do… it was just… this is what you do!

End of story! It was the same off and on the pitch. And it had to be that way, I'm afraid. And Jack was blunt about it. I get that… because I'm that way as well.

The rules are simple. This is the way were going to do it. You might want to do it another way. But it doesn't matter. We're doing it this way, and if you don't like it and you can't f**king do it… see ya. You're offski. Jack didn't hide that fact. It had to be that way. And that's how it was. That's what he did. And it was legendary wasn't it? Put them under pressure and turn them around. And it worked. Like hell it worked.

And of course, what gets people believing is if something works. Even if they would like to do something different! And there were a few who would like to have done it differently or play a pass that he would not want you to play. But you knew that if you did, he would hook you.

I have had a lot of influences in my career. Allan Clarke at Barnsley… and watching Norman Hunter at Leeds… playing for Billy McNeil at Celtic. But two stand out.

Norman Rimmington, who is 93 now and still working at Barnsley, who's the scout that discovered me, if you like. And Jack.

He has been a major influence on how I've done things, and he has been a real positive influence. We have never had heart-to-hearts but we've always gone for a pint together and I just love his company. He has always been really engaging, whether talking about his fishing trips or football. He would invite his fishing mates, or just some people he'd met on holiday or in a pub, to the games and the team hotel. He welcomed people with open arms; he was just a steady, open bloke who was easy to talk to.

And his football knowledge was second to none. He screwed all those big teams by the way we played. As time went on, teams got cute and started sitting back and didn't press on us and we couldn't always play the way he wanted us to play. Unless you can keep regenerating sides like Sir Alex at Manchester United over 25 years, it is hard to keep doing it.

What I loved about him was that he knew, whatever hand you are dealt with, you make the best of it… which I think is a really good life skill. You might want something better, and you can kick up a stink all you like, but you are not going to get it. His attitude was always… let's get on with what we've got and make the best of it. And he did that. It was humble.

We'd turn up with plastic bags with our gear in, the pitches were never great, the travel was always ok; but never once did we complain.

He helped me no end.

Just simple things. I had always played on the left, but he played me on the right and I became a better player for it. I tackled on the right, I headed on the right; it made sense.

And he told me he would never have played me on the left. And he stuck with me, despite everybody telling him otherwise. If you'd had a poll, the vast majority would not have wanted me playing. But it never bothered him. He said, 'f**k 'em all'.

Because he knew Kevin Moran and I were the best partnership. We might not have been the best two players but you look at our record of clean sheets and games we played together, and it stood up. That really was a testament to Jack and his intelligence, football nous and sheer bloody-mindedness. Because there are a lot of people with similar intelligence and football nous who might have said, 'I may have to change this and put David O'Leary in because everyone is telling me to do so'.

Yes, he was probably a better player than me, and various other things, but as defenders, Jack knew he could rely on us and he stuck with our pairing.

ON HIS first night, Jack claims he left the team selection to Mick Byrne.

'You've been with this lot for seven or eight years, you know the form, you pick the team. I'll just sit back and watch and I'll take it from there.' That's what he told the team physio.

But it was Jack who decided David O'Leary would partner John Anderson at centre half, while defender Paul McGrath was played in a deep central midfield, with Liam Brady more advanced. Houghton and Aldridge both started.

Seeds had been planted. Although it would take a few more months to formulate and finalise his plans to shake up international football, he had certainly made an impression on his first official Irish visit.

The good wishes from the public overwhelmed him. Everywhere he went, people wished him well. And he was so instantly recognisable and friendly that people took to him, and he took to them.

Cult status was secured from a very early stage.

With the players, too, he laid down the rules. He forbid the defenders passing the ball to the midfield from that first game. He warned them he would hook them. He was so different to anything they'd ever encountered; they didn't know whether to believe him or not. But very few risked it.

PAUL MCGRATH

Jack comes to me and says he thinks I am too good to play centre half. He wants me in midfield. 'Oh, and by the way, John, you can bring the ball out. You're the captain'. Some days I was John. Some days I was James. I am convinced Jack was doing it deliberately. It was as if he wanted me to get annoyed and correct him. But I never did after that first meeting. I just had a suspicion that this was all part of Jack's plan.

MICK BYRNE

It was a fantastic journey for me over ten years, from the first time I met him at the Westbury Hotel before the Wales game and then spending the next decade with him as The Boss. I consider it a privilege to call Jack and Pat my friends. His sons John and Peter spent so much time with us as well, it was like a family within a family.

And the most memorable moment for me was meeting the Pope and presenting him with a football and an Ireland jersey. Jack actually cancelled training on the morning we met the Pontiff, which was incredible so close to the World Cup quarter-final with Italy.

He was a legend and a World Cup winner before he came to Ireland and he had an aura about him. He was a fantastic coach who was able to work with the top players and tell them exactly what he wanted.

Everything came through him and I did nothing unless it came from him. He had absolute trust in me, and I knew I could trust him.

He is worshipped in Ireland and I love him.

GERRY DALY scored Ireland's first goal under Jack Charlton a month later when Uruguay were the opponents and 15,000 turned out at Lansdowne Road to see a 1-1 draw.

The squad was stretched by withdrawals, and given his limited numbers, Jack's decision to leave out David O'Leary for the end of season tournament in Iceland seemed a big gamble. But when he named the 20-man travelling party, he said he 'knew all about' the accomplished Arsenal defender who had been an Ireland regular for a decade already. He wanted to try alternative defensive partnerships.

When Liverpool trio Ronnie Whelan, Jim Beglin and Mark Lawrenson withdrew, followed by Kevin Sheedy and Liam Brady with knee injuries, he was down to 15 for the games against Iceland and Czechoslovakia in Reykjavik.

So he called O'Leary. His response was to turn down the request and go on the family holiday he'd booked as a result of the earlier decision. It resulted in his international exile for the next three years.

JACK CHARLTON

Before long, the media had interpreted it as a sign of bloody mindedness on my part. Now, I have never held a grudge against anybody in my life. Rows? Yes.

But when I said my piece or the other party had a go at me, I closed the book and forgot it. In football, you simply can't afford to hold grudges. You pick the best players you have, irrespective of personal relationships, otherwise you're deliberately handicapping yourself. I never, at any point, doubted David's ability as a player. Whether he turned out for Arsenal or Ireland he would guarantee managers a level of performance in keeping with his reputation as one of the better centre backs in the game.

But essentially he was a drop-off defender. He didn't believe in getting tight on his opponent, preferring instead to rely on his pace to pick up the bits and pieces. I needed centre backs who could compete with the players in front of them, push them out, deny them time and space to turn with the ball.

David had the opportunity to press his claims in Iceland, and he chose not to take it. That was his business. But I always maintained that I'd play him when I needed him. And I did. The other pertinent fact was that in Mick McCarthy and Kevin Moran, I had two players who fitted my thinking on centre backs perfectly. Here were two guys in their prime; strong, aggressive, exceptionally competitive.

IRELAND WON the Iceland tournament.

It was the first silverware the country had ever won. A new trophy cabinet had to be purchased. Ireland, by now down to 14 players, beat Iceland 2-1 and Czechoslovakia 1-0.

KEVIN MORAN

It was a small tournament in Iceland and he was trying to get us to play his way and there would have been a lot of the players thinking, 'God, this is not really the way that we want to play'. We wanted to knock it about like the other European teams, but then you tend to believe a lot more when success comes with it. Now that tournament was no big shakes but it was the first thing we ever won. He built on win after win; and the draws and the more success we had with it, the more we believed in the way he wanted us to play.

BY NOW Jack was preaching to the entire team about how he wanted them to play. And he was creating a team spirit that would serve him well, buying crates of lager in duty free on the outward journey when he heard there were no pubs in Iceland.

JOHN ANDERSON

It was like the Leicester City philosophy. If everybody does their jobs, we will beat teams. Yes, they'll have more of the ball, but we put them under pressure and they'll make mistakes.

If the ball is there to be shifted, get it shifted; and we reorganise. Do that, keep it tight and you'll get chances. And everybody dug in and chased.

There was definitely a clique under Eoin Hand. All the big-hitters at the big clubs ran the show basically. They had an edge about them. But Jack didn't want individuals with an edge. He wanted people who were going to stick together, and when it got tough would back each other up.

I used to go my mum and dad's house on Saturday night, see my mates and family, and go into training on Monday morning and go home again straight after training; same on the Tuesday. And when the game finished the following night, I'd go back to my mum and dad's and fly to Newcastle on Thursday.

Jack took one look at it for the Wales game and stopped it immediately. He said, 'We meet up and we stay together, and do everything together'.

Everybody had to be in Dublin on the Saturday night, everybody went out together on Sunday, we trained at ten on Monday morning, went to the pictures on Monday night together and we all had a drink together after the match on the Wednesday.

His attitude was, 'I don't give a f**k who you are, who you play for; we're doing it my way and if you don't want to f**king do it my way, there's the door'.

It was more like a club environment; that's what he wanted. That's why everybody had to be together in the team hotel from the Saturday night. And we stayed together. He did use to get names wrong. So we had Paddy Bonner, Ronnie Moran, John McGrath, Billy Whelan, Ian Brady, Roger Byrne…

It added to the laughs and the fun you could have with him sometimes. He just built this club mentality and he told us what he wanted on the pitch. He didn't want full backs knocking it inside to midfield players, he didn't want midfield players coming and getting it. And he said, '… the first one who does that, is off'.

I was usually right back and my job was to knock it down the line, get the ball in behind their back four and then we'd all squeeze up the pitch.

He said to us… 'all these international footballers, especially in the top nations, think they can play. And if you watch them, they like to get the ball off the keeper, and they have time to pick their pass and play'. At the time, we were brainwashed because that's how international football was played. And when Jack said, 'f**k that', at first we thought it was going to be awful and it wouldn't work.

But he was spot on. If you look at the foreign sides, not so much the British sides… but the Dutch, Belgium, Italy, Spain… they'd all jog back together when they lose possession; they wouldn't sprint back together with urgency because they all had the time. Suddenly, *when they came up against us, they were getting the ball off the keeper or in easy areas of the pitch and we were in their faces, and you could see them going 'what the f**k are you doing?'*

AS WELL as winning that first trophy, the Iceland trip was significant for two players who would become stalwarts of the Ireland team under Jack. Packie Bonner was installed as his No 1. And Niall Quinn, a 20 year-old raw Arsenal striker, earned his first call-up.

NIALL QUINN

I walked into the reception of the hotel and Jack was holding court with a few journalists. As I came close to the group, Jack turned to Maurice Setters and said, 'Bloody hell, Maurice. We haven't picked that lanky buggah… have we?'

'Think we had to,' said Maurice.

And there it was.

Elated to deflated in one nanosecond. And it was done in front of the public so you could see the journalists all thinking… 'Christ… now Quinn doesn't even know he's been picked'.

But that was just his way. His whole leadership model was just to make the players feel great about themselves without telling them that they're great.

Whereas some managers would say… 'you're great… you're great, you're great', Jack might say… 'you're f**king hopeless, but you might go and prove me wrong today' and he'd laugh and you'd think… 'I'll show him'.

And then you'd laugh about it afterwards.

He got this wonderful spirit together and he allowed us plenty of rein and he trusted us, unwisely the odd time, but he did that by creating that bond and spirit.

Jack would play cards down the back of the bus and we'd always play hearts. At the most, on your worst day ever, you might lose a fiver but it's a game where you try and chase the leader all the time. And if you went after Jack, he would look at you, give you a look and you just knew there was a chance he might not pick you for the next game.

He'd look at you, steely blue eyes, and you knew what he was thinking and he knew that you knew what he was thinking… so you'd go and hit someone else in the group. Then they would give out at you asking, 'What are you doing?' and Jack would be sat there laughing his head off.

We used to play golf at the hotel in Monaghan where we used to stay. I was playing with Jack and Packie on the first green, playing for a fiver a man. Jack had a five foot putt to win the hole. And he put the ball in the hole by rolling it with the putter along the ground and dragging it in. Packie and I stood looking at each other, as if to say... 'What do we say?'

'Are you going to say anything?'

'No! Are you?'

Of course we were afraid to say a word, so we just walked off towards the next tee. I was afraid of losing my place and he knew neither of us would have the balls to say anything.

What you saw was what you got.

If a journalist wrote something or said something that he didn't like, he made no bones about telling them what he thought. I would never say he was soft, put it that way. But the man, woman or child on the street never felt like that.

He encompassed everybody and connected with everybody.

IN NOVEMBER, 1987 while he was on a farm in the middle of Shropshire, Jack discovered Ireland had qualified for their first major championship finals.

He was on a shoot, convinced beforehand, like the rest of Ireland, that they'd blown their chances in the qualifiers. Any news from Bulgaria was certain to be bad news.

With their own qualifying games done, Ireland needed Scotland to win in Bulgaria. But nobody won in Sofia. Watching the game as a TV pundit in Ireland, Jack's assistant Maurice Setters could not hide his contempt or anger at Andy Roxburgh's negative tactics. And then the Scotland manager sent on Gary Mackay for his debut. His cracking and winning goal was one of the most significant and celebrated moments in Irish sporting history.

Bulgaria 0, Scotland 1 (Mackay).

Ireland were going to Euro 88.

At the very moment that Mackay's shot changed the course of his Ireland reign, Jack had no idea. He was watching the game with a half hour delay and was contacted by a journalist minutes after the actual final whistle.

At first, he didn't believe the news.

'I was lucky enough to enjoy many great days as a player,' Jack later told the media, '... and obviously one has to make a distinction between the playing and managerial sides of the game.

'But I must say the news from Bulgaria gave me as much pleasure as anything I have known in my time in the game.'

Jack had watched Ireland's qualifying opponents Scotland, Belgium and Bulgaria on a trip to the Mexico 86 World Cup finals with Pat. He watched eight games in total; organised the trip himself, and sent the bill for his part of it to the FAI.

Jack came back from the finals with his mind fixed on a game plan he was convinced could shake up world football, and set it in motion immediately.

THE EURO 88 campaign started in Brussels, and was the first major game played at the Heysel Stadium since 39 Italian football fans had been killed prior to Liverpool meeting Juventus in the European Cup final in 1985. Liverpool players Jim Beglin, Ronnie Whelan and Mark Lawrenson were in the Ireland squad.

Ireland earned a credible 2-2 draw, thanks to Liam Brady's last minute penalty.

In the build up to the game, Jack, who had left out David O'Leary and Kevin Sheedy after they'd missed the Iceland tournament, had contemplated dropping Brady to the bench.

Paul McGrath or Mark Lawrenson were vying for the role of his defensive midfielder, and the anchor for the new tactics, not the instigator and creator. That was Brady's job; but it was taking him time to get the message.

In the pre-match press conference, the manager observed, 'Liam is a quality player but he must change his style and do the things I want him to do. If he responds it will be fine, if not, well...

'I don't want passes made from man to man... I want the ball played into space so that we can get the opposition turned.'

Brady was brilliant against the Belgians and although Jack might have called him 'Ian' once too often, he acknowledged the significance of the then 30 year-old breaking John Giles's appearance record by handing him the captain's armband for his 60th cap in the friendly in Poland later in the year.

JACK CHARLTON

We went away to a team that had finished fourth in the World Cup and we got a result. And when Belgium came here in the return match, they never came out of their half and settled for 0-0. The coach was a very experienced guy and he recognised something in our game that said, 'If we try and take the game to them we will come unstuck' and they were the first team to sit back and say, 'You have to be careful against them lot because they do things you might not be able to handle'. And he was correct.

JACK WAS delighted with the result in Brussels, but frustrated when Ireland failed to turn their dominance over Scotland in the next game into a win, drawing 0-0 in front of 45,000 at Lansdowne Road.

The failure of ground staff, under the direction of the IRFU (Irish Rugby Football Union) who rented the place out to the FAI, to prepare the pitch properly for the game probably cost Ireland, and Jack knew it. He told Casey and the FAI to sort out an agreement to give him a pitch fit for football. He was learning fast where football, as he knew it, stood in Ireland's sporting hierarchy and wanted to change that.

Jack's mood, and that of the entire country, changed with a 1-0 win at Hampden Park in February, 1987, courtesy of a Mark Lawrenson collector's item. Injuries had forced him to play Paul McGrath and Ronnie Whelan as full backs. But only the media and supporters found it odd.

The players were learning to get on with it and play for Jack.

And the Green Army, increasing in numbers, were in on it too. With full access to the team's Glasgow hotel, they mingled with Jack and the players for what the manager described as 'the mother of all parties' before he retired at two am. It was still going strong when he departed five hours later to catch a flight home.

RAY HOUGHTON

That was the night for me that we knew we could qualify.

You can see these things in the reaction of the players. I mean… Liam [Brady] had come off injured. I liked Liam, he wanted to win and he was a brilliant player, but he never really showed his emotions; he never let them get the better of him, but that night he was back on hugging people and telling them, 'Well done'.

MARK LAWRENSON

We were sitting there and he went… 'It's Packie in goal… Paul McGrath, Kevin Moran, Mick McCarthy, Ronnie Whelan…' and we're all looking at each other trying to figure out whether he was just naming the 11 or whether he was naming them where he was going to play.

'Mark Lawrenson, Ray Houghton…' he just went on and on.

And at the end of all of this I think it was Ronnie who says, 'Jack, you've named me a left back,' and he said, 'Yes, I have… have you got a problem with that?'

'No… no!'

And he says, 'Paul… you're right back.'

And Paul is just, 'Yeah, yeah, not a bother… that's fine'.

And then we all sort of looked at each other and thought… 'Oh my God, what is this all about?'

But in fairness to him, when we saw the Scotland team, and we saw the midfield with Pat Nevin and Dave Cooper and Gordon Strachan in the centre, they were a little bit like Ken Dodd and the Diddymen. So that was his master plan and after the initial shock we just thought… 'Fine… we better get on with it'.

Because I scored that day and people say that was the start, it is quite nice personally. It was enjoyable because I scored with my left foot but I actually closed my eyes when I hit it.

IT WAS Lawrenson's last game for Ireland, his talents cruelly taken away by a ruptured Achilles. He had instantly taken to Jack's style, whether he was a fan or not, and Jack had big plans for him. Paul McGrath's importance to the cause grew; and concerns about Brady's suitability rose again.

After losing in Sofia to Lasser Tanev's controversial penalty, and that goalless draw with Belgium, they beat Brazil 1-0 on May 23, 1987. It wasn't the strongest Brazilian team of all time, and they barely registered a shot. But Ireland had defeated Brazil in Dublin; Liam Brady notching the winner.

Irish people started to take Jack, and his team, seriously. They then recorded two unconvincing wins over Luxembourg, falling behind in the second game at home to the side considered, for many years, to be the worst in Europe. Ireland then had to beat Bulgaria in the final game at home.

Jack's decision, and gamble, during the fixture negotiations, to pester the FAI for home games for the second half of the campaign would pay off. Bulgaria would still only need a draw with Scotland to secure a place in Germany, but Ireland put the pressure on with a 2-0 win over them in front of just 26,000 at Lansdowne Road, thanks to goals from Paul McGrath and Kevin Moran.

And Brady was brilliant again. This game could have changed the end of his Ireland career and possibly his relationship with Jack. Jack thought he had cracked it. And then, with two minutes left, he was sent off.

'He was playing off the front two, taking on defenders, going to them when they had the ball, doing everything I had asked of him for more than a year,' Jack recalled. 'I remember turning to Maurice and remarking, "The penny has at last dropped".

'And then this gifted man who can calculate a pass to the last roll of the ball, goes and destroys it all. We're leading 2-0, there's only a couple of minutes left, and as he turns away from an opponent... Sadkov, he's kicked.

'What does he do?

'He spins around and kicks the guy back, straight in front of the referee. Off! My heart sinks. Normally, I would blow my top at such stupidity, but in a peculiar kind of way I empathized with Liam in that moment. He had just produced one of the great international performances of the year, had lumps kicked off him in the process, and then with time almost up, he had suffered one foul too many.

Brady's suspension was initially four games, reduced to two on appeal. Many, perhaps even Brady himself, who had played in all eight qualifiers, thought the ban would be irrelevant anyway. But it was left to Scotland's Gary Mackay to change all that and write his name in Irish soccer history. The Irish team was on its way to the Euro finals, and practically the whole country was ready to join them, as captured in songwriter Christy Moore's immortal lines.

It was in the year of eighty-eight, in the lovely month of June,
When the gadflies were swarming and dogs howling at the moon,
Ah with rosary beads and sandwiches for Stuttgart we began,
Joxer packed his German phrase-book, and jump-leads for the van.
Ah well some of the lads had never been away from home before.
It was the first time Whacker put his foot outside of Inchicore.
And before we left for Europe, we knew we'd need a plan,

So we all agreed that Joxer was the man to drive the van.
In Germany the Autobahn was like the Long Mile Road
There was every make of car and van, all carrying the full load
Ford Transits and Hiaces, and an old Bedford from Tralee,
With the engine overheating from long-hauling duty free.
There were fans from Ballyfermot, Ballybough and Ballymun
On the journey of a lifetime and the craic was ninety one
Joxer met a German's daughter on the banks of the River Rhine
and he told her she'd be welcome in Ballyfermot anytime
And as soon as we found Stuttgart, we got the wagons in a ring
Sean óg got out the banjo and Peter played the mandolin.
Oh there were fans there from everywhere, attracted by the sound
At the first Fleadh Ceol in Europe and Joxer passed the flagon round
But the session it ended when we'd finished all the stout
The air mattresses inflated and the sleeping bags rolled out
As one by one we fell asleep, Joxer had a dream
He dreamt himself and Jack Charlton sat down to pick the team
Joxer dreamt they both agreed on Packie Bonner straight away
And that Moran, Whelan and McGrath were certainly to play
Ah but tempers they began to rise, patience wearing thin
Jack wanted Cascarino, but Joxer wanted Quinn
And the dream turned into a nightmare, Joxer stuck the head on Jack
Who wanted to bring Johnny Giles and Eamonn Dunphy back
Ah well the cock crew in the morning, it crew both loud and shrill
And Joxer woke up in his sleeping bag many miles from Arbour Hill
Ah next morning none of the experts gave us the slightest chance
They said that the English team would lead us on a merry dance
Ah with their union jacks all them English fans for victory they were set
Until Ray Houghton got the ball and he stuck it in the net
What happened next is history, brought tears to many eyes
Oh that day will be the highlight of many people's lives
Well Joxer climbed right over the top and the last time he was seen
Was arm-in-arm with Jack Charlton, singing 'Revenge for Skibbereen'.
Ah now Whacker's back in Inchicore, he's living with his Mam
And Jack Charlton has been proclaimed an honorary Irishman

Listen do you remember that German's daughter on the banks of the River Rhine
Ah jeez, well didn't she show up in Ballyfermot last week

Joxer Goes To Stuttgart
– Christy Moore

THE FRIENDLIES in the build-up to West Germany were impressive.

Ireland finished 1987 with a 5-0 thrashing of Israel, and a David Kelly hat trick to boot, and were named World Soccer's highest-rated European team. Ireland won eight in a row, scoring seven and conceding one in home wins over Romania, Yugoslavia and Poland in the spring.

Bobby Robson was getting worried, and wasn't fooled by the goalless draw with Norway in Oslo just 11 days before their meeting.

Liam Brady, suspended for the first two games, admitted defeat in his battle to beat a knee injury just before Jack named his squad of 20. But Mick McCarthy was declared fit, 10 days after knee surgery.

BOBBY ROBSON

The Irish influence took over our training. We knew what Jack's side would try to do. They would attempt to wear us down, try to steamroller us. We worked on long throws-in and things we would have to compete with in the actual game and then try to get the ball down to play our own brand of football. If you don't win the first ball, make sure you win the second ball. No matter how much you want to play, you can't stop them kicking the ball when they have it and this is what is going to come at you thick and fast.

WHEN HE arrived at the Neckarstadion, Jack made a beeline for the England manager, and his former Newcastle players Chris Waddle and Peter Beardsley. It was the first time he had encountered Waddle since Jack had stormed out of his transfer tribunal. Jack greeted him like a long lost friend.

And then he turned his attention to his own players, and how they were going to deal with the English threat, and take their game very much to the favourites.

MICK MCCARTHY

I'd been captain a few times when strangely enough he made the decision to change it for the Euro 88 finals and he made Ronnie Whelan captain. That annoyed the hell out of me, I have to be honest. I didn't get it but it really was a case of having an Irish player, and someone who played for Liverpool I guess, although I was at Celtic at the time.

I didn't like it.

We didn't fall out about it but we did have a disagreement and then I had to accept his decision. We had a number of disagreements over the years. He has an unbelievable warmth in him; he genuinely likes people and they warm to him because he is warm in the first instance. He is blunt to the point of being rude – and there's me saying it. He says it how it is, and as the manager he told you what he wanted and if you didn't do it… you didn't play.

And I have to say that is me and all. People who say it that way don't often like it the other way round, as I have discovered over the years.

It was the time of my life, and that was the same for a lot of us. It doesn't get any better. And what is lovely is how well we are all remembered and respected and liked and loved. We all get well received in Ireland and that's all because of him. He was the band leader.

We just played his tune.

RAY HOUGHTON

I have photographs at home when I scored, and you can see the delight from the smiles of Ronnie Whelan and John Aldridge. You would think those two had scored and not me.

KEVIN MORAN

We knew we could do it before the game.

It was the hardest 90 minutes you will come across, believe me. Before the game we were probably saying, we will do well to keep it down to two or three. Obviously that was the first major game in the championships we played and it was against England on neutral ground when they were overwhelming favourites. It was a great day.

RONNIE WHELAN

Everyone still calls it a shinner. I don't even know why I was there. That was not even my position at throw-ins. On that night, or afternoon... whenever it was, I don't know what happened to that team. We had a lot of gifted international footballers who could play. That afternoon, we decided to play.

Jack didn't tell us to go out and play, Jack told us the same thing; put it in the corners and go up and attack them. But we played some tremendous football that afternoon, probably one of the best performances we have seen from an Ireland team for a long time.

It was just a long throw from Mick. I just decided to get myself on the edge of the box... see what happens. I think Paul (McGrath) was playing and he played a little bit more defensively than me and when it came across, I just thought, 'I might make a right fool of myself here, but I don't really care'.

It was the European Championships... if it goes in I am a bit of a hero. And 23 years on, people still remember it.

They [Russia] were a top class team in those days. Now, you've got all the different countries but back then it covered a lot of countries and they had a lot of very good individuals. We played tremendously well. A lot of people have said that that was my best game for Ireland. It was a position that I had played and was comfortable in. It was somewhere where I felt that I could have more of an impact on games.

TONY CASCARINO

My first contact with Jack was a brief handshake in the lobby of the team hotel, but it wasn't until we started preparing for the game (against Poland in the Euro warm ups) that I caught my first real glimpse of the man in charge.

We were practising set pieces and had moved from corners to free kicks. Jack was explaining to Ronnie Whelan exactly what he wanted done. I was facing away from him with Kevin Sheedy in the wall.

It was hot, the session becoming tedious. Bored with our role as the bricks in the wall, Sheedy and I had just started to shadow box when I was suddenly aware of a hush and Jack's presence on my shoulder. He was not amused.

'What do you think you're doing, you stupid f**king b*****d?'

He was fuming.

'Sorry, Jack,' I choked. 'We were just having a bit of a laugh.'

'A bit of a laugh! A bit of a f**king laugh!! We are trying to get some serious work done here and I look around and you're shadow boxing with f**king Sheedy!'

'Sorry, Jack, I've just...'

*'Just my arse! Pay attention… you stupid pair of b*****s!'*

Sure any chance I'd had of ever playing again from Ireland had disappeared, I was surprised at his good humour later, over dinner. 'And what are you up to today, Cascarino… you silly buggah?' he chuckled. And I was even more surprised when he named me in the team. It was nice to know he didn't bear grudges.

In hindsight, because it certainly didn't occur to me at the time, my performance during those first 32 minutes against Poland was probably the most important of my career. First impressions were important with Jack; had I ignored his instructions or played badly and been substituted, there was a fair chance I wouldn't have won a green shirt again. But when I scored in the 32nd minute, following up a Ronnie Whelan free that was fumbled by the Polish keeper, the manager was happy. And when Jack was happy, your future with his team was secure.

I quickly learned to understand a few basic principles. Well, actually, there was just one basic principle. The manager's instructions weren't open to interpretation. The dressing room wasn't a forum for debate. Jack never pretended he was running a democracy. When he said, 'Jump,' you asked, 'How high?'

THE MOOD in the camp was relaxed and even 10 days of negotiations with the FAI over match fees and bonuses did not distract the players or their manager. Jack left Frank Stapleton and Kevin Moran to reach the settlement with their employers and sponsors. A week before they left for Germany, Jack had taken the squad to Phoenix Park races for the day.

TONY CASCARINO

After a couple of punts and a couple of pints, we all soon forgot the numbing dullness of the training camp. As a mark of appreciation (and, it's fair to say, in the hope we might be allowed another drink), we began singing his praises on the journey back to the hotel.

'We love you Jackie we do…'

At first, he pretended not to bite.

'Shut up! Don't try all that rubbish with me. You're not stopping at a pub for a pint. You lot are going straight back to the hotel.' But five minutes later, there was a huge cheer when the bus pulled into a hostelry by the side of the road.

'Ok, everybody off,' he smiled, 'but let's be clear on one thing; I'm not buying the drinks!'

As an exercise in building team spirit it was brilliant. And if there was one quality that team possessed in abundance, it was spirit.

ENGLAND MANAGER Bobby Robson was getting worried, and wasn't fooled by Ireland's goalless draw with Norway in Oslo just 11 days before their meeting in Stuttgart. He primed his players for Ireland's aerial and physical assault.

He deliberated over the inclusion of Glenn Hoddle for the game until the last hour; refusing to name his team the day before kick-off.

Jack knew his good friend was playing silly buggers, so he did the same.

PACKIE BONNER

I was sharing a room with Gerry Peyton and we were like a couple of schoolkids going on their first trip abroad when we discovered, to our delight, that the hotel backs on to the football pitch where we train.

This was brilliant. You could get changed in your room and make your way down to training so we got our gear on, stole into kit man Charlie O'Leary's room and nicked a football to take out on to the pitch. As we kicked a ball at each other, testing the bounce of the grass, we were suddenly joined by Big Jack and his son John who had taken a wander to familiarise themselves with their surroundings.

'What are you doing?' Jack casually asked. Gerry and I thought we had been caught by the headmaster out of hours, but when we explained that we were just getting a feel for the pitch, he did the most extraordinary thing.

Jack Charlton, manager of the Republic of Ireland, pointed to his son and said, 'Right, give the ball out to the young fella there and we'll try a couple'.

With Gerry and I taking it in turns to go in goal, John Charlton lobbed the ball towards the penalty box and Big Jack, dressed in his tracksuit and his training shoes, would catch the ball full on the volley and rocket it towards us.

With Jack, you knew to expect the unexpected and this was typical of a man who could create the most relaxed of environments for his players. As we sat in the hotel, just before we headed off to the Neckarstadion ahead of the English match, Jack went into his team talk.

We would all be stunned to learn later that Glenn Hoddle had been left on the bench, which was a bit of a relief I think for Big Jack, because he was paranoid about that ball over the top that Hoddle could deliver just about better than anyone else and that would let the supreme poacher, Gary Lineker in on goal. Lineker was the obvious threat but Jack thought that Peter Beardsley was just as dangerous, and talked about him at some length even though the gist was simple. He pointed out that the defenders weren't to let Beardsley turn with the ball as that was a favourite manoeuvre of the Geordie striker. He would try to find space and run at his marker either to play a penetrating pass or simply get a shot away. With the best wishes and tactical thoughts of Jack, we walked out on to the pitch on a beautiful summer's day in Stuttgart for what I would consider to be the biggest game of my career up until that time.

STUTTGART

Saturday, June 11, 1988.

It was the biggest football match for Ireland in 60 years. It may be the greatest result ever recorded.

An England side including John Barnes, Gary Lineker, Peter Shilton and Bryan Robson were the overwhelming favourites. As ever with an English team, and its merry media, they were in the finals to win it. Defeat to the competition's outsiders, who many believed were there just to make up the numbers, was unthinkable.

In the sixth minute, the unthinkable happened.

Ray Houghton scored with a looping header over Shilton, launching himself at the aftermath of a Kenny Sansom slice from Tony Galvin's cross that John Aldridge had nodded into his path ahead of Tony Adams.

What followed was 'the longest 84 minutes I've ever sat through,' said Jack. Ireland rode their luck, but with the combination of solid, disciplined defending and a large measure of good luck kept their lead intact. Lineker and Beardsley missed five decent opportunities between them, not least when Hoddle found his range after his introduction.

And Packie Bonner was in inspired form protecting his goal, particularly in a frantic final five minutes. Ireland actually should have scored a second, but Ronnie Whelan's drive hit the bar.

JOHN ANDERSON

Jack took me to Germany as a sympathy vote because I was injured and I was not going to play. When we beat England, I was sat right behind him in the dug out. It was red hot…

I had never seen or felt anything like it. It was just a sea of green on one side and red white and blue on the other, and the noise when we came out was incredible.

He jumped up when Ray scored and clattered his head against the top of the dug out... nearly sparked him out. I didn't know whether to laugh or cry. He gets out of the dug out, swearing and holding his head, and just says... 'who the f**k scored?'

After the game, he came into the dressing room, rubbed his hands and says, 'Right, we're having a party tonight lads'. And we had the biggest party in the world in the hotel. For two days. How the hell we got a result against Russia, I do not know.

He was totally relaxed about the lads having a drink. If you want a drink with your dinner, have a drink with your dinner. If you want a couple of pints... do it, but don't abuse it. If you abuse it, you'll be on the first plane home.

When we got back from Germany, all the lads got a typed letter from Jack on FAI paper, addressed to the clubs, thanking them for their players' part in the tournament, and wishing them good luck for the new season.

Jack added a handwritten note on mine. He put...

'He was f**k all use because he was injured.

'Hope he enjoyed the holiday.

'Jack'

AS WELL as expecting his players to enjoy good drink, Jack knew the supporters would do the same; win, lose or draw. He wasn't disappointed on that front. There were 53,000 in the Neckarstadion, and double that in the city.

For many, this was the party they would remember for the rest of their lives.

'One thing you can say about the Irish fans is that they will drink all the beer in Stuttgart tonight,' Jack promised. 'But they won't fight.... Irish football fans don't fight.

'I tell you what they do do.... they have the best parties of any people on earth.'

Days later, Ireland travelled to Hanover to face the Soviet Union, who had opened their finals campaign with a 1-0 win over eventual winners Holland.

Paul McGrath was ruled out with a damaged knee, forcing Jack into one of his unorthodox changes in personnel that saw Kevin Sheedy play in central midfield, and Ronnie Whelan as the sitter.

Ireland took the lead with a Ronnie Whelan volley six minutes before half time and before Oleg Protasov's equaliser 15 minutes from time, the first goal Packie Bonner had conceded in 820 competitive minutes, Ireland should have put the game beyond the Soviets.

Strikers John Aldridge and Frank Stapleton both missed the chance to beat goalkeeper, Rinat Dassayev. Although the draw was a disappointment, the Irish side went into their final game against Holland knowing that a point would be enough to take them into the semi-finals in Gelsenkirchen.

Ireland were buoyed by the return of Paul McGrath but unbeknown to anyone but the player, his room mate Gerry Peyton, Mick Byrne, Maurice Setters and Jack, Packie Bonner was playing beyond the pain barrier. The Celtic goalkeeper had suffered a back spasm while washing his hands in the hotel bathroom. Byrne tried stretches and massage, but Bonner was in agony.

He went to Jack's room.

PACKIE BONNER

When I arrived at his room, the door was ajar as though he was expecting me. I knocked, but there was no reply. Very gently, I pushed the door open and there he was... Jack Charlton, already on his way to being an Ireland legend... and he was washing his socks in the washbasin of his bathroom. 'What do you want?' he said without looking up.

'Jack...' I started tentatively, as I didn't think he was a man who took bad news well. 'My back has gone into spasm. I don't think I can play today.'

There was a seemingly interminable pause while I watched the manager of the Irish national football team squeeze the soap out of his white socks.

'Listen...' he began.

He spoke without lifting his eyes up from the basin. 'If you don't play this afternoon, you will be letting yourself down. Not only that...you'll be letting me down and... worse than that... you'll be letting your country down.

*'Now... f**k off.'*

As motivational speeches go, it was brief and to the point.

And I got the point!

THE DUTCH had not yet found their flowing feet and despite needing victory to advance, struggled to break down Ireland's determined rearguard. But Ireland were to be the gallant losers, bowing out to a flukey goal from Wim Kieft who headed Ronald Koeman's mis-hit shot inside the post.

The adventure was over.

'I looked around and I saw the effort the lads produced,' Jack explained to the media immediately after the game, '… and felt that they did all and more that I asked of them.

'It is one of those occasions when commiserations or congratulations are in order. But one thing I am certain, the lessons of the last few weeks and months are going to benefit us enormously.'

When the squad arrived back in Dublin on the Aer Lingus 737, renamed "St Jack", they were mobbed all the way from the airport to the civic reception. Only Pope John Paul and Tour de France winner, Stephen Roche had attracted such crowds. The journey to the city centre took over an hour, and then another hour down O'Connell Street.

Taoiseach Charles Haughey greeted Jack and made him an Honorary Irishman.

'The country feels better this lovely Sunday morning than it has felt for a very long time,' Jack confessed.

'It makes me wonder what the reception would be like if we won something.'

Jack led the players, crowd and even the Garda escorts in a chorus of *Molly Malone*, and promised them this was just the beginning.

7

IRELAND 90

JACK CHARLTON, on one of his first trips to Dublin as Ireland manager, once made the mistake of discussing The Troubles in Northern Ireland.

And once was enough.

He was on a journey from the airport to the city centre when he mentioned to his taxi driver the Bobby Sands graffiti on a wall. His driver went off on a furious rant about Sands who had died on hunger strike. Jack, Ireland's English manager, said nothing more and made a pledge never to mention them again. And he stuck to it.

Jack kept his mouth shut, and veered away from politics when the Republic of Ireland's campaign for the 1990 World Cup started. Their first qualifying game was in Belfast. He was careful in the build-up, refusing to become embroiled in any war of words with Billy Bingham, on this occasion at least. A hostile crowd, with no away fans, because they had been denied access to the fixture, greeted the new face of Bord Failte's tourism campaign. Many in Windsor Park thought him a traitor.

As Jack made his way down the touchline to the dug out, the vitriol and hatred spilled from the terraces of the famous old ground in the first meeting for nine years between North and South. Jack smiled and tried to ignore it. When he got to the bench, he spotted a fan lighting a cigarette, and promptly tried to cadge one. Half a dozen hands reached through the wire fencing to offer him a light.

There were no other gifts handed out that night as the two sides fought out a goalless stalemate.

NIALL QUINN

Jack Charlton started the Peace Process and he was responsible for the start of the Celtic Tiger era in Ireland. And he did it, just by being himself.

If you go back to when he took the job, it was unthinkable for an English manager to come into our game in Ireland and do what he did. Why?

Because English people weren't comfortable coming to Ireland, so it was a big step for him. And Irish people were not as comfortable with English people as they are today and there was an underlying suspicion of them. We were brought up to believe that as kids. I was 14, 15 when the hunger strikes were going on and there were black flags outside houses in the street and everybody in Ireland said Margaret Thatcher was the devil. That was only five years before Jack came, and it had not cleared up by any stretch of the imagination.

It was a risky move for him but one that he took absolutely full on and embraced from day one. He dealt with any political suspicions really well, and in his way. He was blunt and won the people over, not by launching a PR campaign, but by just being himself. Look at the way he asked for a light after he'd been given some shocking abuse by the crowd in Belfast?

It calmed them down because he was laughing it off and dealing with it as only he could.

It was good for him on a personal level to get a job in international football at that stage of his life and he wanted to take it on. He was fresh and enthusiastic, and he would have no political reasons floating around in his head.

Because he kept politically out of it and brought everything sporting into play, we just had people concentrating on what he was doing from the football perspective, and getting pleasure and enjoyment out of it. And the country felt proud of itself again.

The famous Celtic Tiger; its origins are rooted firmly in Jack's appointment as Ireland manager. Economically we went into a crazy place because we started to believe that if footballers could go into a crazy place, and we had this Englishman to get us there, why can't the rest of us?

We could make money in England, we could have commercial interests there, and now, by far, our most important ally commercially in the world is England and English people make up the majority of the tourism numbers that come into Ireland now. The whole thing has changed. I am not saying Jack is wholly responsible for it but his handling of the job and the way he performed in the job and his public persona made us all feel better about ourselves.

When we went to Germany, it was amazing. I couldn't believe what had happened and I went to the airport with the biggest smile on my face, knowing Ireland was finally going to a tournament.

We all watched Northern Ireland in '82 and '86 and now it was our turn. We had some good players but never really jelled as a team. He breezed through the whole thing. It was rough and tough, but it had to be. He had to scatter what was in place to bring in a different atmosphere. The true players were treated better

We even had taxi drivers waving and smiling at us. They had been given us abuse two years earlier, regularly.

I remember walking down the street with Liam Brady, not long after Jack had been appointed, and I remember this taxi driver stopping his car and giving out to us, saying, 'Youse are a joke, et cetera'. And then we played Brazil in a friendly, it was only a friendly, but they were in their pomp, and Liam scored the winner.

People went, 'F*** me, they beat Brazil'. People started to realise it was going places and it was good. Beating England in '88 took it to a whole new place and he became an honorary Irishman that night.

PAT CHARLTON

I hadn't been to Ireland before Jack became the manager of Ireland. When I went to Ireland I would stay with the FAI chairman Des Casey and his wife Mary, who became good friends. On a match day we would travel down to the match and afterwards I would go back to the hotel with Jack and then we would fly home together.

When Jack took the job we were wary at first because of The Troubles. Not many people from the UK travelled to Ireland but we didn't have one bit of bother in ten years.

The only time we had any trouble as a family was when our son Peter travelled on the ferry to Ireland for the match against England, which had to be abandoned. The England fans had found out that Jack's son was on the ship so the captain decided to hide Peter away in his private room for the whole journey to protect him.

When we walked round Dublin, people would stop us every five minutes for an autograph. I only got really annoyed once. I'd seen these shoes in a shop window and I went in to try them on.

Jack came in with me, and the staff were so busy looking around for pieces of paper for him to sign that they forgot about me. Eventually I was stood at the till, on my own, waiting there to buy these shoes, while these lassies fussed round Jack.

Then I said, 'Ain't anybody serving in this place?'

JACK HAD again gambled with Ireland's fixture list, choosing to schedule their three most difficult away games, Northern Ireland, Spain and Hungary, at the beginning of their World Cup qualifying journey. The draw in Belfast saw a shift in personnel too.

With Liam Brady struggling with injuries, and his Euro 88 captain Frank Stapleton now unattached, a newer, younger Ireland was starting to emerge. Dundalk's Steve Staunton, 19 and signed by Liverpool, made his international debut in a 4-0 win against Tunisia in October, 1988 when his new Anfield teammate John Aldridge ended his 20-game international drought to score his first Ireland goal.

David O'Leary was recalled at last for his first game in two and a half years when Ireland travelled to Spain a month later. The fixture in Seville coincided with the publication of the Arsenal defender's autobiography, in which he had been far from complimentary about Jack's management style.

But Jack had always said he would call up O'Leary when he needed him and with Paul McGrath ruled out, he needed him to face Spain. Not that it mattered. The Spanish preserved their unbeaten record in Seville to win 2-0. It was only Ireland's second defeat in 15 games, but could have been considerably worse as the home side totally dominated an Irish side that featured Kevin Moran and John Sheridan in central midfield, with O'Leary partnering Mick McCarthy.

TONY CASCARINO

In the game against Spain Jack ordered John Sheridan, who was playing midfield, not to use possession by playing short passes to either me or John Aldridge up front. 'I don't want you giving it to the centre forwards feet and playing cute one-twos,' he was told.

'If you do it… I'll pull you off.'

I was standing next to John when he was given the order and knew from the tone of Jack's voice that if he tried it even once, he'd be off. So did John. He was absolutely terrified. This, after all, was the same manager who had substituted the great Liam Brady 10 minutes before half time. I was sitting on the bench when he made that decision and though he knew it wouldn't endear him to the crowd, he wasn't changing his mind. 'I know it's Brady's day,' he bellowed, 'but there is a World Cup to prepare for and I've got to get the midfield right! The Germans are running riot!'

THE NEW year brought more new recruits.

Andy Townsend, then of Norwich City, who qualified through his Kerry-born grandmother, made his debut in the 0-0 friendly against France in front of a sell-out 22,000 at Dalymount Park in February, 1989.

But a month later, that decision to gamble on Ireland's fixtures looked like it may have backfired on Jack and his team. They had failed to turn their domination in Budapest into goals, returning from the Nep Stadium with just a point from another goalless draw. Despite the poor return of two points from the three toughest games, Jack was in feisty mood after the draw in Hungary, insisting group leaders Spain could still be caught.

He knew the return showdown with Spain in Dublin was do-or-die for the campaign. What followed was one of the great Lansdowne Road nights.

An own goal from Michel after 16 minutes set up a tortuous 74-minute countdown for nearly 50,000 Ireland spectators and their manager. Ireland dug in, and dug deep, before referee Horst Brummeier finally ended the agony and signalled the start of a long party.

MICK McCARTHY

We beat Spain before we even kicked off.

There is a photo of me shaking hands with Emilio Butragueno, and I have got hold of his hand and I am squeezing it; looking at him in his eyes and he was terrified. We were so wound up; we bashed them.

The team just chased and harried, and kicked and scrapped them, and we beat them 1-0. We were different class. That was a really good Spain team. Of course we respected teams like them and we admired them. But did we like sticking it up them? Of course we bloody did.

I think Jack did respect that belligerence and stubborn streak and fighting qualities, and it is what I like in players, of course. I don't like milky centre halves; I like leaders. He will always say he had good players but even with good players you have to get the best out of them and he got the best out of us.

I remember asking him about players taking off some nights. I said to him, 'You know those two rooms you and Maurice used to share, top of the corridor; the only way in and out? You two must have heard us coming in at two, three or four o'clock in the morning, making noise, thinking we were being quiet.

'Did you really never hear us?'

And he said, 'Of course we bloody heard you. But if I stuck my nose out of the door and saw you, I had to deal with it and what was the point? So we just left you to it.' Managing players. The penny drops. At your club, that's two weeks wages and a serious offence. But he knew we were all doing it and he knew that on Wednesday we would play like hell and give him everything, and we always did.

So he didn't have to go looking for that particular problem.

BY THE end of the 1988-89 season, after Malta and Hungary had each been dispatched 2-0 in Dublin, Ireland were back in the hunt to qualify. The first chants of "WE'RE GOING TO ITALEEE... QUE SERA SERA" were echoing round Lansdowne Road at the end of June. The FAI, who had made £500,000 in the previous 12 months, on top of the £1.3million they grossed from Euro 88, arranged a friendly in Trinidad to finish the season. Ireland lost 1-0 in Port of Spain.

While that end of season trip may not have concerned too many, the consequences of Ireland's next friendly certainly would. The occasion was September 6, 1988 when Jack's old pal Franz Beckenbauer brought his highly fancied West Germany to Dublin.

Now at West Ham, the game, which would also feature senior players Frank Stapleton and Tony Galvin, would be Liam Brady's second start in the 19 games since his dismissal against Bulgaria at the end of the Euro 88 qualifying campaign. It took Jack 36 minutes to decide that one of Ireland's greatest ever players was surplus to his international requirements.

He substituted Brady three minutes after he'd lost his man for the German equaliser, allowing Hans Dorfner to score.

Brady announced his international retirement immediately after the match. Jack was more interested in the late goal Northern Ireland had scored against Hungary that night which had enhanced Ireland's chances of qualification.

He was not particularly bothered about possibly humiliating Brady, and never has been. The pair were back on speaking terms within a few weeks, and Brady did make one final appearance for his country in his testimonial game against Finland. He received a standing ovation before departing in the latter stages of the 1-1 draw.

A MONTH later, in another tense encounter with Billy Bingham's Northern

Ireland in front of another sell-out crowd, Ireland put their first foot on the plane to Italy. Hungary and Spain drew on the same night to leave the final outcome to the last set of matches, but Ireland could afford to lose in Malta, knowing Hungary needed a four-goal win in Seville to take their place in Italia 90.

They made hard work of it against the North, and if future manager Michael O'Neill had buried their best chance with the game still goalless, it could have been even harder. Ronnie Whelan, Tony Cascarino and Ray Houghton scored the goals to secure top spot in the group.

When he had helped arrange the fixtures before the qualifying campaign began, Jack always had in mind a party in Malta. He knew Ireland would win there; he knew the fans would go over in their droves.

The party in Valetta did pan out and Ireland qualified for the 1990 World Cup in Italy. John Aldridge scored the two goals to secure their path, his first competitive goals for his country.

When Jack spotted the Liverpool striker being surrounded by the media in the Mixed Zone after the game, he shouted across, 'Keep him as long as you like… he has kept us waiting long enough for his goals'.

AFTER THE glamorous actress Sophia Loren had paired England with Ireland for the World Cup finals – they would also meet in the European Championship qualifying group for the 1992 finals in Sweden – the planned Dublin friendly against England in March was called off.

Wales took their place and Bernie Slaven got the winner in a 1-0 win, before Steve Staunton did the same against the Soviet Union a month later. Two days after Brady's farewell, and the draw with Finland, Jack was on the River Corrib in County Galway. He had a four-day fishing trip with friends. Although he would inevitably spend some time pondering his final squad for Italia 90, the World Cup could wait.

CHRISTOPHER DAVIES

It was March, 1990 and the Republic of Ireland's B team had just thrashed England 4-1. As I followed Jack Charlton up the steps of the plane at Cork Airport I noticed he was carrying a couple of plastic bags.

'Presents for the missus, Jack?' I inquired.

'No... dooty frees,' he replied.

'Jack,' I said. 'We're travelling from Cork to Dublin... how did you manage to buy duty frees?'

'No f**ker said anything to me...!'

No one would have begrudged Jack any perk of his job, though as he settled down in his seat there was an even more mischievous grin on his face as he opened a newspaper. There was a full-page advert for a certain financial institution with Jack's photo... 'loads-a-f**king-money', he said with a smile.

When I joined The Daily Telegraph in 1987 I was given a choice of countries to cover... Wales, Northern Ireland or Ireland. I had covered Wales for another newspaper and despite having far more outstanding players than the Euro 2016 team (Neville Southall, Kevin Ratcliffe, Mark Hughes, Ian Rush) they had constantly underachieved. Northern Ireland had been to the 1982 and 1986 World Cups, and I decided they had peaked.

The almost 10-year Charlton era was the most enjoyable of my career. By the time he left after qualification for Euro 96 ended in failure I still had no true idea what made Charlton such a great Ireland manager. His tactics were basic. Losing possession in your own half was a cardinal sin. The big man-little man combination up front was almost sacrosanct.

Former Denmark coach, Sepp Piontek once said, 'Jack does a lot of fishing. I'd love to know what he's thinking'. If opposing coaches struggled to find a way to overcome Charlton's Ireland, Jack was also stumped for answers at times, not least when some journalists did a quiz with him. The topic... "The Life And Times Of Jack Charlton".

I think he got eight out of 20 wrong.

'Still won the f**king World Cup,' he said in his defence.

Italia 90 was the highlight of Jack's time as manager.

Before the quarter-final tie against Italy in the Olympic Stadium, Jack was going round the players giving last minute instructions, only to find the noise of Pavarotti warming up for the Three Tenors' performance a distraction. He opened the dressing room door and shouted... 'Shut the f**k up'.

'Boss, you can't say that,' Andy Townsend advised him, '...it's Pavarotti'.

'Never f**king heard of him,' replied Jack.

While Jack was generally a belts-and-braces no-nonsense manager, when Steve Staunton, Ray Houghton and John Aldridge were selected for a World Cup qualifying tie against Spain just 11 days after the Hillsborough disaster in April, 1989 the manager was inevitably asked what his approach to the Anfield trio would be?

'I shall sit down with each of them,' he said.

'Talk to them… see how they are, assess their mood… and make a decision based on what they say.'

All three played in Ireland's 1-0 win.

'What did you say to them?' Jack was asked afterwards.

'I just said… "Alright?" he answered.

'… they said, "Yes"…

'so that was that.'

JACK WAS in a bad mood when Ireland left for the World Cup in mid-May of 1990. It was early morning, so he was grumpy anyway.

And then Opel laid on a Sicilian band to see the players off at the airport. 'I don't like this,' said Jack as he had a coffee at the airport with the press lads. 'It's ruddy ridiculous. Should have been done yesterday.' The moody Ireland manager and his players left for Turkey on Friday, May 25 and would then head to their pre-tournament training base in Malta, and on to Sardinia.

Although Ronnie Whelan, Kevin Moran and Ray Houghton were carrying injuries they were expected to be fit for the start of the tournament. But Houghton's unexpected problem would force a re-think in his view of the final squad.

The squad went straight to the stadium in Izmir on arrival. Now Jack was pleased. The competition was getting close. And the conditions would be perfect preparation for what they would face in Italy.

Just 200 Ireland supporters squeezed in among the 40,000 fanatics in the Ataturk Stadium, in temperatures reaching 106 degrees. It was the warmest May Day Izmir had known in 50 years.

Predictably, it ended goalless and Jack was unhappy with the lack of pressing in his side because players were trying to preserve energy in the heat. But some had enjoyed a good workout; the McCarthy-O'Leary partnership had worked well, and Tony Cascarino got a start, if not an entirely satisfactory one. Gary Waddock played on the right of midfield, but failed to impress the manager that night.

When it came to naming his final 22, Jack decided to gamble on the fitness of Ray Houghton, Ronnie Whelan, Kevin Moran, David O'Leary and Andy Townsend. Whelan was the only major doubt, but his fitness would improve as the tournament progressed.

The contingency plan, if one of them didn't make it for the opener against England in Cagliari, was to call up Alan McLoughlin who had scored 15 goals for Swindon, including the winner in the play-off final against Sunderland and who could play on the right or central midfield.

But that meant giving some bad news to Gary Waddock.

'Eventually I decided that Gary Waddock would have to go,' Jack resolved, 'and that nearly broke my heart. When I told him that he was coming to Turkey with us, he must have felt that all his birthdays had arrived together. Yet here I was, less than a fortnight later, obliged to inform him that it was a false start and that he would not, after all, be a member of the World Cup squad. It was one of my most difficult moments as Irish manager.'

Jack broke the bad news while the squad was waiting in the airport. There was no other time or place available to him.

'To his credit Gary put a brave face on what must have been a crushing disappointment. He wished both Alan and the team the best of luck but decided that he didn't want to remain on with the party as an official guest of the FAI.'

Waddock got the first plane back home.

Jack didn't blame him.

MICK MCCARTHY

I was sitting with Niall Quinn and Bernie Slaven at the airport in Malta, and a few of the lads were messing around riding on the luggage carousel. We saw Jack pull Gary to one side. You could tell what he was telling him; he was pulling him out of the squad. Gary was a great lad, a teammate of mine at Millwall, who had come back from a career-threatening injury and a spell in Belgium to play for Ireland.

He decided to go home, but before he left he went round all the lads and wished them all the best. That said so much about Gary. And then a few days later, Alan McLoughlin joined us and I don't think there was a happier, or more surprised footballer in the whole world.

I got Ruud Gullit's shirt for Gary. I asked Ruud before the game if I could have his shirt because I wanted to give it to someone as a gift. When I got back to Millwall, I gave it to Gary Waddock because I wanted to get him a memento from the finals.

THE IRELAND players were not impressed with their Malta base, which had seen better times since Jack and Pat had been visitors there several years earlier. In the middle of nowhere, and looking a little run-down, it quickly earned the nickname "The Betty Ford Clinic".

The purpose of the training camp was hours of acclimatizing work, relaxation and a couple of nights out. Maurice Setters took the first day of training in Valetta as Jack was confined to bed with a stomach bug. There had also been trouble with the food when the squad arrived, to such an extent that FAI logistics man Eddie Corcoran was sent to the kitchens to sort it, and ended up as the team's chef for the remainder of their stay.

Ireland beat the home nation 3-0 on another sweltering afternoon. Jack may have upset the locals when they misinterpreted his pre-match remark that it was 'a game he could do without'. It was part of the agreement for using the Maltese facilities, so Jack had no choice. But he was treating the game seriously. Chris Morris, Ronnie Whelan, Ray Houghton and Mick McCarthy were all ruled out, so Alan McLoughlin, who had flown in from London, made his debut with John Sheridan in central midfield. Niall Quinn scored the opener and subs Andy Townsend and Frank Stapleton added two more for a result that flattered the hosts.

It was Stapleton's 20th Ireland goal, breaking Don Givens' record. Jack was happy for the legendary Irish striker, though he did not imagine him in his plans for the weeks immediately ahead. He also felt the squad needed a night out, and told them to be careful, advising… 'don't get involved in hassle, stay in groups, and frequent only those places where there are a lot of people. Above all, I don't want anybody bringing trouble back to the hotel'

Same night, the manager drank the 'best part' of a bottle of whiskey. Maurice Setters took training the next morning at 11 o'clock to 'get the booze out of their (the players) systems' while Jack had a lie-in. He poured himself another whiskey that night, when he retired to his room to give himself time for 'thinking and plotting'. He was fast reaching the conclusion that Ronnie Whelan had no chance of playing against the English. When some reporters gave Whelan a hint of his manager's thinking, he did not take it mildly.

'He was furious,' Jack recalled in his World Cup diaries. 'He came knocking on the door of my room protesting that if I have excluded him from our plans for the England match I should at least have had the good manners to tell him first. I informed him that I said nothing of the kind. I repeated that I felt he was losing the race against time for the England game but that if he could prove me wrong in training, I would be first up to shake his hand.'

The moment Jack and the Ireland players landed in Italy they knew they were in "WorldCupLand". Armed police, dogs, cameramen, FIFA officials and the unofficials were all there to greet them off the tarmac.

An impromptu press conference was called at the airport where Jack was informed Ireland were one of the last teams to arrive in Italy. When they left the airport, a helicopter hovered above the team bus and an entourage of motorcycle outriders and police cars front and back took them to their hotel complex on the beach just outside Cagliari. The players were billeted three to a chalet in the woods. Although Eddie Corcoran would have to work his magic with the chefs again, it was a promising start.

JACK CHARLTON had known Bobby Robson for years.

He had shown nothing but sympathy and compassion for his old friend in the build-up to the finals, when the tabloids used the England manager as collateral in their circulation war. But when he discovered Robson was not going to name his team until the final hour before kick-off, he was not impressed.

So Jack decided if Bobby was going to play silly buggers at his press conference, he would do the same. He told Robson to call him with his team, so they could discuss. He told the Irish press gathered at the Sant'Elia Stadium for the final briefing before Ireland's first game that he was not impressed.

Jack was kidding. Privately, he was quite pleased he didn't have to name his team 24 hours before the match, as was usually the case. He still had one or two decisions to make.

The day before the England game was spent relaxing and sunbathing, with Ray Houghton ordered to put more sun cream on, or get himself in the shade. After the mayor of Cagliari had made a presentation of mini World Cups and medals to the players, they headed to the stadium, for their final training session.

MICK MCCARTHY

The night before the England game he called me to one side and said, 'Come on... I want to go for a walk'.

I thought for all the world he was going to strip me of the captaincy and drop me. There had been a lot of scrutiny and the usual questions about whether I should be playing. I was nervous as hell as we headed out of the hotel doors and went for a walk on the beach. I was convinced he was going to give me the curly finger, the nine o'clock news and tell me I was going to be left out.

So he started the conversation... asking what I thought of certain players, the make-up of the team, and he started to go through what looked like the starting line-up. We got to the centre halves, and he said... 'What do you think? Are you playing? You... Kevin Moran or David O'Leary?

'What's your thoughts?'

It seems bonkers now.

So I said, 'Well, if you check the stats, I think you'll find Kevin and I have been your best partnership.'

'Aye... aye,' he said.

And that was it. He didn't tell me the team but that was his way of reassuring me I was in. If I was fit, Jack played me. And I learnt that loyalty from him because that is a big leap of faith. I learnt that if players had played for you and played well, they kept their place. Perhaps they would have a month away and they might not have played, or not played so well at their club, so straightaway the media is on it and they might want to see someone else in the team,

But it did not matter to Jack. You stick with them, always. He never once wavered in his support. And if I played well in the last game for him, I played in the next one. And I love him forever for that. You don't often get that unwavering support.

AFTER A late breakfast and the traditional walk around the hotel grounds, when Jack talked to the players about their individual roles for the night ahead, and then a light lunch, Jack went to bed in the afternoon.

He slept soundly for two hours.

Charlie O'Leary stuck the *Sean South* tape on the bus PA as it approached the stadium. Before the Irish team arrived, the mass of green had greeted the English players with a standing ovation. Bobby Robson was so touched by it he sent a message to the FAI to thank the Irish fans.

Almost as soon as they arrived, Ireland discovered the England team.

JOHN CHARLTON

We bumped into Steve McMahon when we arrived and he told us he wasn't playing which meant Gazza was. He (Gazza) was sitting in the dressing room on his own when I walked past and he said... 'John... go get yer fatha'.

I asked him what the problem was, and he said he was nervous and needed to speak to him. So I went to get my dad. He saw Gazza and walked into the England dressing room and had a word with him and tried to calm him down, telling him to go out and play his normal game. 'But just don't play too bloody well!' he said.

ENGLAND SCORED with their first attack after only nine minutes when Gary Lineker sneaked between Chris Morris and Mick McCarthy.

Ireland then struggled to cope with a strong wind, which would affect England after the break, when a thunderstorm hit the stadium. Alan McLoughlin entered the fray for his first competitive match and Robson sent on McMahon.

And with virtually his first touch the Liverpool midfielder lost possession to Kevin Sheedy who swept an unstoppable low left foot shot past Peter Shilton.

THE MOVE to Palermo was not a smooth one, and the hotel was remote and basic, as the players were quick to tell Jack. And he told Maurice Setters, because his assistant had booked it. Eddie Corcoran had to work his culinary magic with the local chefs again.

As well as his pre-occupation with Egypt, who had impressed with their defensive organisation in the 1-1 draw with Holland, Jack was becoming increasingly irritated by the media's obsession with Ronnie Whelan.

He had missed the opening game completely but, when asked, Whelan told reporters he was fit. But his manager disagreed and had already decided he would not start the second game. When Whelan found out, he was furious once more.

'Somebody suggested that I should go and talk to him but I wasn't having any of that. At that moment, I didn't feel any responsibility to explain my decisions to him. I would do it when it suited me. For the present, he could fret it out and stew in his own juice,' Jack said in his memoirs.

With reports circulating that the pair had had a bust-up, and unable to sleep, Whelan wandered round the hotel reception looking for Jack and found him in the restaurant with Setters, Noel King and Maurice Price. Any suggestion of a private meeting was dismissed immediately, much to Whelan's annoyance, before the player was allowed to say his piece.

'He told me that he couldn't understand my selection. And that he felt he was at least deserving of a place on the bench. I probably shattered him by telling him that the thought of it never entered my head.'

RONNIE WHELAN

What made it worse was that you knew nobody else cared, apart from family and friends. Nobody was listening because everybody was on the bandwagon. 'We're on a roll here, we're having a brilliant time!' It was like being at a great party but you're only drinking water and everyone else is having a ball. Because deep down I knew that the lads were getting on fine without me. The fact was, Andy (Townsend) had come into the team and was doing a good job, he was doing the job that Jack wanted.

And Jack was thinking, 'Why should I break this up? There is no point in breaking it up.' That is how the game works and there was no getting around that. The show was moving on.

MICK MCCARTHY

I did have one blazing row with Jack in Italy.

We had played the night before and we were going to do something to prepare for the next game. We did one lap of the pitch and he wanted us to start training and I said, 'Hold on Jack... I'm not warmed up. I need to stretch and warm up properly'.

He said, 'You'll be alright'.

And I said, 'No I won't... I need to stretch'.

It was the start of the session, so there were people watching in the stands and I stood up to him. It started to get quite heated and we were just about toe-to-toe. He didn't like the fact that I had challenged him. Eventually, he let us have a stretch, but he was not happy about it.

I thought that was the end of it but we went back to the hotel after training and he pulled me to one side and gave me a right going over, effectively telling me not to do it again, and then he started to walk away.

And I said, 'Hold on, no... no, no, no. Let's just clear something up here, you've given me your opinion... now I'll give you my opinion'.

So I said to him, 'What happens if I get injured because I haven't stretched properly?' And you know what he said to me?

He said, 'Well… I'll just get someone else'.

'No f**king chance,' I told him, 'I have worked my bag off to get here and I am not getting injured in the warm up… just because you decide we're only doing one lap, when we normally have three or four.'

I was 31, I knew my own body, and I knew what I needed to do to get warmed up properly. I didn't see why I should jeopardise my chances of playing at the World Cup because he couldn't be bothered. He let me finish.

Then he said, 'Is that it?'

And I said, 'Yes… I've said my bit… you said your bit'.

'Good,' he replied, shook my hand, walked off and it was never mentioned again.

And there was the night the girls came and stayed.

He showed his teeth that night. We were staying in a camp, and the lads were in the bar with the wives, well after curfew. He went ballistic with everyone that night, even those not in the bar.

IRELAND DESPERATELY needed a fully fit Ronnie Whelan to break down the Egyptians. They stifled the very few Irish attacks and dragged out the 90 attritional minutes in baking conditions. It was a poor game even by a poor World Cup's standards.

'I was furious,' Jack insisted. 'On my way over for the press and television interviews, I thought about doing the diplomatic thing, making excuses for them and praising the way in which they defended. But I said, 'Bugger it, I'll call it as I saw it. The Egyptians, I said, had adopted a diabolical approach to the game and had reflected no credit on anybody.

'I hadn't shaken hands with any one of the Egyptians after the game; in fairness they didn't go out of their way to shake mine, and I realised that my post-match comments wouldn't win me any new friends in Cairo. But there are times when one must be brutally honest.' The loss of a point, coupled with England's scoreless draw against Holland in Cagliari, left the group in a dangerous state.

Jack was deeply unhappy with Tony Cascarino's loss of form. He needed goals, and he decided Niall Quinn might get them for him.

TONY CASCARINO

When the team to play Holland was announced, I was named as one of the substitutes. Furious, I called Jack aside to confront him about his decision. 'Give me one good reason why you've left me out,' I demanded. 'In all the games I've played for you I haven't let you down once! You said yourself after the...'

But Jack wasn't listening.

His face had turned crimson. 'You were f**king crap!' he exploded. And then he started reaming off a litany of mistakes, and I realised that nothing I could say would change his mind.

And for the next five years, as long as Jack had an option, that's how it was. As long as Jack had the option of Niall, I was second rate. And nothing – not my goal against England in Dublin, or my winner against Germany in the summer of 1994, or some of my great performances later at Marseilles – was never enough to change his mind.

WHEN JACK walked into his pre-match press conference before the Holland game in Palermo, he was not in the best of moods.

The reaction to the Egypt game had been less favourable in Ireland, while the English and Italian press had a field day with 'El Grupo Morte'... 'The Dead Group'. Just before he was about to meet the press, he read one back page headline from England... 'Jack Ass'.

Then the manager and his captain spotted Eamonn Dunphy among the press corps. Jack had discovered very early in his reign that some players did not speak to him, and did not want to. Dunphy stuck the knife in to Mick McCarthy in particular on too many occasions.

When Jack heard Dunphy had said he was 'ashamed to be Irish' on TV after the Egypt game, it confirmed opinions in the camp. It was actually a slight misquote, but that didn't matter. The damage was done, and so was Dunphy.

Sent over by an Irish newspaper to cover the Holland game, he attempted one of the first questions of the press conference. As soon as he opened his mouth, Jack interrupted, advising he would not be answering any of his questions because, he exclaimed, Dunphy was not 'a proper journalist'.

This was red rag to the bullish Dunphy, who was backed up by several other journalists in the room. Jack walked out.

He advised the regular journalists that he would see them at the team hotel.

Though Jack subsequently regretted his actions that hot afternoon.

'I didn't realise the repercussions, the aggravation and how famous I would make him,' he said. It was not the first time he had blanked Dunphy and suggested their diffferences of opinion could be settled outside the room.

But it was the last.

JACK NAMED the team to face Holland at ten o'clock the next morning. He had decided to go with Quinn for Cascarino, with Ronnie Whelan back on the bench.

Frank Stapleton and John Byrne decided to test their manager's patience after lunch. Jack was sitting in the hotel grounds with Maurice Setters, when they spotted the pair down below in the harbour, in a boat, both bare-chested and hatless. Jack waited for them on their return, and was distinctly unimpressed when they pointed out they were not involved that night.

'We're all in this together,' was the message from a furious Jack, who had spent most of the 1970 finals in Mexico going through the same emotions as the fed up pair.

'WHEN WE got to the stadium, I shook hands with Leo Beenhakker, the new Holland manager, and asked him, jokingly, for a cig and when he reached into his pocket to get me one, I told him to hang on until the end of the game.

'Come to think of it now, that was one cigarette I never did collect.'

Jack and Maurice spent hours studying the Dutch. Jack knew Ireland had to control Ruud Gullit to stand any chance of controlling the game. It was one pre-match team-talk dominated by the opposition. He told the players to take cold showers as temperatures in the dressing room started to rise.

His last request was for a few moments of quiet reflection while every player took in the enormity of his role in the game that would decide whether they were heading back to Ireland immediately, or not.

Ireland versus Holland was one of the occasions that has always stood out for Jack. Maybe it was the colour – orange against green in that stadium – or maybe it was the noise, threatening the Richter Scale when the Ireland players turned to face the Tricolor for the National Anthem rather than towards the FIFA dignitaries.

It probably wasn't the game, although Jack took a lot of personal satisfaction from his side's equalizer. Created through pressure.

Having booted Charlie O'Leary's medical bag when Gullit was allowed to run through and open the scoring after just nine minutes, Jack was encouraged by his team's first half performance. John Aldridge had a goal disallowed for a close offside call, then Niall Quinn was denied a penalty.

With 25 minutes remaining and the Dutch being held at bay, Jack made two substitutions, sending on Ronnie Whelan and Tony Cascarino, who he decided should partner Quinn.

Then came the goal. Packie Bonner's long punt was knocked back by Benny Van Aerle to keeper Hans van Breukelen and the viciously spinning ball hit the Dutch keeper in the chest, ricocheting into the path of Niall Quinn who tucked it home. Shortly after Ireland's equaliser, news reached the two benches that England were beating Egypt. It meant both teams were through.

Although Jack made no attempt to tell his players, insisting the game was there to be won, Mick Byrne had other ideas. When Ray Houghton went down for treatment, the loyal Ireland physio told him the news. And then Ruud Gullit walked up to Mick McCarthy, suggesting a truce, and the final ten minutes petered out without incident, much to the irritation of the referee.

NIALL QUINN

The game was played out farcically but no one told me so for about 10 minutes so I was just running around still trying to score my second goal, but thankfully that wasn't going to happen even with the game half-stopped. I remember meeting van Breukelen later and he said to me you should be buying me drinks for the rest of my life because I dropped that ball to you, and he was right.

PACKIE BONNER

I was not, under any circumstances, to roll the ball out to Mick McCarthy or Kevin Moran. According to Jack, they couldn't play, which wasn't to denigrate them. In his eyes, centre backs were for heading, tackling and getting the ball away from danger. But in the sapping heat that day, Mick kept dropping back and demanding I play the ball out to him, and each time he did, I refused.

It was starting to get heated between us. Eventually, I had the ball in my hands and I cracked. How else can I explain the mad expression I pulled as I told him to... 'Get the *f**k up the pitch!' My adrenalin was flowing and I launched one of the longest kicks in my life up the park. I hadn't realised my mad face had been caught on camera and that, even to this day, people still think it was just my motivational desire to spur the lads on.*

AFTER MUTED celebrations by the standards of the trip, and a quiet night with their wives and families, with U2's Larry Mullen joining the entourage, the Ireland squad moved on to Rappel, a resort just outside Genoa.

The day before the showdown with Romania Jack had two injury concerns surrounding full backs Chris Morris and Steve Staunton. As long as the pair were massaged back to fitness by the magic hands of Mick Byrne he had decided upon his team. Unchanged again, with Ronnie Whelan on the bench.

Jack tried to put on a video of the Romanians' previous matches for his players, but they wanted to watch the Brazil-Argentina match instead. After the Brazilians' shock exit, he tried again to show his men the 'Hagi highlights', but the majority drifted off to bed, or the pool-room.

IRELAND'S GREEN Army invaded Genoa's Stadio Luigi Ferraris on Monday, June 25, 1990. Jack was so concerned by the sweltering conditions in the stadium that he refused to allow the players to warm up on the pitch. They merely walked round in their training kits.

Perhaps it was no great shock that Ireland started the game sluggishly. An early injury to John Aldridge, which forced him to put on Tony Cascarino, did not help the manager's mood. At one point he turned to Maurice Setters and asked if the players had eaten too much at lunch?

Ireland had the better chances of another difficult-to-watch game but Niall Quinn and Cascarino headed wide. At half time Jack told the players to wrap their heads in wet towels, and many sat, shirts off, backs against a wall desperately trying to cool down as he gave his second half instructions.

But there was nothing cool about the second period. Jack fell foul of Brazilian referee Ramos for vigorously objecting to Paul McGrath's yellow card, only Ireland's second of the competition. Jack, who was already embroiled in a battle with an overly eager cameraman near the dug out, was told to sit down by the officials.

Ramos blew for full time. Thirty minutes of weary extra time followed and the tie headed to penalties. Jack was in the centre circle prior to the spot kicks, but he left the final list to his players. His one order to those who would step forward was simple… make a decision and stick to it.

He watched most of the penalties on the big screen, turning away from the action because he could not see it from his lowly position through the sea of bodies.

Ireland matched Romania penalty for penalty with the first four kicks.

Then second half substitute Daniel Timofte stepped forward, and struck the ball fairly well to Packie Bonner's right. The Donegal stopper guessed correctly; the ball bounced away to safety.

And then David O'Leary moved forward from the centre spot. Jack, like everyone in the stadium, and everyone back home in Ireland, waited to see who was marching forward. He admitted to being 'a little taken aback' when he saw O'Leary striding towards the penalty box. 'It wasn't the best penalty I've ever seen but for my money it was the most vital.'

NIALL QUINN

The Romania match will always go down for me as the best game I ever played in. Not so much because of the quality of the play; you will see better matches, but in terms of the adrenalin and the emotion and the release at the end when we won, when David O'Leary's penalty went in. It was just incredible. The highs and lows that I experienced during that game were just ridiculous really.

It was the hottest day you could imagine. I was full of energy at one point and then thinking… 'I'm not going to last' when we haven't got the breakthrough. When we got to the latter stages I thought someone was going to have to drag me off. It is the most physically demanding game I ever played in. It was incredible

Every day after training I had a little punt with the lads and I would go in goal for three penalties each and if they scored all three I would give them a tenner but if they missed one I would get the money. Sometimes there would be 40 to 50 penalties and it would be the same faces trying to get the money all the time.

RAY HOUGHTON

We were struggling to find five people to take them. I remember going up to Tony Cascarino and saying you are taking one and he said, 'I don't really want to'. And I said, 'If I am taking one… you are taking one'. I had never taken a penalty before in any competition, or in the league in England. Finally he agreed to take one but we were struggling to get the numbers. Everyone always remembers David's penalty and the fact Packie made the save, but others had to take penalties as well.

PACKIE BONNER

Rarely a day goes by without me at some point reliving the feeling that I had after the penalty save. An unremarkable game in itself that could have gone either way concluded with one of the most remarkable finishes in modern Irish football history. I sometimes characterise it as the moment that Ireland really 'got' football.

MICK MCCARTHY

Most of us were absolutely exhausted when we got back to the dressing room. There were a few tears, and then someone brought the beers in and the celebrations began. I remember the Italian media caught up with us outside, asking how we felt about facing Italy in Rome for the quarter finals. They still had Uruguay to play but of course they didn't have a clue when I said they shouldn't count their chickens before they hatched!

MCCARTHY HAD been silent with his colleagues' complaints in Genoa, but soon found the moaning going through the roof once the squad arrived at their new base near Rome. The hotel was in Nemi, a village in the Colli Albani hills, where the US squad had been based. The initial inspection was so unsatisfactory, the team headed to another hotel nearby for a quick look, but that was even worse.

MICK MCCARTHY

We stayed where Scotland had been staying and we all went to our enormous rooms, with mirrors and sofas and all sorts, and we came back downstairs all talking about how fantastic it is, and how come Scotland have been staying here, what's going on? Blah, blah, blah. And Jack comes over and says, 'Yeah and they f**king flew home last week'.

But it was different when we got to Rome. I did go to see him then. You could not get a cat in, never mind swing it. Packie and Gerry Peyton were sharing a room, and they are both huge, and by now we all have two massive kits bags, full of freebies from the trip, and you could not move in there.

It was ridiculous and the FAI suits and their wives were living in luxury, while our two keepers were virtually sleeping in a dorm with a bed that was far too small. It was comical seeing them perched over the edge, their feet sticking out.

I see it even more now as a manager. Everything has to be perfect for the player, and anything that is perceived as wrong becomes an excuse for not performing. It never existed then and we just got on with it because there was usually no point complaining. Jack used to wash his socks in his hotel room sink and dry them on the radiators.

All that superstar treatment nonsense didn't wash with him. But I took him to Packie and Gerry's room and even he kicked off.

He threw the FAI out and we all got double rooms. When he needed to do it, he sorted it out and we all appreciated that.

WHEN JACK had met Mick Byrne for the first time, shortly after he was appointed, he became aware he was a deeply religious man. He promised he would take the popular figure to see the Pope in Rome. Jack reckoned even he couldn't take Ireland to the World Cup final.

On the night of the Romania triumph, Mick Byrne was eager to remind Jack of that Papal conversation. 'Boss,' said Mick. 'You remember…you promised to get us into see the Pope… don't you?'

Monsignor Liam Boyle was a regular member of the Irish travelling party and together with Bishop Tony Farquahar, they pulled some strings and got the Irish entourage an audience with Pope John Paul II.

PACKIE BONNER

Big Jack liked Monsignor Liam.

The priest paid for his own flights and hotel bills but, through time, Jack allowed him into the dining room when we were eating our meals. He became a part of the entourage and very much bought into the feeling that we were 'all in it together'.

Jack treated him as an equal and had a healthy disregard for piety that extended one night to a squad game of Trivial Pursuit.

Monsignor Liam was in the chair as quizmaster as, given his calling, he seemed to be the most impartial. 'How many players are on the pitch in a Gaelic football match, Jack?' he asked. Charlie O'Leary, being on the same team as Jack and who was an authority on all things Irish, jumped in quickly and told Jack the answer. Jubilantly, Big Jack said with relish, 'Fifteen!'

Monsignor Liam smiled before answering, 'You're wrong'.

Jack was disgusted.

'What do you mean I'm wrong? Ask Charlie!'

Liam didn't balk. 'Then, Charlie's wrong. It's thirty.'

Charlie and Jack had obviously thought he meant players on one team and argued the point vociferously without fear or favour. 'It's fifteen, Liam! How am I f**king wrong! How can you have thirty players on one side?'

CHARLIE O'LEARY

If it hadn't been for Jack Charlton, none of us would have had the audience with the Pope. And if it hadn't been for Jack, I certainly wouldn't have met him face-to-face.

When we were waiting for the Pontiff to come and meet us, I was on the second step in the group, hidden away behind Dr O'Driscoll and Fran Fields, who were with the FAI party. Jack was practically leaning on me.

As his Holiness came towards us, Jack tapped the doctor and Fran on the shoulders and pushed me past them and forward to meet the Pope. Because Jack had thrust me forward, I am sure the Pope thought I was the top man in the party, so he ended up talking to me and making a bit of a fuss of me. Chris Hughton told me he was talking away to me and asked what he'd said to me. I was so overawed by the whole occasion I had no idea what he said. It was just a blur.

When Jack took over, I was like the liaison officer for the teams visiting Dublin and that was the job I had for his first game against Wales.

Jack asked John Givens if he knew anyone who could help him with the team and he recommended Mick Byrne. Jack saw me, asked John and Mick about me, and I joined as the kit-man for the Uruguay game and I was there for the next 10 years until the last game against Holland at Anfield.

Jack never boasted. I never once heard him say, 'I've won a World Cup' and he certainly didn't project himself as a football genius. He was just an ordinary soul who was very, very good at football management.

JACK WAS not alone in expecting the meeting with the Pope to be brief and personal. They all went in their team tracksuits, with Jack wearing green to everyone else's white, and took along some gifts. On arrival they were taken to a large auditorium and sat close to the front of the stage with families, officials and the media close by. The team was given a standing ovation by the audience and once the Pontiff arrived he made a speech in English, then Italian, then German…and it went on.

MICK MCCARTHY

When we had our picture taken with him, there was this almighty scramble among the lads to get near him. I wasn't too worried because Mick Byrne and I were making the presentations to him, but you could see lads trying to get near him.

His Holiness wanted to meet Packie because he'd been a keeper as a young lad growing up in Poland. Then he got in the middle of us and threw his arms round Charlie O'Leary and started chatting to him.

We gave him a signed shirt, which I was delighted about, because it was one of mine. I was asked to step forward, give him the shirt, shake his hand and kiss his ring.

It was over in seconds and I'll never forget it.

ANDY TOWNSEND

The Pope made a bit of a fuss of Packie because he'd been a goalkeeper in Poland. When he came into the private room he told Packie, 'I will be keeping a special eye on you and keep my fingers crossed for you'. As you know we lost 1-0 and Packie spilled Donadoni's shot to Schillaci for the winner.

We were in the dressing room and we were all disappointed. Jack was trying to lift us. He said, 'You gave everything, I can't ask any more. I am proud of you, we will have a great night tonight and a good drink and we'll enjoy it.'

A few of the lads are still sitting there not moving, one of them was Packie. Jack cajoles him to get into the shower and as he walked away, he turned to me and said, 'The f**king Pope would have saved that'.

THE FINAL two days before the quarter-final with Italy could not have been more relaxed. After nearly a month on the road, and seven games, Jack was not pushing anyone. John Aldridge, Tony Cascarino and Steve Staunton were the main injury doubts but they were all passed match-fit on the morning of the game.

The night before the Italy game, Jack got the videos out again, this time concentrating on the dangers that were Toto Schillaci and Roberto Donadoni. This time the players were rapt in their attention, and no one missed it or messed about.

JOHN CHARLTON

A consignment of Guinness came to the team hotel from Ireland, so we set up the barrels on the hotel forecourt and sat there, the afternoon before the game, having a drink. It was mainly for the backroom staff and any fans that were hanging around, but the lads were able to have a couple if they wanted a drink.

The players went up about ten, half past, when we got a message from Mick McCarthy to keep the noise down because some of them couldn't get to sleep. My dad took us inside to keep the noise down before we retired to bed in the early hours.

TONY CASCARINO

I asked him years later why he had let us have a beer the night before the quarter-final against Italy, because I knew there would be a reason. And he said because otherwise we would have all had sleepless nights, taking sleeping tablets, or going for later walks. A couple of beers and everyone was relaxed.

He had a different way of thinking. Remember when Glenn Hoddle made Teddy Sheringham go in front of the press and apologise after the World Cup in '98 because he'd had a drink. Jack couldn't believe it. 'He should be backing him and tell him to go out and have a beer, not humiliate him like that.'

ON THE day of the Italy game, Jack had one of his premonitions that things would not turn out well for him and his country. A deeply superstitious man and manager, he grew edgy when Charlie O'Leary put the wrong tape into the machine as the stadium came into view.

Instead of *Sean South From Garryowen* some 'dreadful dirge about lowering a body into the ground' was played. Jack was not happy.

His sense of foreboding grew. And little that occurred in the following couple of hours in the Stadio Olimpico changed his view that Ireland would not be allowed to beat Italy on home territory. Both sets of players watched the Yugoslavia-Argentina game in the centre circle, as it was played on the stadium's big screens. The winners would play the South Americans and Diego Maradona in the last four.

Ireland started well, but Italy started better.

The hosts seized on an un-Irish pass from Kevin Sheedy to John Aldridge. Fernando De Napoli intercepted, and Ireland were caught unaware. Donadoni cracked a shot from the edge of the area that Packie Bonner spilled.

Schillaci reached the rebound before any player in white and green and hammered it into the net. Schillaci hit the underside of the bar after the break and the Italians controlled most of the rest of the game.

A Paul McGrath shot limply flied across Dino Zoff's goal. But that was it. Ireland were out.

The journey back to Nemi was long and tortuous and as Jack looked round the coach, he saw the faces of men who had left a month's sweat on a field in Rome. Defeat left its mark but there was pride too, and just a trace of bitterness at the way the game was handled.

But soon the despondency lifted and as the bus edged through the hotel gates the team discovered that the party was already underway. Many of the supporters who had brought such credit to the country had preceded them. For them, as much as the players, it was an occasion for celebration.

MORE THAN half a million people lined the streets of Dublin for the team's homecoming. Jack spent most of that journey from the airport to the city centre castigating children and teenagers for getting too close to the bus. He was, like his brother after the 1966 World Cup win, convinced someone was going to suffer serious injury under its wheels.

KEVIN MORAN

The whole of the country turned out. We got knocked out in the quarter-finals. England were unlucky to lose in the semiwfinals on penalties and when they got back I think there was half a dozen people or something to welcome them. The welcome we had was unbelievable. It was incredible. And it is a memory that will live with me for the rest of my life.

MICK McCARTHY

After we'd got back, me, Packie, the two wives, Jack and Pat, went down to Malahide for a Chinese meal. We were dropped off by the cab outside Gibney's so we had to walk up to the restaurant through the village. Packie and I were walking at the front, the three wives next, and then Jack.

Everyone in the street and in the cars was stopping to look at us, and Packie and I are waving at everyone, feeling quite pleased with ourselves, that we've been recognised after playing quite well at the World Cup.

But when anyone shouted out, it was always... 'HIYA JACK'... 'WELL DONE JACK'... 'GOOD MAN JACK'.

There was no Packie or Mick mentioned.

In the restaurant the starters came, and he'd ordered soup. But then he ended up taking something from everyone else's starters, just so he could try them. At the end of the meal he said, 'I'll get this'.

Then the owner came over and said, 'That's on me... I've got the bill, Jack'.

'Oh go on then,' he said, smiling across at us.

'If you insist.'

We were playing for Jack. He had a way to make us win. And when a manager has that, you will follow him. Sometimes you will follow him whether you like him or not, but I always got the sense that everyone liked him.

I love the bloke.

And I think all the others did. You might not always agree with the way it was done, but we liked him. He was a great personality.

He was one of our own; it suited him. I see that wonderful statue down in Cork airport, him fishing and standing there. It's a fabulous statue and you can see the shiny marks round his shoulder and on his cap where people have touched him for their photo.

That says it all really.

IRELAND 94

JACK CHARLTON took one look at Mick McCarthy and knew the Euro 92 dream was about to be wrenched from him.

On the final whistle, the Turkish manager Sepp Piontek had told him England had lost in Poznan and that Ireland were through. And then he reached the tunnel and saw Mick. Drenched in sweat, eyes closed, head leaning back against the wall of the tunnel in the national stadium in Istanbul, Jack's captain was no longer smiling.

'What's wrong, Mick?' asked Jack.

'You've not heard, then?' McCarthy said.

'Gary Lineker has scored a late equalizer... we're out.'

Ireland's comfortable 3-1 win over Turkey, and John Byrne's rare two goals, meant nothing. England were going to Sweden.

And Ireland were staying at home.

'I HAVE never seen such a distraught dressing room,' Jack recalled.

'I remember nobody moved for ages. The players just sat there with their heads buried in the hands. They were devastated. I tried to pick them up, but deep down I was numb too.

'We were unbeaten in the group and building a good squad after Italy and it was at its strongest. Players were in their prime at top clubs, they could play in different positions and it didn't weaken us, and no one had really got to grips with us.

England came home miserable failures from Sweden.

'Lineker threw his armband at Graham.

'Given that Denmark went on to win it, and they'd only sneaked in after Yugoslavia were thrown out, we all felt it could, and should have been Ireland.'

The squad that failed to reach Euro 92 was arguably Jack's strongest. As players had moulded into his way of thinking in a green shirt, the team had evolved, and with experience had come confidence and self-belief.

The FAI and players had certainly benefitted from Italia 90 too. The players had each picked up a tidy £50,000 each from the bonuses, the players' fund and more bonuses for beating Romania, that were negotiated just days before the finals.

BUT ONLY one team could qualify from Group 7 for the Euro 92 finals, and Ireland had drawn England again, along with Turkey and Poland.

The campaign started brightly enough in October , 1990 with a 5-0 thrashing of Turkey at Lansdowne Road, which extended the unbeaten home run to 22 games and saw John Aldridge's first Ireland hat trick. But the dramatic build up to the game had exposed Jack to one of the great issues he would have to manage with a sensitivity and understanding for which he was hardly renowned.

When the team bus arrived at Lansdowne Road to face Turkey, Paul McGrath refused to get off. Once Jack was made aware, he went to see McGrath.

It was clear he had been drinking and he was in no fit state to play. Jack tried to cajole McGrath off the bus, but to no avail. He was not going to play. Eventually, less than an hour before the start of the match, McGrath was helped off the bus, and he was taken back to the team hotel. Just 20 minutes before kick-off, McGrath was officially withdrawn from the team.

The whole drama had unfolded in front of the public and Jack was forced to defend his player after the match, saying he had been withdrawn with 'a twinge'. He never mentioned it again.

McGrath's drinking and mental state was a recurring problem. Measures were put in place to keep him away from drink, and trouble. The mini-bar was emptied in his hotel rooms prior to arrival; his travel itinerary from the UK was prepared so he could be met by Mick Byrne at Dublin airport and not by the wrong sort of company; and in the World Cup in America, someone slept outside his room so he was not led astray.

The players looked after him too; Andy Townsend in particular would see that McGrath was safe, but often, on the nights he started off with the rest of the squad, he would escape their guard and fly solo.

He didn't drink to socialise; he drank to reach oblivion. And of course, Paul McGrath would occasionally find ways to beat the systems Jack put in place.

PAUL MCGRATH

I was never scared of Jack's anger because he would always soften. Jack could read me the Riot Act for ten minutes, spitting fire with every word.

Then it would end with him putting his arm round me.

TREVOR O'ROURKE

When Paul McGrath went missing myself, Mick Byrne and Paddy Daly, a retired Garda officer, who also used to work for the FAI looking after the referees and his officials, were sent out to track him down. I drove round the pubs of Dublin, Mick in the back and Paddy in the front, working with the local Gardai trying to locate Paul. There were sightings everywhere.

*We eventually caught up with him in a pub in west Dublin and took him back to the team hotel. You might have expected Jack to give him the biggest b*****king of his life. He just put his arm around his shoulders, took into his room and he was in there for an hour just talking to him. He knew when someone needed that arm round the shoulder. He knew when they needed a slap.*

Paul McGrath was the glue holding everything together. Jack needed him and he looked after him. On Paul's part, and I know he has said this, Jack was the fatherly figure he needed. Someone who understood him and looked after him. They were good for each other.

I think he tapped into the way all of our sport is played; gaelic football, hurling, rugby are physical, man-to-man sports and you just expect your team to give it a go, no matter how good they are. Jack liked that. A great number of Irish people were not great followers of soccer, myself included when he took over, but they know how they like their sport to be played and I think Jack's 'put 'em under pressure' style suited that.

I don't want you to get the wrong impression here, but we had a lot of laughs, and it did invariably involve a drink or two. Wherever he went, Jack was well treated, but that was part of his charm. People liked to please him.

We were doing a Q&A with Dessie Cahill in Galway and we were there early in the day, walking down Shop Street. People were coming out of shops and walking up to Jack and giving him gifts and by the time we got to the end of the street, myself and Des were weighed down with shirts and jumpers, and sides of salmon. It is hard to believe but it's the truth. People just wanted to give him stuff and thank him.

Early on in the reign, Jack wanted a pint before we ended up at the airport. So I took him into Hill 16 which would not be the most salubrious part of Dublin but he was not bothered in the slightest. And they absolutely loved him and it became his local in Dublin. The publican, Tom O'Connor, always looked after him and made sure we got nice quiet seats and no one ever bothered him. Not that they did bother him. Jack was quite happy posing for pictures and signing autographs, if anyone asked, but he wasn't pestered in Hill 16 and I think he just liked that idea of going somewhere where he could have a nice quiet pint.

It was much more relaxed between the press gang and Jack in those days. One of the first things John Givens and myself would do when we were playing abroad, was find a good pub. Then he told the press lads to meet him in the boozer we'd found and that's where he held his press conference. And that became the ritual. He'd be talking away, moving salt cellars and pepper pots as he discussed tactics on the table over a beer.

MCGRATH WAS the greatest player he had as Ireland manager, Jack insists. 'Whatever clubs I managed, if I could have had Paul, I'd have had him. Even though he did have his problems. I would have probably had to look after him there as well, but I would willingly have done that. I think most managers who have had him would say that.'

The first time he saw him, Jack played one of the game's most gifted centre backs as a sitting central midfielder. He knew he was too good to play at the back in his team. And McGrath was brilliant at it. Jack's first piece of advice to McGrath was not to snarl at opponents, but just smile at them.

'That will intimidate the buggers even more,' he advised him.

Wherever Ireland played, if McGrath played, and played well, which he invariably did, then Ireland played well. Recognising his brilliance, no matter what his off-field difficulties, Jack persevered with him from the first day he spotted him wobbling under the influence on a trip to Poland. He knew when McGrath had had a drink, and he tried desperately to keep him away from it.

He gave him more rope than any other player. And he even took him fishing. Every player understood.

McGrath was back for the Euro 92 home game against England in November, 1990 when their new manager Graham Taylor surprised everyone, expect Jack, by leaving Paul Gascoigne on the bench. It was the same decision Jack had expected Taylor's predecessor Bobby Robson to take in Cagliari just five months earlier. Ireland should have won comfortably, putting on a performance that Jack rated as the best demonstration of his pressing game in his ten years in charge. But they fell behind to a David Platt goal against the run of play just after half time and needed a Tony Cascarino header to share the points.

The two sides achieved the same 1-1 result at Wembley in March, 1991. Jack was unimpressed when told Graham Taylor would be announcing his side only an hour before kick-off.

'It's not psychology at all,' he told his press conference. 'It's playing silly buggers… and I don't like it.'

Ireland once again fell behind early to the English when Steve Staunton sliced a clearance past Packie Bonner. But Niall Quinn scored one of the great goals of his career, on his way to taking Frank Stapleton's goal-scoring record, sending 20,000 Ireland fans in Wembley into yet more delirium.

But Ireland squandered more chances and failed to turn another dominant performance against England into a victory. The best chance fell to Ray Houghton in the dying minutes but he put his shot wide when it looked easier to score. 'That's the chance which could cost us a place in the European finals,' Jack said afterwards.

The campaign unravelled in the double header against Poland.

The old problems with the Lansdowne Road pitch resurfaced for the home leg in May. What was particularly galling for Jack was that the pitch was supposed to be improved, as some of those profits from the World Cup adventure were put to good use.

It wasn't that the pitch was prepared for rugby this time; it was just in better shape for a beach volleyball competition. Almost the entire near side of the pitch by the West Stand was sanded and Jack was furious. 'It's just not good enough. It's probably the worst I have seen it for a long time. We accepted that they were to put down a new surface but it's a sight worse than it ever was.'

No surprise that the showdown with the Poles, which was a rare midweek two o'clock kick off at a windswept Lansdowne, ended in a goalless stalemate. Ireland were profligate in front of goal again, missing a string of chances that would have sealed a victory, and kept them ahead of England on goal difference at the top of the group, following their win in Turkey.

They had no better luck when the campaign resumed and moved to Poznan after the summer break and two friendly draws with Chile and the United States. Roy Keane made his Ireland debut in the home game against Chile but he would miss the trip and boisterous welcome in Boston, as well as the Under-19 World Championships in Portugal, under the instructions of his then Nottingham Forest manager Brian Clough. Jack and Maurice Setters were not amused.

Jack cobbled together two Ireland teams, for the autumn friendly in Hungary which resulted in a 2-1 win, and the Sir Matt Busby Testimonial at Old Trafford which attracted a 35,000 crowd for the 82 year-old and a rare appearance by George Best at the ground in a pre-match five-a-side game.

Taking charge of the proper team for the 54th time in Poland in October, 1991 Jack changed the system to employ five midfielders, including Roy Keane, following Ray Houghton's withdrawal through injury. Tony Cascarino was to lead the attack, with David Kelly and John Aldridge on the bench.

For 69 minutes the change worked perfectly. Ireland led 3-1 at that stage, thanks to goals from Paul McGrath, Andy Townsend and Cascarino. Later Jack admitted the lack of options on his bench were to prove costly. He didn't have the personnel to cope with Poland's late resurgence, and Jan Furtok and Jan Urban scored the two goals that left Ireland needing a miracle, and a massive favour from the Poles in the final round of games in November, 1991.

The Turkish team may have been the qualifying group strugglers at that stage, but that did nothing to dampen the enthusiasm and passion of their supporters. Their team even went ahead after 12 minutes when Riza Calimbay notched one from the spot, following Packie Bonner's foul on Orhan Cikirkci.

John Byrne, who had not played a competitive game for nearly five years, scored two in his finest night as an Ireland player and Tony Cascarino added the third as Ireland battled against the crowd and a spirited Turkish side to ensure they finished the Euro 92 campaign unbeaten.

But they were to be unrewarded too. England had pipped them thanks to Lineker's 77th minute equaliser in Poznan.

On his way out of Poland that night, Jack was left to reflect on those missed opportunities against England. They may have played their pressing game to perfection against the Old Enemy, but the inability to turn dominance into goals, and points, cost them a place back at Europe's high table.

'A lot of teams in Europe will be glad this evening to discover that we haven't qualified for the finals in Sweden. Ours is a difficult game to handle and I think even the English will agree that they are a very lucky team to be playing in the finals.'

RAY HOUGHTON

We qualified in '88, we qualified in '90 for the World Cup, and everyone was thinking we are going to qualify for everything now. But with only one team going through, it was a bit more difficult and we were in a hard group with England. But we were disappointed. And the most disappointing thing was we didn't lose a game but we didn't qualify.

ANDY TOWNSEND

I remember watching England in Poland and our boys were in Turkey, and at one time we were winning and England were losing and I thought, 'Yes... we're going to get there'. And it was agony... pacing up and down, watching all that on television.

THE YEAR ended with confirmation that Jack would be remaining in charge for the next campaign at least. Still working without a contract, still planning for the World Cup and how to shape an ageing squad with players like Mick McCarthy, Packie Bonner, Kevin Moran, David O'Leary, Paul McGrath and John Aldridge coming to the end of their careers for club and country.

'I'm not daft enough to plunge into the task of breaking up a team which still ranks among the best in Europe,' he said.

'Some people go on and on about the fact our players are getting old. That, of course, is undeniable, but for me age is just a statistic on a birth certificate. The more realistic criterion by far is the form of players.'

GEORGE HAMILTON

I'd first met Jack when I was working with BBC Radio in London. Then it was Radio 2 on a Saturday afternoon, with second half commentary from a First Division venue that had to stay secret till everybody had kicked off at three o'clock. That particular week, I was in St James' Park for a Newcastle game.

The BBC Sportsroom had an enviable reputation and the pick of the crop when it came to co-commentators. Jack was between jobs, as they say. Not long out of Sheffield Wednesday.

He was genial and affable when I met him at the ground. Of course, everybody knew him. Though by then a thirtysomething, I was still star struck. This was the guy, after all, who'd come from nowhere to play a starring role at the back for Alf Ramsey's team in 1966 when I was imagining the bright red of those England shirts on the black and white TV back home in Belfast.

St James' Park in 1983 can't have been much different from the way it was when Newcastle United were winning the old Inter-Cities Fairs Cup. Radio 2's commentary position was to one side near the front, where an angled partition interfered with the guest's legroom. My abiding memory is of Jack, somehow, shoehorning himself in. Not a word of complaint, though.

If there's one thing you can say about Jack Charlton, he just gets on with it.

Little did I think then that not only would I be back in Ireland myself, but that Jack, the big, good-natured Geordie, would now be the man in charge of the national team that I was tasked with following.

The form of football that evolved in Ireland when soccer and rugby were being codified is also fast and furious, but neither gaelic football nor hurling has found a public abroad beyond the Irish diaspora. They're games enjoyed at home; the fanaticism of the fans contained by the extent of local rivalries.

It took the team moulded by a World Cup winning Englishmen to give the Irish the opportunity to showcase their unique exuberance on a broader stage, and they took that opportunity with relish.

They wore their green shirts with pride, and represented their country with honour in stadia right across the globe. Big Jack revelled in his role at the heart of it all.

And the Irish loved him back.

JACK CHARLTON didn't mean to keep upsetting Billy Bingham. But he did keep upsetting him. The draw for the journey to the World Cup finals in the United States had again pitted the two Irelands together. Albania, Latvia, Spain, Denmark and Lithuania made up the group.

Jack, by chance in Belfast when the draw was made, dismissed Northern Ireland's challenge without even knowing he had done so. He said it would be between Ireland, Spain and Denmark, but Northern Ireland didn't even get a mention. Their manager Bingham, and an entire country, were hurt by the snub, and Jack's apparent arrogance and ignorance. But Jack just expected to beat everyone in the group.

The year did not start well following the disappointment of missing out on the European Championship finals in Sweden. Ireland suffered their first home defeat in six years and 26 games when Wales won 1-0 in a friendly at the RDS.

Home wins over Switzerland and the United States followed before Ireland took the unusual step of starting a World Cup campaign, before the European Championship finals had even been held in Sweden. John Aldridge and Paul McGrath grabbed a goal apiece to see off Albania and open the USA 94 campaign with two points.

Albania, as Jack was to discover on his travels, were in disarray as a nation and a football team. They arrived in Dublin without footballs and the Under-21 team did not have enough kit for their fixture, so borrowed the necessary shirts from Adidas' Irish representative.

Jack then took his squad to the United States for a mini-tournament featuring a return game with the USA in Washington's RFK Stadium, and Italy and Portugal in Foxboro Stadium in Boston. For the record, Ireland lost 3-1 to the hosts, after a long, long flight during which rather a lot of alcohol was consumed. They were then outplayed by the Italians, losing 2-0 before recovering to beat Portugal by the same scoreline.

But it was the events on a bus, in the wake of a long night on the town for the players, that was to earn more notoriety than anything on the fields of play.

Several seeds were planted in Boston that fateful morning and not by or with Jack. And not all the shoots grew into things of beauty. In fact they were to turn into something very ugly ten years later.

Mick McCarthy, now player-manager at Millwall but still captain and still Jack's leader, was among those to share his views with Roy Keane, who had been injured in the first game against the States. A future Ireland captain, and then still a teenager and a drinker, the pair clashed as Keane was late getting on the bus.

TONY CASCARINO

We played the USA in a friendly and then hit the town, where a great night was being had by all until the alarm call next morning. Some didn't go to bed. Shattered and dishevelled, we crawled onto the coach in various states of undress. At 7.30 am departure was delayed until 7.45am, and then 8.0 am, when everyone was accounted for except Roy. Jack was seething and immediately dispatched Mick Byrne to try and locate him.

F**king hell! 19 years-old, his first trip away and he is nowhere to be found! Ten minutes later, when he finally arrived, Jack went for him. 'Where the f**k have you been? Do you have any idea how long we've been waiting?' It was an absolute savaging but Roy didn't blink.

'I didn't ask you to wait, did I?'

And that was it.

End of conversation. He walked straight by and sat down. We couldn't believe it. No one stood up to Jack like that! It was incredible. We were absolutely p***ing ourselves.

AFTER RESUMING qualifying action with a 4-0 home over Latvia in September, thanks to another John Aldridge hat trick, Denmark, the newly crowned European champions, were the next opponents in October, 1992. Ireland, now captained by Andy Townsend, came away from a monsoon in Copenhagen with a point from a goalless draw. They achieved the same result in Seville a month later. That performance was so nearly capped with a winner from John Aldridge, but he was denied by an offside decision even Spain boss Javier Clemente admitted was wrong. It was also the night Roy Keane came of age in an Ireland shirt with the first of many superb performances for his country.

Tolka Park hosted Ireland's customary home game with Wales in February, but Maurice Setters was left in charge of the team. Jack missed the game because he decided to go to Albania to watch Northern Ireland. He faced criticism for missing his first senior game but was more than justified when he saw the conditions awaiting Billy Bingham's squad with his own eyes.

For all their public sparring, Jack was a welcome addition to the Northern Ireland travelling party and spent the night before the game with Bingham. The trip to Tirana was a depressing eye-opener for Jack, who took his own salmon, chicken and game pies for supplies. Albania was a no-go area for westerners then and the poverty and ramshackle nature of the capital had extended to the hotel where Jack and the Northern Ireland players were staying.

They were put on the tenth floor and as the lifts weren't working, had to walk up the stairs in darkness. Neither was anything in any of the rooms. It earned Albania a serious rebuke from FIFA, and a 2-1 defeat. The hotel had improved significantly when Ireland visited and the players stayed on the second floor. Thanks to Colonel Wally Hayes, an Irish officer serving with the United Nations in Tirana, the squad was taken swiftly through customs and a translator was waiting at the hotel.

Every player was given a kitbag with toilet roll, candle, towel, bar of soap and a bottle of mineral water. Jack has also insisted the FAI took their own cook along, with his own utensils.

Despite the impasse away from the cameras in Tirana, Billy Bingham was still seething over Jack's comments from the previous year when he pulled into Lansdowne Road in March, 1993 with his team. He demanded respect because, he insisted, Northern Ireland were still very much in the hunt for qualification. He got nothing in the build-up.

'Let me put it this way,' said Jack. 'I won't be losing any sleep. I'm not exactly in a flap about Northern Ireland.'

Bingham got little sympathy during the game, and while he was shaking Jack's hand at the final whistle, "One team in Ireland" chants of the triumphant home crowd echoed around Lansdowne Road. Bingham was furious.

And he left empty-handed. A rampant Republic tore the North apart, going three-up within the opening half hour. Jack could barely hide his disgust, however, that his team had not recorded a more significant victory over the not so noisy neighbours. His mood did not improve a month later when Denmark held Ireland to a 1-1 draw in Dublin. Niall Quinn scored late to claw back a game that Ireland should have once again won comfortably.

Jack was happier with conditions in Tirana but was still recovering from his first visit to the city when he had to go back. The hotel may have improved, but he knew it was glossing over the appalling deprivation across the city. After going behind after just seven minutes, Ireland were relieved when goals from Steve Staunton and Tony Cascarino secured three more points.

ANDY TOWNSEND

The actual truth as to how I was appointed captain was that we were warming up for a friendly, I can't remember where? Mick had just retired and I assumed Paul McGrath would get the armband. Jack came over to me as we are warming up and he said, 'Mick's *knackered now… and Paul doesn't want to do it, so you'll have to f**king do it'. I was skipper at Villa and Chelsea and I got on well with all the lads and my first thought, rightly or wrongly, was always to my own game and I didn't have to point and shout at others. I just had to play well and be there for every game and be fit, and if I was not fit still play. He knew he could rely me.*

He was not a manager to take liberties. It was always do this and do that, and there was never any opportunity to talk to Jack and ask him to soften it. He was adamant we would do it his way.

Jack always came across as the gruff Geordie and he would not take any bullshit from anybody but he made it a treat to play for Ireland. He was clever enough to realise that if he made it a prison camp, his main men wouldn't come and if they didn't turn up, we would not be as formidable as we were.

I will be honest, it was important to the players to be social. Players came in limping. Yes, we might have been better if we had been slightly more professional but it was important for the boys to come over, and have a skinful and Jack knew that. Monday morning was just a five-a-side and shooting practice because he knew we had been out on the Sunday. But he also knew that come Wednesday night, we would be focused and more often than not get a result. It takes an intelligent manager to understand that.

THIS WAS the well documented week Paul McGrath went missing, turning up in Israel via Cork rather than in Tirana. Although Jack's patience had been tried again, he welcomed McGrath back with open arms. It had taken a phone call from McGrath to his manager and brief reconciliatory talks between the pair to restore some trust. But McGrath was back in the squad for the trip to Riga within the week.

Three days after returning from Albania as group leaders, an under-strength Ireland suffered a 4-2 defeat home to Hungary in David O'Leary's testimonial, notable only for Roy Keane scoring the quickest ever goal at Lansdowne Road. Jack quickly erased the game, and took the squad on a much more important journey into the unknown in the Baltics; to face Latvia, and then Lithuania.

McGrath scored in the first leg in Riga, adding to John Aldridge's early opener to secure another vital away win. A week later Steve Staunton grabbed the winner in the Zalgiris Stadium in Vilnius to see off the vastly improved Lithuanians. They were also the early autumn visitors to Lansdowne Road, going down to strikes from Aldridge and Alan Kernaghan.

Although he had actually castigated his players for being overly reliant on the long ball, the 2-0 win left Ireland needing at least a point from their two remaining games; Spain at home, followed by Northern Ireland away. 'If we fail to make it, we will only have ourselves to blame,' said Jack.

Spain boss Javier Clemente delivered a bone-shuddering defeat at the home of Irish football.

Spain swept Ireland aside in an astonishing first 25 minutes, scoring three simple goals. Ireland, without John Aldridge who failed an early morning fitness test, had no answer to the visitors apart from John Sheridan's late consolation goal. It was the first competitive defeat in Dublin since Denmark had won in Eoin Hand's last game in charge eight years earlier.

They now needed to go to Windsor Park to get a point, hoping that Spain would see off Denmark in Seville on the same night.

The Troubles had shown no sign of abating since the two nations had last met in the previous World Cup qualifying campaign. In fact they had worsened considerably when they met for the decisive showdown in Belfast in November, 1993. There had been an increase in violence in the weeks leading up to the game.

The IRA blew up a fishmonger's shop in the Protestant Shankill Road in Belfast, killing ten people, including the bomber. In the course of the following week, 14 people died in reprisal attacks by Loyalists. That included eight people mown down in The Rising Sun public house in Greysteel on Halloween night.

FIFA made a late decision, after many lengthy discussions with the two associations, that the game should go ahead in Belfast. Billy Bingham, preparing for his retirement game, also stirred up home fans with his pre-match remarks. Still angry by the reaction of the Dublin crowd to Ireland's earlier group win, and by the defection of Alan Kernaghan to the south, he accused the Republic's players of being 'carpetbaggers'.

NIALL QUINN

Belfast '93? That was a tough night. Trick or treat, that's what the crowd was singing, which is what the gunmen had shouted when they walked into the bar (in Greysteel) and killed those poor people.

That was a horrible night. The atmosphere was dreadful, the crowd calling Jack 'an effing Fenian traitor' and hurling racist abuse at Paul McGrath and Terry Phelan. But we got through it. Sport won in the end. My best memory of the night was Alan McDonald, since tragically deceased at such a young age, who was the Northern Ireland captain that night. He came into our dressing room after the game and gave the most fantastic speech congratulating us and wishing us well on behalf of all true sportsmen in Northern Ireland.

It was the most poignant speech I've ever heard in a dressing room after they had lost the chance of going to the World Cup, and bearing in mind the state of affairs in Northern Ireland was at its worst. But, also at that point we were worrying about how the hell we were going to get out of there!

TONY CASCARINO

Niall Quinn was selected to start up front, as he had for most of the campaign; while I watched the drama unfold from the bench, as I had for most of the campaign. Jack was popping and hissing like a pressure cooker from the moment the game kicked off. The game was balanced on a knife edge. We were taking control but weren't creating chances, and with every second that passed Jack was becoming more and more irate.

In the 73rd minute, disaster struck when Jimmy Quinn rifled a volley past Packie to put the North one in front, against the run of play. The ground absolutely erupted. Jack spun around in disgust and immediately ordered me to get stripped.

It was a very cold, blustery night and experience had taught me to wrap up well on the bench. Pumping with adrenaline I ripped off my coat, kicked off my tracksuit bottoms and unzipped my top; and discovered that all I was wearing underneath was a plain cotton T-shirt.

For the first, and only time in my career, I had left my jersey on its peg in the dressing room! 'Oh f**k! What am I going to do?'

Jack was getting impatient and kept glancing over his shoulder.

'Come on! What''s keeping you?'

Until the penny finally dropped and he knew there was something amiss. 'Where is your bloody shirt?'

'I don't know, Jack,' I spluttered. 'I think I've left it in the dressing room.'

His face turned purple. I thought he was going to have a heart attack.

'You f**king idiot!'

Charlie O'Leary, our kit man, was immediately dispatched to the dressing room, but as he raced down the touchline I couldn't help thinking, what if the dressing room is locked?

What if the geezer who has the key is enjoying the game from the stands? Deciding I would retrieve the situation myself I turned to Dave Kelly, who was also on the bench.

'Dave,' I said, panicking, 'just give me yours.'

'What? Do you mean swap?'

'Yeah, just give me yours.'

Jack flipped. 'What! You can't do that! You'll have us thrown out of the tournament, You f**king idiot! Charlie... Where is Charlie?'

I have always believed that if Alan McLoughlin had not equalised with a volley from the edge of the box as we were waiting for Charlie to return, there's a fair chance Jack would have chinned me, or at least changed his mind about sending me on. But Alan's goal was enough to secure the draw, and with Spain winning 1-0 in Seville, an extremely tense and difficult evening ended in celebration.

THE IRELAND players had flown to Belfast from Dublin after spending the week at the Nurermore Hotel in Monaghan, which was closer to the border. Once again, no away fans were allowed in and only one national anthem was played. *God Save The Queen* was belted out with some fervour. The game was scrappy and tense, and goal-less at half time. Then Jimmy Quinn struck for Northern Ireland in the 73rd minute.

Bingham did a little jog of delight in front of the dug outs and started to conduct the Windsor Park crowd in the choruses of "One Team In Ireland". His assistant Jimmy Nicholl turned to Maurice Setters and shouted, 'Up Yours!'

But that euphoria for the North was short-lived. In fact it lasted less than three minutes. Jack's substitute Alan McLoughlin, sent on to be a nuisance, equalised after chesting the ball down on the edge of area and delivering a low volley beyond the reach of Tommy Wright in the home goal. Attention then switched to Seville, where there were four minutes of the game remaining.

Spain were leading 1-0, and held on with ten men to hand second place to Ireland, rather than the Danes. The wait was short but it was agonising. The Ireland contingent went crazy when the final score finally came over.

Jack spotted Bingham talking to his players, and walked across to him intending to shake his hand.

'Instead, in a moment I still find difficult to understand,' he admitted, 'I pointed a finger at him and blurted out, "Up Yours too, Billy!"'

'He just looked at me and turned away, dumbfounded. And I realised I had gaffed, yet again. Afterwards, I made it my business to seek him out, barging in on his press conference with the remark, intended to be jocular, "It's all right, Billy, I've not come to flatten you".

'And Billy, competitive to the last, says, "It's OK Jack, you wouldn't be able to manage it, anyway."'

PHILIP QUINN

THE voice on the end of the phone was challenging, almost belligerent. 'Who gave you mah number, son?'

I muttered something apologetic and stumbled on. 'Have you applied for the job of managing the Republic of Ireland, Mr Charlton?' I stammered. There was a pause. A lengthy one. After a bit, just as I was about to hang up, the World Cup winner spoke up.

'Have I applied? No I bloody well haven't.' And that was it. Completely cowed, I thanked 'Mr Charlton' for his time and hung up. As investigative journalism went, it was a pretty shambolic effort.

He regarded me as the 'little baldy fellah with the glasses', which was about right, and gradually warmed to my presence. One time with his Irish side based in the Nuremore Hotel in Carrickmacross, Jack fancied a few holes of golf. We went out as a two-ball, with a handful of clubs apiece and played for a fiver. Jack gave the ball a good clout but his chipping was hit and miss, and he lost his temper when he moved the ball 10 yards with one club, after smashing it 200 yards with another.

In between shots, he spoke about the good fishing spots nearby, and made some irreverent comments about the Irish players – it was all off the record - pausing only to reach for a club and give it a lash, as he didn't hang about over his shots. We were level coming up the ninth when he lost a ball, and his temper. We shook hands and he stormed off. I never got that fiver.

Before his last game as Irish manager, the Euro '96 play-off against Holland at Anfield, we were staying together – team and press – in a Cheshire hotel.

In a corner of the bar was a game of table football and Jack fancied having a go. We told him he could play the winners so he waited a bit while battle unfolded.

When it was his turn, he insisted he controlled the midfielders and forwards. 'I love getting a go up front,' he said as he flicked his big hands and whirled his 'men' after the little white ball. With his face alight, Jack was like a little kid again. We couldn't get him off the table.

THE REPUBLIC of Ireland manager and his players were given a security escort out of Windsor Park and touched down in Dublin just after one o'clock in the morning. The Taoiseach Albert Reynolds and more than 3,000 fans were there to welcome them. Reynolds thanked Jack for the result, and qualification. USA 94, said the Taoiseach, was just the lift the whole country needed. Jack, for his part, left the players to the celebrations. He had a sore throat, a sore head and had not enjoyed the night or the performance. He went to bed without even supping a pint.

JACK STOOD in the middle of a very large crowd in the Phoenix Park, in Dublin in July, 1994 waved his flag, and smiled a strained, polite smile. This felt like a celebration too far. Ireland had come back from the United States with nothing to celebrate, other than a memorable win over Italy.

They had underachieved in the World Cup finals and he knew it.

The previous year had ended badly. Just days before they were drawn against Italy, Mexico and Norway in their USA 94 group, Niall Quinn had snapped his cruciate. Jack's first choice forward looked certain to miss the finals. Subsequent efforts by the big striker to get fit were curtailed by Manchester City chairman Francis Lee who refused to accept the medical opinions Quinn had sought in a desperate bid to be in Jack's 22.

Quinn's fitness aside, preparations for the finals had gone well on and off the pitch although Jack was forced to miss the special FIFA conference for the 24 finalists in the Sheraton Hotel in New York in February because of a viral infection.

He had to field an understrength team for a game with Russia in March, which had been arranged just days before the English League Cup final between Manchester United and Aston Villa, though the absence of players like Keane, Irwin and McGrath at least gave Jack the opportunity to blood Jason McAteer, Gary Kelly and Phil Babb, who were soon to become the "Three Amigos".

There were then promising friendly victories, not least in Tillburg where a Tommy Coyne goal defeated Holland, the side that would eventually curtail Ireland's World Cup adventure in Orlando's Citrus Bowl.

For Kevin Moran's testimonial match, Jack had his doubts about Ireland's friendly against an English Premier League XI even though the team included Alan Shearer and Andy Cole up front. Ireland won 5-1. 'I read one of the pre-much tributes which stated that no braver man ever played football and I would wholeheartedly agree with that,' Jack said.

He had booked Bolivia to play in Dublin as part of their European tour but Manchester United pair Roy Keane and Dennis Irwin needed a rest. Of more concern was Paul McGrath's shoulder injury that ruled him out. When the team trained at Oriel Park in Dundalk, McGrath looked out of condition and was carrying the shoulder that had been causing discomfort for nearly three months. In his absence, Ireland beat the Bolivians 1-0.

Jack was forced to gamble on McGrath's fitness when he named his final 22 for USA 94. 'The man has been so influential in the development of the team, so reassuring to those around him when he is playing well, that it is a risk we must simply take,' he observed matter of factly.

BEFORE THE end of May, Jack was made a Freeman of Dublin.

Initially, when he had been informed of the impending honour, he had remained unfussed. Since his successful days with Leeds United he had grown accustomed to calls to attend this function and that function. 'It was only when I got to the presentation area in College Green that I knew I was guilty of a monumental miscalculation,' Jack remembered in his World Cup Diaries. 'And there were thousands of Dubliners out there on the street to prove it.'

There were so many people, and on the stage sitting with the city dignitaries were some of his best Irish friends, including Des and Mary Casey. All of his players were there, of course, and some older players like Con Martin, Tommy Eglington and Arthur Fitzsimons.

'The Lord Mayor, in his address, referred to me as a special Englishman and, to be honest, I felt a bit special just then. What appealed to me most was the fact that I was the first Englishman to receive the honour in this century. The last apparently was a plumbing contractor who undertook a major scheme in the city in the mid-1850s.'

The signature immediately above Jack's belonged to no less a person than Mother Teresa of Calcutta. And further back, John F Kennedy and Nelson Mandela had entered their names into the book. Only 62 people in history had received such an honour from the people of Dublin.

'I paid tribute to the squad and deservedly so. I was stepping up and accepting the kudos but essentially it was a collective award, a tribute to the players and backroom staff who had worked so hard to get us where we are.

'I am sure that people back in Ashington would have been chuffed to discover that one of their own had made it to the top in Dublin and the miner's son had joined some of the most famous people of the century on the city's roll of honour.'

AFTER THE Freeman ceremony, Ireland travelled to Hannover for a testing showdown with Germany who were preparing to defend their world crown. Jack was apprehensive about meeting such esteemed opponents on their home turf, particularly in front of more than 54,000 fans.

But he need not have worried. Ireland had a great night and the 3,000 Green Army foot soldiers who made the trip had a ball back at the ground where Ireland had played the Soviet Union in Euro 88. Jack had selected Alan Kelly in goal, denying Packie Bonner the chance to break Liam Brady's appearance record, and he had given Jason McAteer the chance to impress. The young Bolton midfielder, who was not even in the plans until Jack had seen him in action at Sunderland before the season's end, took it. Paul McGrath's suspect shoulder was also put to the test.

Rather than ease McGrath into action, Jack picked him to start and told him his place on the plane to America was on the line. Paul McGrath responded as only Paul McGrath could. He was outstanding as Gary Kelly scored his first Ireland goal to double Tony Cascarino's first-half strike, and they won 2-0.

The small blip of a 3-1 defeat to the newly formed Czech Republic in the final farewell game in Dublin on June 5, 1994 failed to dampen the spirits of Jack, his players or the nation as the finals loomed. It was a flat Irish performance, and a rare home defeat, but too many players, McGrath included, had entered the fray unwilling to put their fitness in jeopardy. The Republic of Ireland football team finally left Dublin for the United States on June 6, 1994.

A couple of thousand well-wishers, including the Taoiseach, were on the tarmac or peering out of the airport buildings to wave them off. Jack and Maurice Setters got an Aer Lingus upgrade, but the players did not. Unfortunately the 200-plus Irish fans waiting in New York to greet the players did not see them, as they were kept from the exits and whisked on to their internal flight to Florida.

Jack fretted about just about everything prior to landing in Orlando. He worried about the weather, the flights, the hotel, the presence of the English tabloids as all the British nations had failed to qualify.

But once he did land, he started to relax.

In his World Cup diaries, Jack mentioned that the team hotel was a good mile from the highway, and that there was enough privacy around the place for the players to go walking. 'There's even a small lake where they can go and throw stones if they wish.'

The team had the top floor of the hotel all to itself, which was a bonus. Another bonus for the manager was the fact that the hotel only had one bar. Jack allowed his lads to visit the bar to conduct media interviews. But alcohol was banned.

However, Jack did find a container in his bedroom that was covered with a cloth. 'When I examine it I find it's a keg of the nicest Guinness you've ever tasted,' he wrote in his diary. 'I invited some of the press lads to the room and we sampled the hospitality.

'Whatever about this weather, I think I am going to enjoy this hotel.' Others were not in such happy form. A young Roy Keane was distinctly unimpressed even before he left Dublin, as he explained in the first of his two autobiographies many years later.

ROY KEANE

On the flight Jack and Maurice, the coaching staff and the FAI officials, and their wives, took their places in first class. We were back in economy class with the fans and the journalists. No space, no privacy, no respect. A small thing? Not really. Shouldn't the whole FAI party, players included, travel together? In first class?

To prepare us for the heat and humidity, our training camp was in Florida at Orlando. The facilities laid on by the Americans were perfect. But I thought the training put on by Maurice Setters was s***. I was used to the well planned, always interesting and relevant routines put on by Brian Kidd. By comparison, Setters hadn't a clue.

After two or three days of duff training, morale was beginning to dip. One day Jack disappeared, leaving Setters in sole charge. The sun was blazing down. Even walking to the training ground you began to sweat heavily. He ran us into the ground. Then he set up an eleven-a-side game on the full pitch. This became a farce. Knackered, we didn't know whether to laugh or cry. Everyone was pissed off. Andy Townsend, the captain, told Setters we'd had enough. I'll tell you when you've had enough, was Setter's response. We just downed tools. Next thing, Andy walked off the pitch, followed by the rest of us. Mutiny.

The press was there, although at first I don't think they copped what was going on. Setters started shouting at nobody in particular. Andy repeated we'd had enough. The news finally reached the media. 'Bust-Up in Irish Training Camp' was a hot story. 'Keane in Bust-Up in Irish Training Camp' was an untrue story. I'd simply followed the herd, although I completely supported the walkout. I was mystified as to how my name came to feature in the story. When we finally returned, Jack called a team meeting to find out what had happened. Then he proposed a solution. Setters and I would hold a press conference to clear the air. 'Everything was fine,' would be the message.

Instead of saying that I hadn't had a bust-up with Setters – that in fact it was skipper Andy Townsend acting on behalf of all the players who'd had the row – I went along with the party line. Good old Roy!

Charlton was clever with the media. On this occasion his plan worked perfectly. I became the story. Nobody asked why he had been absent from training.

ROY KEANE was 19 and full of hope when he made his debut in 1991. But he was already disillusioned with the FAI. Jack embodied all he disliked about the Dublin blazers and the way they controlled the game, and the players; and way Jack controlled his game, and the players.

Whatever his opinion of Jack as he matured from that skinny, shy but insolent rake at Nottingham Forest into one of Ireland's greatest ever players, and an enigmatic and divisive figure, he never said anything to Jack's face.

Keane's saved the venting for his first memoir, with the added spice of Eamonn Dunphy as his ghost writer.

As for Jack, Keane was just another player, and one of the hundreds he dealt with in his career. And Jack was always happy to help any of his players, including Keane. Once he called Keane into his room and said he'd been impressed with how the Corkman was handling the intense speculation surrounding his future. Jack added that he'd heard Blackburn were on the verge of signing him, but advised against it, and told Keane to join Manchester United. Same day Jack put in a call into Alex Ferguson.

There was no sign of Keane's deep unhappiness when representing his country. Keane was not even among the top three players Jack would pick from his Ireland years – McGrath, McCarthy, Townsend got that accolade – but then he had not yet developed into the world class player who led Ireland to the 2002 World Cup finals, and was then sent home. And Jack backed Mick. Enough said.

ROY KEANE

Not knowing exactly what was expected of me, apart from the effort I was happy to provide, I kept my head down and did my best to work out if there was any more to Charlton's magic formula than there appeared to be on first acquaintance. Time would prove that there wasn't.

I had mixed feelings about playing for Ireland. I relished the ninety minutes of football when match day came, but the rest of it left me cold. Of all the set-ups I'd been part of, going back to Rockmount AFC, through Cobh Ramblers and Forest, the Irish international camp was by far the worst organised. From training facilities to the training itself, travel arrangements, the kit we trained in, medical facilities – you name it, the Football Association of Ireland got it wrong. Finding something as basic as a tracksuit was a problem. If you were lucky, you might end up with an XL top and a small-size pair of tracksuit bottoms. Or vice versa.

Coming back to this shambles from a professional club in England was a shock. Coming from Manchester United, where Alex Ferguson ensured that every detail was attended to with a meticulous care, deepened my sense of frustration. Worse than the shambolic preparation was that perverse sense of pride everyone appeared to feel in the fact that the Irish did things 'differently'. Unlike the international teams we were competing against, we could be ill prepared and unprofessional and boast about it!

Nobody seemed to enjoy telling anecdotes about the eccentric FAI set-up more than Jack Charlton.

JACK BELIEVED that his team was ready. He fully believed that everyone had done everything in their power to have the team ready for their opponents, and the oppressive heat and humidity awaiting them.

'We're getting near the end of the hard work and I bet the lads thought the day would never come,' he continued writing in his World Cup Diaries. 'We've done the graft, we have sweated in cloud and sun, and we're as ready as we will ever be.'

Like every other manager counting down the days, Jack also received a fresh directive from FIFA dictating that players could only take water during games once they stepped off the field. Jack was dismayed. 'What about the central players? How are they going to get to the line while the game is in progress? It would be laughable if it weren't too serious.

'If players are not allowed to take liquid, they will dehydrate in this weather. And if they dehydrate seriously, they are liable to die.'

Working too hard in the intense conditions was a hidden danger that Jack remained conscious of, long before the first game of the tournament against Italy in New Jersey. But, one day, he was stopped in his tracks when he looked over at Roy Keane who was 'doing nothing', just standing there on the pitch.

'When I ask him if he has a problem, he tells me that he has a bit of a groin strain,' Jack included in his diaries. 'More than that, he informs me that he's had it for a couple of days – and I see red.

'I ask him if he's heard of me preaching over and over again that if anybody has an injury problem, they don't train.

'He tells me that he intends to run it off, and I inform him that he will run off nothing of the kind. Roy is not the easiest person to deal with. He is basically a shy lad who will never volunteer conversation, and unless you approach him, you'll learn nothing. But on this occasion at least I think he takes the point.'

JACK WAS in a surprisingly good mood as the Italy match approached. His only concern was the on-going battle with FIFA over ensuring his players were properly hydrated.

Jack seemed to be the only manager voicing such concerns. But while he was sick of hearing his own voice, he knew he was right. On the morning of the Italy match, he sent his agent John Givens out to buy plain, white baseball caps and every player was given one before walking out into the searing heat of the Giants Stadium.

On match day, more than 5,000 fans arrived from Ireland in a fleet of 20 planes. Estimates on the day put the number of Irish supporters among the 74,000 sell-out at around 40,000. It was an official invasion by Jack's Army.

Another one of the greatest ever days in Irish football history had officially commenced. Eleven minutes into the game Denis Irwin pumped a ball high into the Italian area; keeper Gianluca Pagliuca advanced from his line to deal with the ball but Franco Baresi, one of the most graceful defenders to play the game, attempted a headed clearance.

Put 'Em Under Pressure, Jack said.

So Tommy Coyne did. And Baresi could only manage a half-clearance. He played the ball into the path of Ray Houghton. So Houghton hit it.

Over Pagliuca!

Into the net! Still, like his strike against the English in Stuttgart, one of the greatest Ireland goals.

When he emerged from the dressing room after the game, beaming from ear to ear, Jack was smoking a cigar nearly as big as his forearm. His team had defeated the eventual finalists, but it was no fluke. Packie Bonner hardly had a save to make, and John Sheridan had the best chance of the game to double Ireland's lead but his late shot hit the underside of the crossbar.

The Italian players were somehow gracious in defeat. 'We lost and that's it,' said Roberto Baggio, who would have to come to terms with much harsher disappointment at the end of the month when he missed the fateful final spot-kick against Brazil. 'On their first chance of the game they scored a goal and it made things easier for them, harder for us,' he continued. 'As the game went on, we couldn't shoot because they were trapping and pressing us.'

But victory came at a cost and the lack of water throughout the first game – and too much afterwards – inevitably led to an on-going battle between Jack and the match officials. Dutch referee Mario van der Ende refused to allow bottles to be thrown onto the pitch and stepped in when Ray Houghton was offered refreshment by the touchline. To his astonishment, when Jack approached a FIFA official at half time to register his concerns, the individual concerned refused to take action, and then promptly drank from the water bottle Jack was holding.

Jack may have sworn at him at that point. The lack of water also ruined Tommy Coyne's chances of being fit for the second game against Mexico.

The Celtic striker was selected for the drugs test. He eventually provided a sample after a three-hour wait. Coyne, who had spent the first hour still in his playing kit, was plied with fluids as he tried to speed up the process. In fact, he took on so much liquid that he made himself ill. No surprise that Jack was angry, and still complaining about the treatment of Coyne, and the rest of the players in the tournament, in the build-up to the Mexican showdown in Orlando. He told the FAI to lodge a formal protest to FIFA.

'I'll tell you something,' he told the press. 'If the television people had insisted on games being stopped for a minute for commercial breaks, there would have been no objection, so why can't the needs of players be taken into consideration?'

FIFA general secretary Sepp Blatter dismissed Jack's observations; in fact pointing out that no other team had complained.

'The Irish seem to overdo this,' said the now-disgraced football powerbroker. 'They were complaining about drinks before the tournament had even started. There is no question of players not being allowed to drink. We don't want to have any influence on the health of players. But we don't want bottles thrown on to the pitch.'

ANDY TOWNSEND

We'd been told there was a good chance there would be more Italian fans than Irish. But as we got nearer the stadium in New Jersey, there was coach after coach full of Irish fans, and it became apparent that there were going to be more Irish, possibly 60-40 in our favour. Then outside the stadium and as we walked out for the warm-up, it was inundated with Irish fans, we hardly saw any Italian fans. I was walking out with Jack and Cas, and Jack turned to him and said, 'F**king hell Cas… you're the only Italian in here'.

RAY HOUGHTON

There were a lot of rumours at the time that I may not be playing. I worked hard through the summer and Jack rewarded me by playing me. And thankfully on the day I went out and did the business for him and scored a goal.

IN THE middle of the month, on a drive from Washington Airport, Jack, Des Casey and an old friend from England David McBeth called into Arlington Cemetery, and paid their respects to the grave of John F Kennedy.

New Jersey had been suffocating. Washington was even more oppressive, however, and Jack knew that it would be a breeze for the Mexicans to play in such extreme heat, though he feared for the Norwegians as much as his own boys. Jack was seated in the VIP area of the RFK Stadium during the game.

'At regular intervals a hostess comes along and offers us iced drinks. And on two occasions, once in either half, they come round with chilled napkins to place on our heads,' he noted in his diaries.

'I turn to Des and say, "Damn it to hell, but who are these people to put the safety of players on the line while they sit around in the lap of luxury with their iced drinks and chilled napkins? It is not right and I will continue to rant on about it."'

Jack left the game early but on arrival back at the airport discovered that a bad electrical storm had left all flights either cancelled or deferred. He was offered a seat on a plane to Charlotte and took it, but once there failed to make his connection to Orlando and spent the night trying to snooze on a hard, plastic seat in the airport.

Back finally at the team hotel, the manager asked not to be disturbed until he had helped himself back to full strength. He was eventually awakened with some bad news, on the double. Tommy Coyne was indeed in a bad way after his ordeal in trying to pass water after the Italian win, when he remained togged out for three and a half hours gulping down too much liquid in the hope of producing a sample. Also, Andy Townsend's knee was up 'like a balloon' and the initial diagnosis was that he was suffering from poison ivy – the Irish captain apparently had leaned against an ivy fence during an after-match drink in New Jersey

ON JUNE 21, too far into the tournament for Jack's liking, he was informed that he had 'won' his battle with FIFA. A faxed message stated that the governing body was prepared to allow water bags to be thrown onto the pitch.

But not everything was to his liking. Roy Keane's head, for starters, was irritating him. 'He has had his hair shaved tight in what I can only surmise is his latest concession to fashion. Now here he is, in scorching sun with no headgear on, charging about when he's supposed to be resting his leg.'

Jack had warned all of his players carrying any injuries, or bangs of any degree, to rest up. He decided to give Roy a piece of his mind. 'And guess what? Within another five minutes, I spot him out on an adjoining pitch whacking balls in at Packie Bonner. I might have known Packie would be involved, for no matter what I say, both he and Alan Kelly will insist on running and throwing themselves about in training. But Roy and his dodgy leg are a different matter.'

The stay in Orlando was of course not without incident, but one particular night almost brought Tony Cascarino's World Cup stay to an end. The striker, who struggled for fitness throughout the finals, had managed to smuggle a young lady into the team hotel but he was 'outed' by security who informed Charlton.

TONY CASCARINO

He knew it was me.

He went ballistic. 'You're injured, you're no use to me, then you bring a bird back. I should f**king send you home,' he raged.

A group of journalists had moved into range. I thought, for f**k's sake Jack, keep your voice down. We don't want them to get wind of it. But how do you tell Jack Charlton to shut it when he's frothing from the mouth with rage?

'I'm really sorry, Jack,' I grovelled. 'I promise this will never happen again.' But there was no calming the storm. He grumbled at me for a bit and then seemed to calm down.

And then he said, 'Well I hope she was worth it.'

WHEN JACK opened the blinds in his hotel suite on the morning of the Mexico game, his heart sank. He thought back to Miami and the runaround the Mexicans had given Northern Ireland in a pre-tournament game. He thought of water bottles, pedantic referees and dehydration. He had no idea what he was letting himself in for.

The training of the last fortnight, and beyond, had been specifically for this day. And yet nothing could really prepare a team of Irishmen for a game in 120 degrees heat against a bunch of Mexicans. If there were any shadows to chase in the Citrus Bowl, Ireland were chasing them. And anything Ireland did to slow down the game appeared to backfire.

Denis Irwin was booked for taking too long over a throw-in after just 20 minutes. That also meant he was ruled out of the final group game against Norway.

Just after that, the linesman on Jack's side of the pitch attempted to stop the Irish bench throwing water bags on the field. The fourth official intervened and told his colleague he was mistaken. But it was not be the last Ireland heard of him.

With the players starting to tire in the dying minutes of the first half, Mexico went ahead. Phil Babb lost possession near the penalty area and the ball fell invitingly to Luis Garcia, who lashed it inside Packie Bonner's right hand post.

Twenty minutes into the second half, Denis Irwin made an uncharacteristic error and Garcia benefitted again to score a second.

Jack then decided to bring on two substitutes. What followed became one of the most bizarre and hotly contested substitutions in World Cup history.

Jason McAteer got on the pitch, alright. He replaced Staunton. But because the fourth official could not pronounce Aldridge's name properly as he read it down the internal phone to a FIFA colleague, the striker could not get on to take Tommy Coyne's place. A little man in a blue suit and a yellow hat refused to let Aldridge on. Jack, who was nearly twice the size of the official, stepped in, demanding action.

Aldridge came close to a total and utter meltdown.

When an irate Aldridge did eventually make it on to the pitch, he left the man in the yellow hat – and millions watching – with no doubts about his thoughts. The cameras, and the microphones, picked it all up and he was still shouting cheating allegations as he made his way on to the pitch.

JOHN ALDRIDGE

When I saw it afterwards, I was embarrassed with the antics but at the time it was very frustrating. I was supposed to have gone on when we were 1-0 down but in the meantime they had made it 2-0. We brought two players off and could only put one on. So we were 2-0 down with 10 men on and I got dragged back off. So my frustrations boiled over to the point where everyone saw it.

THANKFULLY IT did not affect his performance. Aldridge pulled a goal back with six minutes to go, but it was not enough to rescue Ireland. And when Jorge Campos pulled off a brilliant reflex save in his garish, fluorescent kit after that, Ireland left the Citrus Bowl empty-handed.

The Irish party was due to go to Disneyland the next day, but the players came to Jack and told him they did not have the stomach for it. Jack was not in disagreement. With the Norwegian game looming, Jack took time out with Pat and went shopping for presents for their grandkids. Arriving back in the team hotel with bags in hand he was surprised to find a gang of journalists on the lookout. He was quickly informed by two newsmen that he was in 'trouble'.

FIFA had decided to ban the Irish manager from the bench for one game. They also fined him 20,000 Swiss francs, which Jack soon discovered was about £7,000 sterling. John Aldridge was also fined for his part in the sideline face-off. A statement was issued by FIFA explaining that the Irish manager was being disciplined.

'Already there are stories going out in the papers which have me swearing at the referee and insulting people generally,' Jack logged. 'Rubbish! I can say that during the Mexican game I never approached any of the three match officials.'

Back in Ireland, good-natured supporters decided to stand by Jack and Aldo. Pub collections, Jack was informed, had already raised more than £10,000. Jack was appreciative, but stubborn as usual. 'If there is a fine to be paid, I'll pay it myself... I can afford it.'

A bigger concern for Jack was Paul McGrath. He looked to tire faster than anybody else in the heat against the Mexicans, and he admitted that he had difficulty getting up for the high ball because of his shoulder injury. Jack told his favourite player that he was considering dropping him for the game the next day. McGrath pleaded to hold onto his place. Jack received little sympathy from FIFA, who denied there was a vendetta against him and the Irish team.

FIFA spokesman Guido Tognoni said that while the Ireland manager and his staff had complied with the correct procedures surrounding John Aldridge's substitution, they had insulted officials at the same time. 'Jack is a crazy man, we like him and we need characters in the game but he must learn where to draw the line. Charlton has been critical of us but that is his opinion. We are tolerant and try to help as much as possible.

'It is disappointing that in February Charlton missed a seminar for managers. He was reported to be sick. Four years ago before Italia 90 he missed the same kind of seminar. We feel it is important for managers to be there and understand our guidelines.'

JACK WATCHED Ireland take on Norway in the TV gantry, sitting next to son John, with a two-way radio between himself and the dug out. While Maurice Setters sweated and kicked every ball by the dug out, Jack sipped a G&T and before the game at least, waved cheerily to the fans through the window.

He may have been physically distant from the action, but, as Maurice and the bench could testify, he was there in more than spirit. Unable to do anything from his high vantage point, the only advantage was being able to keep in touch with Italy's game against Mexico that was also playing out as a stale goalless draw, meaning Ireland would qualify. Jack had pulled Paul McGrath to one side on the pre-match walk round the hotel grounds. He told him he was going to risk him and put his 'nightmare' performance against Mexico behind him.

McGrath was arguably Man of the Match against Norway.

If Norway manager Egil Olsen was also aware of events in New York, he hid it well. His team needed to win but barely threatened and, in fact, the best chance fell to John Sheridan who chipped narrowly over. The game ended 0-0.

In the dressing room Jack was congratulating his players on their efforts when he was informed that the Irish supporters were still holding up in the stadium waiting for him to come back out. They wanted to hail Big Jack.

HE DECIDED to get back to Washington the next day, to watch Belgium play Saudi Arabia, which ended up as a wasted exercise since Holland turned out to be Ireland's next opponents in the knockout stages. They were also going to be playing the Dutch back in Orlando.

It was a city Jack had had enough of, but getting back to Florida from Washington in double quick time was not so easy. There were more electrical storms on the loose. 'The captain tells us that if we don't get out before ten o'clock we're stuck in Washington for the rest of the night,' Jack wrote in his diaries. 'The next announcement on the tannoy is that the flight has been cancelled and we're all off the plane. All flights to Orlando the following day are fully booked up and they can't get me a hotel room in Washington.

'I tell them that I am the manager of the team still involved in the World Cup and I just have to be in Orlando the following day. So the guy goes back to his computer and tells me that there is a small plane leaving for Atlanta around midnight and that I can get a connection there for a flight to Florida at seven the next morning.

'In my desperation, I take it and so begins one of the most uncomfortable nights of my entire life.' Jack remained confined in Atlanta Airport for the night, and found himself snoozing on the same hard plastic seating once again.

WORD REACHED the Irish manager that the collection back at 'home' had now reached six figures. However, with the Citrus Bowl looming once again, the fines were the last thing on Jack's mind.

He was calmed by reports that the weather was forecast to be tolerable for Ireland and the Dutch. But he was bothered by his team selection, and struggling to predict which of his players would 'show up' and play like their old selves in the hottest conditions.

Jack didn't get it right, for once, not really. But the defeat to the Dutch was largely down to two uncharacteristic mistakes from two of his favourite characters.

Terry Phelan and Packie Bonner, two of the most consistent players of Jack's reign, made the two critical first half errors that swung the game for the Dutch.

Phelan's indecision in dealing with a routine attack in the tenth minute let in Marc Overmars, who crossed for Dennis Bergkamp to open the scoring. Bonner, who had been under pressure from understudy Alan Kelly throughout the tournament but who had retained his manager's loyalty, dropped a tame one from Wim Jonk.

It was a cruel and catastrophic spill from the man from Donegal who, at the same stage in the World Cup four years earlier in Genoa, had written his place into Irish sporting history with his penalty save to deny Daniel Timofte.

PACKIE BONNER

Mistakes happen. You can't blame this, you can't blame that. It just happens in a split second. But obviously I was very very disappointed. While I was elated to save the penalty in the World Cup in '90, I was devastated to lose such a goal and we were knocked out possibly because of it. Coming back from America, we were probably a bit embarrassed about it because we didn't do as well as we did in Italy and obviously there were a lot of people who were a bit disappointed that we didn't go further.

As clichéd as it sounds… it was just one of those things. In all honesty, I cannot say how that goal happened – it just did and I was wounded by it. I was in complete shock in the dressing room afterwards and the tears flowed. It was the lowest point in my professional career.

IT SEEMED particularly cruel that Bonner, a stalwart from day one and one of Jack's most reliable and loyal players, had made the catastrophic error which ended another World Cup dream. It's also worth noting Bonner recorded one of the funniest stories of his time with Jack in his autobiography, *The Last Line*.

Jack's XI had provided the opposition for Bonner's testimonial and the keeper wanted to make a presentation to all the players, and the manager who had taken part. He bought Jack a bottle of Scotch, but wanting to add something personal, and a bit different, also forked out for a brand new CD Discman player.

'As Big Jack approached the podium, I had the contraption out of the box to show it off a bit. He stopped and looked at it and I could see the puzzlement on his face.

"What the f**k is that?" he asked, staring at the state-of-the-art sound machine and before I could explain he said, in a loud voice, "What the f**k am I gonna do with a toaster?"

It brought the house down.

CHARLIE STUART

When the Republic of Ireland played out a boring scoreless draw with England in a friendly at Dublin's Aviva Stadium in June, 2015 the most rousing applause of the afternoon and heartfelt affection from the 50,000 capacity crowd came ten minutes before kick off time when Jack Charlton was suddenly introduced to the fans.

The roars of approval from both sets of supporters lasted for three emotional minutes. Many of those present were not even born at the time when Charlton had decided to quit the Irish job almost 20 years previously. But the love affair continues for what I described all those years ago as, 'the most popular Englishman ever in Ireland'.

When the Irish Press *newspaper Group for whom I worked for over two decades went into liquidation in June, 1995 my colleagues staged a lock-in at our premises at Burgh Quay in the centre of Dublin. My late colleague Michael Carwood, the then Sports Editor of* The Sunday Press *suggested we approach Jack for some type of moral support for the hundreds who had been made redundant and thrown on the dole with no redundancy package. We asked the big man, who came from a mining background in Northumberland, for some type of moral support.*

The reply was instant and made headlines in Europe and America. By good fortune, Jack's full Ireland international squad was in Dublin to play in the Chris Hughton testimonial game at Lansdowne Road that June. After the match Jack suggested that the team coach with all the players on board would come to our newspaper headquarters and wish those partaking in the lock-in the best of luck.

I recall driving my car from Lansdowne Road to the office with a Garda escort and the team bus just behind. The camera crews were there on arrival as Jack and the players stepped out of the coach and up the steps to shake the hands through the windows with those involved in the lock-in. That was protest and publicity at its best – thanks to Jack.

Jack and his patient wife Pat often loved to spend part of the winter in Altea, a lovely old Moorish town on Spain's Costa Blanca. They had a lovely home there and were gracious enough to let friends, myself included, stay there. We were greeted by English ex-pat friends Brian and Dee Cremin who kept an eye on the place and welcomed us saying, 'Any friend of the Charltons are friends of ours and you will have a great time'.

When my wife Maura and I discovered that Brian's mother was Irish, we had to include him in the "Green Army", so we presented him with an Ireland football shirt before we left. Once home, we sent an essential kit for an Irish supporter in Spain – baseball cap, scarf, badges, T-shirt, flags etc.

And you can imagine Jack's surprise when his old pal Brian collected him from the airport on his next visit, greeted by Brian in full Irish fan regalia.

JACK CHARLTON… Ashington, Leeds, England, Ireland, player, manager, friend. Thanks for all the memories.

JACK WAS prickly but philosophical after the Holland match. He had been annoyed by the inevitable questions about his future in the build-up; and he dismissed them before they got out of hand in the wake of defeat.

'The hardest decision I will have to make is to get out while I'm still ahead of the game. When that will be is anybody's guess, but I'll tell you something, I hope to know before the press.'

Jack was not the only one who was reluctant to be paraded before the Irish public on their return. Unlike after Germany and Italy, this didn't feel right. Other than their first win against Italy, Ireland had underachieved in America.

But he knew it was for the fans who had been unable to make the trip, who had still held the street parties and followed the team's every move from afar.

'We were out of the World Cup. We were a bit depressed. And then they tell us that we've got to come back to a party. Anyway I had a word with a couple of the FAI officials and they said, "Look, you should come back".

'So I said, "okay I will come back."'

And so, despite having to take a flight back to Dallas the following morning to join the ITV World Cup team, Jack Charlton stood in the middle of a very large crowd in the Phoenix Park in Dublin in July, 1994, waved his flag, and smiled a strained, polite smile.

'I'm sorry we didn't win the World Cup for you… but we did wor best,' Jack told the attendance.

IRELAND 96

JACK CHARLTON ended his reign as Republic of Ireland manager in the back of a Dublin taxi. It was here, after a meeting with the FAI in which he had agreed to resign, that he was to say farewell to the Irish public.

Jack had been called to Dublin by his bosses, whom he felt seemed overly eager to move him on after the failure to qualify for the Euro 96 finals in England. He had always said the campaign would be his last. But he was in no rush to quit; in fact he quite fancied seeing it through to exactly ten years and then go.

The FAI had other ideas. It had been a long day. But it had also been an extraordinary one. Everyone in Ireland seemed to know why Jack was in town. And everyone wanted to wish him well.

Very few asked for an autograph or photo that day. The majority just wanted to thank him.

MICHAEL FLATLEY

Jack is a legend. Many pubs in Ireland have three photos up on the wall. The Pope, John F Kennedy and Jack Charlton, and not necessarily in that order!

Huge respect to Jack.

He's an Irish hero!

JACK HAD told FAI president Louis Kilcoyne that he would announce his resignation when Ireland lost their Euros play off to Holland at Anfield on December 13. That night, Kilcoyne told him not to be so hasty, but then called within days of Jack and Pat returning from a break at their Spanish home.

He wanted a meeting, so Jack reluctantly flew to Dublin. He was picked up by his Irish based agents Trevor O'Rourke and John Givens at the airport, and then went to Merrion Square to meet Kilcoyne, Joe Delaney, Michael Hyland and Pat Quigley.

His old friend Des Casey, by then vice-president, and the man who had made those first phone calls a decade earlier, was absent among the FAI powerbrokers.

Although upset and surprised he had not been granted a kinder exit, Jack knew it was time to walk, before he was pushed. As his taxi sped through the streets to the airport, a noisy motorcade fell in behind him to say their own farewell. Jack, nestled into the back seat, reflected on his nine, nearly ten years, in charge.

He leaned back and looked out of the window.

'Success is relevant to where you're at. I took a team that had never qualified for a World Cup or a European Championship and qualified in three out of four,' Jack reflected, 'and we were looking to qualify for four out of five.

JOHN GIVENS

We went into that last meeting as Jack's advisers, but it was very last minute. He'd never mentioned it to us beforehand, just asked us to pick him up from the airport.

He never told us if he had any intention of resigning. It was just decided very quickly in the meeting; a mutual resignation.

We went to his favourite boozer, Hill 16, for a pint. He seemed relieved, I'd say, but maybe a bit surprised by the speed of it. I think he quite fancied the idea of ten years, and I think he'd earned that. He knew the FAI wanted control back from the manager and I don't think he had the enthusiasm for the fight. We were having a laugh at some of the great times. And then suddenly he said, 'Oh f**k… we better tell Maurice'.

The World Cup in Italy changed the perception of the Tricolour. Nearly every house had one for Italia 90 and since then, if you have a flag in your house, no one bats an eyelid. Before that, if you had the Irish flag outside your house, it had a totally different meaning. That was a significant change down to Jack.

He was very involved in the supporters becoming so favourable on their travels.

I remember Jack telling the FAI, 'Tell them they are the best supporters in the world, and they will be'. He said they had done it at Sheffield Wednesday and it worked. And look at the reputation of Irish supporters now.

We had an office in Palmerstown and the River Liffey was out the back, so we got a fishing rod so, if ever he called in, Jack could go out the back and throw the line in for half an hour. He never caught anything; in fact, I don't know if there was anything to catch but he enjoyed himself.

Jack started doing talk-ins across the country, and when we were out on the road, if we ever crossed a bridge, he'd insist on pulling over to look at the river, and if he ever saw anyone fishing he'd go down and have a chat with them.

There was one incident at Croom in County Limerick where Jack saw this fella, went into the river, took the rod off him, had a few casts and handed the rod back. I am sure the man went home, or down to the pub and said, 'You'll never guess who I was fishing with' – and no one believed him.

After gigs, we would only be gone 100 yards and Jack would be asleep and then, if we were coming back from say, Cork, and I'd ask to pull over, we'd swap, and 100 yards later, I'd be asleep. But we had some great laughs on those trips. I remember one night we stopped at a chipper in Monasterevin in Kildare about one in the morning and the fella said, 'Aw, Jack, I'll have to get my grandma'.

So he goes to wake her up; but not upstairs, he had to run up to her house, 50 yards up the street. And sure enough, ten minutes later, after we've finished our fish and chips, he brings his grandma in, in her pyjamas with a coat wrapped round her, to meet Big Jack. And he loved it. He had this great ability to always look like he was enjoying himself.

One of the first gigs he did was for Opel who paid for him to go to London where he was Guest of Honour at an event for the West Cork Tourism Board that was sponsored by Murphy's. Before we went in, he was concerned that he'd never been to West Cork, but I just said, 'Don't worry… just say you've never been… but you've been invited and you're looking forward to going'. So when he got up to do his speech, he said, 'I've never been to West Cork, but I've been invited and I'm looking forward to going. I love going over to Ireland. And I do love the Guinness'. And someone whispered across, 'No, Jack… it's Murphy's (the sponsors)'.

And he said, 'Sorry, the Murphy's Guinness.' It was front page news the next day and to this day, he wouldn't know the difference.

Over the years I lost count of the number of people who would just come over to Jack, wherever we were, and just put out their hand and say, 'Thanks, Jack'.

PETER BYRNE

There is a line on Jack Charlton's CV which puts him apart from other football managers of this or any era – his casual acquaintance with a couple of Popes.

Jack and his assistant Maurice Setters were the only non-Catholics in the Republic of Ireland entourage that set down in Rome for their World Cup quarter-final tie against Italy in the summer of 1990. But it didn't stop them attending Mass on the eve of the match in the hope that heavenly intervention might perhaps redress a perceived imbalance between the two teams. That sadly didn't work but earlier in the week the Irish party experienced their own little miracle in the Eternal City when the squad was granted a private audience with Pope John Paul and Charlton got to speak with the leader of 1.1 billion Catholics for a couple of precious minutes.

Fast forward fifteen years, when I accompanied him on a return trip to Rome as part of a team making a television documentary entitled Italia 90 Revisited. *Once again favours were called in at the Irish College in Rome and, once again, arrangements were put in place for Jack to meet with the Pope as part of the papal public audience each Wednesday.*

In this instance, the practice was to position special guests at the front of a semi-circle with the Pontiff and his assistants moving relatively quickly imparting the spiritual blessing which would live long in the memory of those privileged to be in the front row. By now, Pope Benedict was in office with his demure, saintly presence offering a contrast to the occasional earthiness of his predecessor. Standing just a couple of paces behind Jack, it was impossible to disguise the sense of awe as Benedict approached with people so humbled in the moment, that they couldn't utter a word when His Holiness every so often appeared to be receptive to a response. Not Jack Charlton.

Where others were incapable of delivering a word, he appeared anxious to start a dialogue before the Pontiff moved to the next person, but not before casting a curious backward glance at the man he had just left.

When we eventually disentangled ourselves from the hordes gathered in St Peter's Square, I asked Jack what he had said to the Pontiff and was astounded by the reply. 'I told him he was the third Pope I had seen but that one of them, John Paul's predecessor, was dead at the time, adding that it had nothing to do with me'. It was a good hour or so before I regained my equilibrium.

As a national sporting icon in the closing phase of his professional career it was inevitable that he would get to know many men of the cloth on his travels around Ireland. And never once did I find him disrespectful. His remarkable exchange of words with the Pontiff has to be seen in that light but it served to illustrate the element of self-confidence that identified his time in Ireland.

In many ways Big Jack and the Irish were a natural fit. He liked their propensity for the outrageous, their passion for sport and perhaps most important of all, the prospect of having a manager who would demand the respect of football people across Europe.

JACK HAD confirmed in August, 1994 that he would be staying in the job for at least two years. Well, the FAI announced as much.

On the day of their annual general meeting, Jack went fishing, leaving the announcement to general secretary Sean Connolly. Jack, for his part, never felt the need to make a formal declaration to carry on. The same rules applied for him; no contract, no fuss, he had a job to do.

And it started against Latvia in September, 1994 for a new-look Ireland, without Bonner, Moran and Houghton, but with John Aldridge, now 36, still included as he started to knock in the goals for Tranmere Rovers. Ireland won 3-0 in Riga, with Aldridge scoring two. That was followed a month later with a 4-0 stuffing of Liechtenstein in Dublin, and a brace each for fit again Niall Quinn and strike partner Tommy Coyne.

Even the November trip to Belfast, just a year after their previously fraught visit, passed without incident or discomfort. Under a "NO CEAESFIRE" banner at the railway end of Windsor Park, the visitors tore Bryan Hamilton's team apart. It should have been more than the four scored by Aldridge, Keane, Townsend and Sheridan, but it would suffice.

Ireland had nine out of nine points going into 1995.

'Very satisfactory,' said Jack, in a much calmer post-match press briefing than on his last visit. 'But I don't think it was a good performance.'

While the game north of the border passed without incident or aggravation, the visit of England for a friendly on February 15, 1995 was to be one of the most depressing nights of the Charlton Era.

Terry Venables was putting together the England team that he felt could challenge for the European Championship title as they prepared to host their first tournament since 1966. It was a strong England side against an Ireland team somewhat weakened by Roy Keane's withdrawal.

David Kelly scored in the 22nd minute and then the English supporters housed in the upper tier of the old Lansdowne Road main stand went ballistic.

In scenes of quite appalling violence, they threw broken chairs and ripped-out wooden balustrades at spectators below.

The visitors made all the right, appalling noises afterwards. Gary Lineker said the English 'fans' were an embarrassment, lunatics and fascists. Alan Shearer said it was a 'sad night for football' and FA chief executive Graham Kelly said they were 'an embarrassment'.

Jack, an Englishman and honorary Irishman was baffled by the scenes. After remonstrating with one young Irish lad who had thrown a bottle into the melee, he was jostled and harangued by English supporters.

'I've never experienced anything like that. Never. Never known anything like that in a lifetime of playing football. It just seemed to be beyond control.

'I don't know what it was all for.'

TERRY VENABLES

I don't know how many troublemakers there were, but the FA had received only 4,000 tickets to make up ten per cent of a 46,000 crowd inside Lansdowne Road. The minority chose to rubbish our game and reputation. I don't know the reasons behind their actions, whether it was political or sectarian or a challenge to the IRA, only that the rioting – for it was bad enough to be described as that – turned horribly violent, with seats and all sorts thrown from the top of one stand to the tier below.

I never suspected such a thing could happen, something I had not experienced before or since. It was a friendly match, and the first time we had played in Dublin since a November, 1990 qualifier.

When the Republic scored and then we were disallowed a 'goal', the violence erupted and the referee called the teams off. Jack Charlton was as distraught as I was. We were two Englishmen ashamed of what was going on above us.

WHILE VISITING fans were welcomed back to Lansdowne Road for the next game, there were to be stringent restrictions on those brave enough to make the journey. For the first time in three visits, Northern Ireland supporters were among the Dublin crowd.

And after the 4-0 drubbing in Belfast, the hosts were expected to coast to victory again. Iain Dowie and Co had other ideas, however, and he cancelled out

Niall Quinn's goal to earn a 1-1 draw. Though Ireland were back on course as they reached the halfway stage of the qualifying campaign with a 1-0 win over rivals Portugal the following month.

KEVIN MORAN

There was maybe a little bit of doubt settling in from that particular game. Let's be honest about it, after beating Northern Ireland 4-0 away, we should not really be happy just to sit back and accept a one-all draw at home. But the performance against Portugal at home was one of the best for a number of years. When you saw a performance like that, and after we'd gone to Northern Ireland and beaten them 4-0, the team should have been on a high going into all these games.

IT ALL seriously unravelled in June, 1995 with the fateful trip to Liechtenstein.

He may not have been a happy camper in the Ireland camp, but Roy Keane was one of Jack's most influential players. After Manchester United's 1-0 FA Cup final defeat to Everton, the future Ireland captain was booked in for a hernia operation. He would miss the qualifiers in Eschen's Sportpark, and the visit of Austria a few days later. Liechtenstein managed to avoid defeat for the first time in a competitive match on Sunday, June 4, 1995.

And still, no one who was there knows how?

In all, Ireland managed 40 goal-scoring attempts, 16 of them on target. Goalkeeper Martin Heeb, a 5' 9" groundsman at the stadium during the day, defied attack after attack.

Jack was never particularly chirpy in defeat. His post-match press conference in Eschen was brief. 'I'm frustrated,' he said. 'I have never seen a game like that, it was so frustrating. We had some great chances but it seemed written in the stars that we weren't going to score. The damage is done and we have made it difficult for ourselves. The other countries will be delighted with the result.'

Then there was an awkward silence.

'Can I go now?' Jack said. The other nations were indeed delighted with the shock result. And the Austrians were delirious the next week when they came from behind to win 3-1 in Dublin.

Jack was again forced to bite his tongue before the media. 'I had a feeling something like this would happen,' he said. 'It has been a dreadful week and I don't know what it all means.' It didn't really matter after the reverse fixture in Vienna when a Peter Stoger hat trick gave the Austrians the same 3-1 victory.

The night before was not one of Jack's finest as Ireland manager. He had bought a share in a Harry Ramsden's fish and chip shop, jointly owning it with the company and a group of Irish investors. It opened on the Naas Road in Dublin in December, 1995 and he took the squad there the night before the Austrian game.

GABRIEL EGAN

Some years into his time in Ireland, I was invited to do a piece with him on the team he'd just announced for the game the following day. Work duties over he produced the bottle of duty free and two glasses. Agitated he couldn't settle as he looked in vain for his notes on the Austrian team he had scouted some weeks earlier. Then he dropped the bombshell and told me he decided to quit. I countered by saying, 'No… you will miss it too much'. He insisted he'd had enough and gave me an expansive insight into his thoughts on international football. He said, 'Coaches are not stupid people… they have worked out how we play and are now doing to us what we have been doing to them'. He went through his Ireland team player by player and said he would have to devise a new way to play if he were to stay and felt he did not have the players to do that.

Apart from getting the best out of footballers Jack had a knack of getting people onside. I recall being in Newcastle with him and his lovely wife Pat. Jack was taking us all out to lunch; his treat and indeed we did enjoy a one 'n' one from the back of a chip van; high end dining indeed. Walking through a flower show with him a little lady said, 'Oh Jack… when will you come and manage England… we need you?' He smiled at her, pointed to me and said, 'He's my boss he won't let me'.

He could have people eating from his hand without even trying. I asked him to do co-commentary with me on an FA Cup game at Elland Road once. He wished to know would he be doing me a favour or was it an earner? I made it clear we could organise a fee and he was sold. On the day other broadcasters were amazed to see the Big Man coming onto the gantry to join me. First freebie of the day for Jack was to bum a fag from a young technician nearby, regular occurrence… 'Of course Mr Charlton'.

The young fella then arrived up with a packet of ciggies and presented them to the legend before him. Jack came smartly dressed in a blazer but was feeling cold. He proceeded to disappear down into the bowels of the stand only to reappear in a brand new club bench coat. He always emerged a winner.

Another day before an International friendly against Spain a colleague and I left the training session in Seville and headed for a cafe to get a coffee. As we sat in the window I spied Jack and the staff strolling back to the hotel for the mandatory media conference. I went to the door and shouted. He did not wait for a written invitation to stroll inside and spent the next half hour telling the assembled Spanish diners about the virtues of sardines and other fish tapas on offer. The massed ranks of media had to wait to put their questions sometime later.

PAUL MCGRATH

By 1995 we had all become comfortable and a little careless. The players headed off in the afternoon to the pub or wherever; I'd be stuck in my room with a sentry on the door. The final insult arrived on the bus journey to Dublin when, after stopping at a community centre in Ballyfermot for no apparent reason, we were then headed into Harry Ramsden's fish and chip outlet for an official opening. Jack was a shareholder in the restaurant and watched happily as most of us took up the "Harry Ramsden challenge".

The price for meeting the challenge was a free dessert. After Harry we went to Lansdowne Road for our final pre-game training session. The following day "Fortress Lansdowne" fell like a house of cards. In our last four competitive matches, we had conceded 10 goals.

NIALL QUINN

We all shuffled into Harry Ramsden's. Jack was a shareholder. Packie or Paul or somebody cut a ribbon and officially opened the place. So the night before the game, after a week of drink, I settled down to fish and chips. Gary Kelly took the "Harry Ramsden's Challenge" and ate a fish about a yard long and a mountain of chips and anything else they challenged him with. He thought there'd be a certificate but he got a free dessert instead, which he duly ate.

Jack herded us out pronto. Twenty minutes later, it's dusk at Lansdowne Road and we're all waddling about the pitch, groaning, full of fish and chips and trying to do a training session the night before this must-win game. We're burping and farting and creased over with laughter.

Our main thought was it's been a happy era and it's ending soon. Sometimes you don't need a weatherman to know which way the wind blows. It was all over for Jack.

JOHN ALDRIDGE restored some normality to the qualifying campaign when Latvia were comfortably dispatched in October, 1995 and he went within a goal of Frank Stapleton's goal-scoring record with his double. But there were to be no more Ireland goals for the Scouse striker.

Still without Keane, and also deprived the services of Andy Townsend and John Sheridan, Jack took his side to Lisbon with speculation again rife over his future in the build-up. They were totally outclassed by the Portuguese and lost 3-0. And Niall Quinn picked up a second booking in qualifying which would crucially rule him out of the play-off.

Once again it was Holland. This time the meeting place was Anfield.

JACK COULD not pick his best Ireland team.

Guus Hiddink could pick his best Holland team. They were the better team on paper and they were the better team on the night. Patrick Kluivert, at 19, was nearly half the age of Paul McGrath. He led him a merry dance on the Anfield turf and scored the two goals that sent Holland through to Euro 96, and a group draw with hosts England and Scotland.

Jack, flat cap and long blue coat, cut a lonely figure at times as his team failed to respond to the Dutch. But then he knew they couldn't. Holland were too good on the night.

Jack was back in the dressing room when a Merseyside police officer knocked on the door and pleaded with him to go back outside. The 15,000 Ireland supporters were refusing to leave. They had once again, with their Dutch counterparts, contributed to a wonderful, electric atmosphere in a sea of green and orange in the famous old English ground. And they wanted to see Jack, and perhaps say goodbye.

He grabbed a Tricolour and a scarf and as he headed up the tunnel with Maurice Setters. *The Fields of Athenry* echoed round Anfield.

JOHN ALDRIDGE

It was a very emotional night.

For me personally, it was a dream to play at Anfield and I'd imagined before the game beating Holland and scoring the winner in front of The Kop so we went to the Euros in England. But we were second best on the night; Kluivert was a different class and it was a really difficult night for us. The fans were fantastic and it was a great atmosphere but it was a tired performance from us and we were not great.

I think we all knew when he went out to the fans, that that was going to be it for Jack. It was a sad night for me. I remember going back to the pub in Wootton near where I live with my family, and friends who had come over from Ireland, and it felt like the end and that it was never going to be the same.

What a meeting that was the night he came to Oxford. He asked me if I fancied playing for Ireland, and I said, 'Yes… definitely'. Then I recommended Ray Houghton… he didn't even know he was eligible… and what a tremendous player he went on to be for Ireland.

They were the best days of my life as a footballer. We all became massive friends and our friend was the manager. All right, Roy Keane might have felt differently towards the end, but we all had so much respect for him. I used to love watching that Leeds team he played in, and that respect was cemented when he became the Ireland manager. Jack was great to work for. What you saw was what you got… there were no airs and graces. And it was Jack's way or no way. We believed in him.

I didn't like to do the running. I was a goal hanger but I would have gladly given up my goals for Jack and the team.

He had been at the World Cup in Mexico and decided how he wanted us to play and he didn't want us to play across the back four or the midfield four because it could be intercepted, and international teams would swarm all over you like the Red Arrows when they got the ball.

*From my point of view, that meant when the full backs got the ball I had to bend my run and get in the corners, and when I got the ball I had to bring in the likes of Ray Houghton or Kevin Sheedy. And Jack used to tell me, when their defenders get the ball, you chase the b*****ks off them. I was the first of the line to chase; that was my job. We played in their half, and it was clever. They talk about the pressing game now, but that was how we played under Jack.*

*He was very old fashioned in many ways, but he was very clever. We knew as a team what he wanted and what he would not accept and if you did as you were told, you'd play… if not you'd be out. He treated you like a man. If he saw someone drinking a Coke, he'd say, 'What are you drinking that s*** for? Guinness is better for you'. He didn't mind lads having a couple of pints.*

He gave us a lot of leeway, maybe too much, but he just let the lads get on with it. We wouldn't start training until Monday afternoon, but some lads started to come in on a Saturday evening so they could get a Saturday and Sunday night out of it and meet up with the lads. And it was like a family, and I think Jack made sure it was a relaxed, fun place to come, so that the lads wanted to come over and play.

On the Tuesday, I used to feel guilty if I'd had a skinful, so I'd be running my nuts off to get a good sweat on, and Jack used to b*****k me and shout across, 'Aldo… stop f**king running… save it for the game tomorrow'. Sometimes I used to wait until he'd gone in just so I could do a bit extra away from him.

Two days before we were due to play Italy, the lads were getting restless so Jack said we could have a couple of pints each when the Guinness truck came to the hotel in Rome.

The Guinness was set up round the pool with all the media people hanging round, plus the Italian police who were guarding us. The cops couldn't believe that the Ireland players were drinking two days before we were due to play Italy, and that the manager was in the thick of it.

We started playing the penny game, which basically involved putting a penny on your forehead, hitting the back of your own head until the penny falls off.

By this time, a couple of pints had turned to five or six. Jack heard the commotion, so came over and asked what the game was?

And being the ultra-competitive person that he is, Jack said he wanted a go. So Jack took his coat off to get ready and sat down. Then, Andy Townsend placed the coin on Jack's forehead – only he took it off at the last second, without telling Jack.

And Jack was winding his arms up like a windmill to hit himself and was belting the back of his own head while of course the lad, and the Italian cops and the press, were absolutely p***ing themselves.

He must have hit himself about ten times, full pelt as well, and then twigged and tried to grab Andy and clip him round the ear.

When I had my testimonial at Tranmere, Jack showed up as a surprise without telling me. That really meant so much. I love him to bits.

JACK ISSUED a statement, through the FAI, which was released before he set off for Newcastle. 'I have felt for some time there was a need for change. Ten years is a long time in the job. They have been brilliant years. I have enjoyed every minute, the 'craic' has been great, but everything must come to an end.

'I'd like to thank the people of Ireland and the FAI for making these ten years the happiest of my life. I have many friends in Ireland. The country is in my blood now and I intend to spend a lot of time here in the future among my friends.

'I don't know who will take my place, but I wish him the best and if he needs my help at any time in the future, I'm available at the end of a phone.

'Thanks for everything.'

CHARLIE O'LEARY

The one thing I want to say about Jack is that I have never met anyone with as good man management skills. When he came in the FAI were not as professional as Jack might have been expecting. He straightened them out in many ways. We were sent ten footballs for the first training session. The balls had seen better days, the leather was coming off them and you could see the lining underneath.

Jack was not happy.

I said, 'Mr Charlton', because I called him 'Mr Charlton' back then. 'These are the balls I have been given.' Jack told me the players were complaining and walked away. I rang an official at the FAI and told him a little white lie and that training had been cancelled because the players weren't happy with the footballs. He said, 'I gave you ten balls' and I told him they were like ten balloons.

He told me to give them away and sent out twenty new balls immediately. The next day, we started training with the new balls. I could see Jack looking at me, and he nodded, as if to say, 'He understands what I need when I tell him'.

He told us that once he'd been out on the training ground at Middlesbrough and one of the secretaries came out because he needed to take a phone call. He said he wanted someone else to take the call, but no one was prepared to do it.

He pointed to me and said, 'He's proved you can make decisions without me'. And then he looked at me and said, 'Just make sure it's the right decision'.

I might have been the kit-man but I was a very important part of his team and I was always shown great respect. He put me in charge of the music on the bus. Jack didn't understand some of the songs but he loved the marching music in particular. We were playing Poland away and a song came on, which would be more to the British Army than the Irish Army, and it was a very dull song and slow.

When we were beaten he said to me afterwards, 'Never play dirge like that again'. The funny thing was the next day he was humming the song.

Sean South of Garryowen *was his favourite.*

It got to the stage where it had to be played. It's a rabble-rousing song full of life, if you forget about the words; it was lovely. There was a spot, just as we reached the gates of

Lansdowne Road, and I would put the song on so they were all hyped up by the time we arrived.

He'd often invite his friends to travel on the bus, and we met some lovely people. But it wasn't just the friends. I remember there was a little girl in a wheelchair with her mum who had come up to see us and get some photos and autographs at the team hotel. Before we set off, Jack asked if they were going to the game and because they were, he was insistent they came on the team bus and he arranged for them to be looked after at the game. When we arrived at the ground, the mother threw her arms round Jack.

I knew a taxi driver who was dying of cancer and we took him out of hospital to go home because there was no hope. Jack found out and insisted that he go to visit him, on the condition that no one was told about it. Unfortunately the local priest turned up and he was a Leeds United fanatic so he spent the whole time talking to Jack as this fella was propped up in bed. The following Sunday, the priest got up and told everybody that Jack had been to the house, thanks to me, and I got more than a few requests for Jack after that, but I had to tell them it was a one-off.

As far as time was concerned he was extremely generous.

About three years ago I was out in the garden when someone told me Jack and Pat were at the Westbury Hotel in Dublin. I went along and we were chatting away and I asked them what their plans were while in Dublin? Because John Givens was away, they had no plans so I told Jack my son John keeps peregrine falcons so I asked Jack and Pat if they fancied coming along, because, as you know, Jack is an expert in everything.

The following day he came to my son's house and he loved the birds and he was there all day, inviting the neighbours in and basically taking over the place.

He was absolutely brilliant.

It was like a patron saint coming to town.

JACK CHARLTON travelled with Pat to Dublin in June 2015 to open the Jack Charlton Suite at the new Aviva Stadium. At half-time during the Ireland-England game, he was introduced to the crowd. The standing ovation from both sets of fans was emotional and warm and just wonderful. Jack, who had been apprehensive about the trip, was overwhelmed, maybe even tearful. He sat at the game with Paul McGrath.

PAUL MCGRATH

The reception was just amazing. It was lovely to see him and Pat again and spend some time chatting with him, because I hadn't seen him for a while, so it was nice to know he's ok. It was quite an unusual thing for me making sure that people were not grabbing Jack and spinning him round for autographs and so on and that for once I was the bodyguard.

I think he enjoyed it but Pat was getting a bit worried. We were in the new Jack Charlton suite, and there were quite a lot of famous Irish people around, but everyone wanted to speak to or have their picture taken with Jack. I don't think the people upstairs understood how many people would want to grab a piece of him so there was quite a lot of pushing and shoving and Pat was getting pushed and pilloried too so I took a hold of her hand and she was okay. I like to think that I could be pulled and pushed around at 56 a couple of times, and that would do, but Jack seemed to handle it fine.

I had a father son relationship with him and I have been scolded once or twice by him. We had that type of relationship and I appreciate everything he did for me. I don't think I would've won half as many caps for Ireland and I don't think many managers would have gone to the lengths he did to get me to play for Ireland. He is one of those people who lights up a room immediately and he has done that since he came into the Ireland set-up. He took our team to another level and made us renowned as men, taking us to our first finals and then the first World Cup. He did an awful lot of good things for this country and that will never be forgotten.

I don't think any other manager would have taken the time to do the things and put the stringent measures in place to keep me as part of the team. I don't think many managers would have wasted their time. But it was not all about the football, it was also about caring for someone and trying to make things better for them.

He has that lovely side to him and I have seen it so many times. He just wanted to make things easier for me. As far as I was concerned, he was willing to take the rough with the smooth and make the best of what he could with me. I can never forget that.

I think I still owe him a few more shifts as his bouncer to make up for it.

ACKNOWLEDGEMENTS

'IT ALWAYS SEEMS IMPOSSIBLE UNTIL IT'S DONE.'
— NELSON MANDELA

THE BIGGEST thank you goes to Lesley for putting up with me all these years and certainly for putting up with the last few months of the book, and that never-ending attempt to get to deadline day. As a long-suffering journo's wife, she is well versed in the huffing and puffing and keyboard bashing. But it has been relentless and she hasn't batted an eyelid as the late nights got later and later.

She has, to her credit, been amused on the numerous occasions I have burst out laughing and insisted on telling another story from Jack's life.

Thankfully Lesley has met Jack and Pat Charlton and she's been to Ireland many times. So she understands...

Like the Charltons, we count ourselves lucky to have so many Irish friends who welcomed us with open arms and made us feel so at home.

Without her support, as she does her proper nursing job, and willingness to sacrifice time together as a family, I could not have pulled this off.

They reckon you could not get through the production of a book without your family, and in our case, the entire family have become involved to a degree none of us could have imagined.

So thank you Rachel Thompson, Thomas Young and Harry Young for your assistance – but you did ask – and the same goes to Georgia Wilson and Ryan Huntley. I might be wrong, but I think you enjoyed it really! And to Harry, I promise we'll get that holiday, mate.

My dad Iain has become editor extraordinaire over the last six months and demonstrated a degree of pedantry and attention to detail that surprised us all. Who knew? I can't thank him enough, but then I know he DID enjoy it. He also kept me right on that file back-up thing.

Thanks too to my mum Eleanor, who kept the cakes and the cuppas of Northumberland Tea coming (thanks Bill and Helen). They both provided a haven and temporary office in Yorkshire, where I was able to scatter the many books and notes, and take over the place for a few days, again.

The all-too brief visit from Australia of 'Our Kid' Andy and his wife Kelly enabled us to share a few beers and a barby, but also to tap into his great knowledge of that there internet and how best to put it to use.

When I was approached by Liam Hayes to write a book about Jack Charlton, I was very keen to get permission from Jack and his family first. I am so glad we waited. None of this would have been possible without Jack and Pat, and the help and support of the Charlton family. Thank you to John Charlton in particular for the countless hours he has given up and always having a warm welcome in the bar at Cambois beach, not to mention his wife Deirdre, and Debbie, Peter, Tommy, Gordon, Emma – and not forgetting John, Niamh and Roisin Charlton.

There were not enough pages or hours to fit in all the interviews which might cover Jack's 81 years, and tell his story, but the very mention of his name, and his and the family's authorisation, opened so many doors and released so many phone numbers. People just love him.

Thank you to John Aldridge, John Anderson, Jimmy Armfield, David Armstrong, Ray Bailey, Peter Beardsley, Packie Bonner, Mick Byrne, Tony Cascarino, Des Casey, David Croft, Terry Curran, Fred Dinenage, Michael Flatley, Paul Gascoigne, Steve Gibson, Frank Gillespie, David Hodgson, Norman Hunter, David Hutton, Chris Kamara, Mark Lawrenson, Bill and Helen Logan, Mick McCarthy, Glenn McCrory, Paul McGrath, Gary Megson, Ante Mirocevic, Mac Murray, Charlie O'Leary, Trevor O'Rourke,

Niall Quinn, Duncan Revie, Kim Revie, Lady Elsie Robson, Arthur Scargill, Graeme Souness, Andy Townsend and Chris Waddle.

Knowing that the book needed solid, well-written testimony from across the years, how could I not turn to some of the best football writers in the business?

These are journalists who still work on the premise that the size of your contacts book is more important than the number of 'followers'. They became friends with Jack while writing about his career, and were lucky enough to join in the fun and grab a beer or two with him along the way.

It's my good fortune that these friends and colleagues were not only willing to contribute, but every one told me it was a privilege and an honour to do so. And they have, as anticipated, provided faultless copy.

I will forever be in debt to Bob Cass, Christopher Davies, Gabriel Egan, Peter Ferguson, George Hamilton, John Helm, Jim Mossop, Philip Quinn, Ray Robertson, Charlie Stuart, David Walker, and, the doyen, Peter Byrne. Without Peter's support, and his brilliantly written and detailed diaries and autobiography, this latest account of Jack's life would not have been possible.

That is also the case with John Givens who has overseen the operation with his customary guile and expertise, demonstrating why the Charlton family have trusted him and Trevor O'Rourke for so many years.

Other people have been generous with their time and help and I would like to place on record my thanks to George Caulkin, Gordon Cox, Peterjon Cresswell, Ian Dennis, Cathal Dervan, Paul Dews, Joanne Falconer, Bryan Falconer, Matt Fowler, John Gibson, Mark Hannen, John Hickson, Ann Kamara, Kevin Kilbane, Liz Luff, Andrew Merriman, Dave Nath, Tony O'Donoghue, Paul O'Hehir, Chris Pennal, Vicki Pennal, Terry Robinson, Andrew Smith, Richard Sutcliffe, Steven Thompson, Greg Thornton, and Debi Zornes. Thanks also to the NHS and Belmont Library, Durham. And Lauri, thank you for the guidance on spelling Middlesbrough correctly

Finally, my editor Liam Hayes has been the perfect guide for my first attempt at a full biography. The book has evolved somewhat since our first discussions some years ago when we set out with a much smaller cast-list. If the late additions, changes and dodgy deadline hitting were exasperating, he never showed it. His patience, calmness and understanding have been invaluable and I won't forget his support for me, long before this adventure started. And many thanks to the team at Hero Books.

His appreciation of Jack's impact in Ireland has also made his editing of some of my ramblings easier, I'm sure. I sincerely hope the end product is somewhere close to the excellent books he's written in the past.

Mick McCarthy was right. It has been a privilege. And I was right. It was hard work.

Unfortunately, after more than 60 years in the game, it simply isn't possible to interview everyone Jack managed, worked or played with. But the beauty of managing a successful Ireland team is that many of the lads have written autobiographies, so I hope they don't mind us borrowing the best tales, where necessary.

BIBLIOGRAPHY

1966, My World Cup Year, Sir Bobby Charlton
Andy's Game, Andy Townsend
Back From The Brink, Paul McGrath
Billy Bremner, Richard Sutcliffe
Captain Fantastic, Mick McCarthy
Cissie, Cissie Charlton and Vince Gledhill
Field Sports, An Introduction, Jack Charlton and Tony Jackson
Full Time, Tony Cascarino with Paul Kimmage
Gazza My Story, Paul Gascoigne
Jack & Bobby, Leo McKinstry
Jack Charlton's American World Cup Diary, Peter Byrne
Jack Charlton, The Autobiography, Peter Byrne
Jack Charlton's World Cup Diary (Italia '90), Peter Byrne
Keane, The Autobiography
More than a Game, Con Houlihan
My Autobiography, Bobby Robson
Newcastle United, The Ultimate Record, Paul Joannou
Niall Quinn, The Autobiography, Niall Quinn
Revie Revered and Reviled, Richard Sutcliffe.

The Last Line, Packie Bonner
The Team That Jack Built, Paul Rowan
Three Times A Quaker, David Hodgson
Walk On, Ronnie Whelan
Born to Manage, Terry Venables

Jack and Pat love receiving letters. They get dozens every month, mainly just asking for photos or books to be signed. Many, from Ireland will include little stories, such as the priest from Limerick asking for a book and photograph of the pair of them to be signed. He recalled that day, and the impact on the nuns and sisters. There was pandemonium for days.

But he doesn't get any from ex-players, or journalists. Perhaps this book, for the many who have not contributed directly, is an opportunity to put that right. If you have enjoyed these stories, and have your own involving the great man, which Jack will enjoy recalling, we would dearly love your letters to pass on to him.

Write to:
DearBigJack@gmail.com
Twitter: @DearBigJack

Colin Young
September 1, 2016

ABOUT THE
AUTHOR

COLIN GEORGE YOUNG was born near Glasgow in 1970 and, with his parents Iain and Eleanor, and younger brother Andrew, moved to Riccall, near York at a very early age. He was educated at Archbishop Holgate's Grammar School and after turning down a return to university in Scotland, joined the *Yorkshire Evening Press* as a trainee reporter where he worked for four years.

After an invaluable and enjoyable stint as Hull City writer, then of the Third and Fourth Division, for the *Hull Daily Mail*, Colin has worked for several national newspapers in the UK as a North East football writer for the last 20 years. He has seen one League Cup win by Middlesbrough in that time. He has also covered the Republic of Ireland football team for the *Irish Daily Mail* as a football writer and columnist.

He has been married to Lesley for longer than they care to remember, and between them they have five children, Lauri-Beth, Rachel, Vicki, Thomas and Harry. He is also 'Grumps' to Beth, Jack and Darcey and chief walker for Charlie. He posts David Bowie songs on social media every day, to the annoyance of family and friends, and loves *The Wedding Present*, bacon sandwiches before the boys' matches on a Saturday, Tetley's (tea and bitter), Scotch Pies, Irn Bru, Kenneth Mathieson Dalglish, watching Harry play cricket for Littletown CC, the cities of Glasgow, York and Durham, a day out at Bamburgh Castle, beach and fish and chips in Seahouses, walking with Bob Cass, and Lesley, and Charlie and a good football tale. He hates…let's not go there.

If he had not written this book, he may not have heard his favourite story ever.

Charlie O'Leary was relentlessly teased by the players. And he was there for every game, bar the first one when he was working for the Wales FA.

Inevitably the subject got on to sex and Charlie, a religious and very Irish Irishman, was inevitably never entirely comfortable.

But asked one day what sex was like for a man in his 70s, he casually replied, 'It's like playing snooker with a rope'.

Thank you, Charlie. And thank you, Jack.

* Author photo back cover: Andy Commins